An Introduction
to Comparative Sociology

Also by Jon Oplinger

*Quang Tri Cadence:
Memoir of a Rifle Platoon Leader
in the Mountains of Vietnam*
(McFarland, 1993; paperback 2014)

An Introduction to Comparative Sociology

Jon Oplinger

McFarland & Company, Inc., Publishers
Jefferson, North Carolina

LIBRARY OF CONGRESS CATALOGUING-IN-PUBLICATION DATA

Names: Oplinger, Jon, author.
Title: An introduction to comparative sociology / Jon Oplinger.
Description: Jefferson : McFarland & Company, Inc., Publishers, 2020. |
    Includes bibliographical references and index.
Identifiers: LCCN 2019053891 | ISBN 9781476680965 (paperback: acid free paper) ∞
    ISBN 9781476638799 (ebook)
Subjects: LCSH: Sociology.
Classification: LCC HM585 .O75 2020 | DDC 301—dc23
LC record available at https://lccn.loc.gov/2019053891

BRITISH LIBRARY CATALOGUING DATA ARE AVAILABLE

ISBN (print) 978-1-4766-8096-5
ISBN (ebook) 978-1-4766-3879-9

© 2020 Jon Oplinger. All rights reserved

No part of this book may be reproduced or transmitted in any form or by any means, electronic or mechanical, including photocopying or recording, or by any information storage and retrieval system, without permission in writing from the publisher.

Front cover illustration by Andrei Dobrescu (Shutterstock)

Printed in the United States of America

McFarland & Company, Inc., Publishers
  Box 611, Jefferson, North Carolina 28640
  www.mcfarlandpub.com

For Jean

Acknowledgments

There are always large debts. My wife Jean has been unfailingly supportive and, as always, my wisest critic. Close friends and colleagues Stephen Adams, Elizabeth Cooke, and Margaret Wycoff have offered insightful comments and greatly augmented the clarity of this text. Wycoff's technical assistance has been indispensable. Together, they have relieved me of the burden of foolish mistakes. I wish also to express my gratitude to Judy Loeven for her enthusiasm and the sure editorial eye she has brought to this project. I am indebted to the efficient work of Sarah Otley who as interlibrary loan officer at Mantor Library is my conduit to the larger world of scholarship.

Table of Contents

Acknowledgments	vi
Preface	1
One. How to Explain Society: Different Views	3
Two. Reliable Knowledge	35
Three. Culture	41
Four. Social Organization and Stratification	52
Five. Economics: Symbolic Exchange, Technology, Wealth and Colonialism	68
Six. Strategies of Political Control	77
Seven. Demography	84
Eight. Urbanism	90
Nine. The Sociology of Religion	97
Ten. How to Manufacture Deviance	106
Eleven. Collective Behavior	129
Twelve. Sociology of War	135
Thirteen. Social Change	145
Fourteen. Globalization	161
Coda: The Consolations of Sociology	168
Principal Sources and Further Reading	171
Bibliography	177
Index	179

Preface

According to the ancient sage Callimachus: "big book, big bore." While I don't agree with that assertion, I have no quarrel with what follows by implication: that all good books are short, or anyhow, most good books.

This is a short book. And I intended it to be short. That is one reason I am inclined to call it a primer. The other reason is that, because of the narrow constraints of length, I am forced to discuss sociology's central concepts and the thinking of sociology's founding theoreticians in a straightforward manner, devoid of abstruse hairsplitting. All of the subject areas standard to an introductory text are covered plus two that are not standard, but which in my view are all important: the mass production of deviance—the Great Witch Craze is one example—and the sociology of war. The mass production of deviance, warfare, and the preparation for war are so much a part of the nation state that these topics should be included within the canon of sociology. Resolutely cross-disciplinary, the text draws upon the insights provided by anthropology and history as well as, obviously, sociology. This approach reflects graduate training in anthropology, archaeology, and sociology and an undergraduate degree in history. My fascination with these disciplines has never left me. The comparative method, the foundation of cultural anthropology, is emphasized more than in other texts. This method proceeds by the simple process of examining society across time and culture. By comparing, in other words, what is different, what is similar, and what is missing. I hope that you will agree that such an enterprise provides an illuminating understanding of a vital and compelling subject: human society.

To guide the student, important concepts and terms are in boldface type. Sources for major works are found in the body of the text so that reading is unencumbered by footnotes. However, there is both a full bibliography and an additional and extensive reference source listing, chapter by chapter, of texts used in this study and further reading.

ONE

How to Explain Society: Different Views

Throughout the course of some 200 years of development, the discipline of sociology has developed techniques to objectively determine what is going on in society and a number of theories to explain why that might be so. To be very sure, sociology is not like classical physics in the accuracy of its predictions. All the same, sociologists do make predictions, and often these predictions are correct. The track record of sociology is far better than the untutored conventional wisdom of common sense for the simple reason that sociology is a system for making good guesses about the workings of social life.

Although there were brilliant observers of the social scene during antiquity and the Middle Ages, the discipline of sociology did not take recognizable form until the nineteenth century. In that most optimistic and confident of centuries, it was assumed that society could be understood, engineered, and fixed. All would be well if only the men in power would listen to sociologists, which, of course, they did not. There is an air of messianic certainty about much early sociological writing and for some the truth of sociology became a matter of religious conviction. This phase did not pass as quickly as it should have, but by the end of the nineteenth century academic sociology had been established and grown distinct from anthropology. Simply stated, if you studied social behavior in some far-off place among people who were not of European descent, people who were, in the parlance of the time, primitive and savage, you would have called yourself an anthropologist; on the other hand, had you stayed home and, within the context of industrial society, studied people who were also regarded as primitive and savage—poor in other words—you would have called yourself a sociologist.

Alfred North Whitehead has famously said that a discipline that has not forgotten its roots is doomed. In actual fact much (but certainly not all)

An Introduction to Comparative Sociology

of what early, pioneering, sociologists have written is profound, insightful, and theoretically solid. It is toughminded work that enabled the following generation to establish sociology as an academic discipline. Admittedly, there isn't anything in sociology comparable to *On the Origin of Species*. Karl Marx's *Das Kapital*, surely one of the most influential books ever written, perhaps rises to that stature. However, the fact of the matter is that few sociologists have read the entire difficult, three-volume tome, which was nevertheless seized upon by revolutionaries as having supreme authority in economic and social matters. The consequences of this zealotry have not been kind to Marx's theory, but his perspective on social relations, **dialectical materialism**, provides a formidable analytical tool.

All of the major theories of the nineteenth century, that of Marx included, were in some respect evolutionary theories which meant something different than Darwin's "long argument" or what is denoted by the term today. For the social theorists of the time, it meant progress. It implied, or stated directly, that the forces of history would infallibly move human society to a better state. The twentieth century has undercut this innocent view.

As a result of their upbringing, academic training and the inclinations of personality, theorists within the discipline of sociology fall into two broad camps identified as either **conflict theory** or **functionalism**. These camps derive from very different sets of assumptions about the nature of society and the forces that determine how it works. These theoretical perspectives shape the understanding that sociologists have of the causes and outcomes of the human condition.

It is useful to begin with two dominant theorists of the mid-nineteenth century—**August Comte** and **Karl Marx**—because most of the theorists of the late nineteenth century and twentieth centuries can in some degree be aligned with the very different theoretical perspectives these two men developed. Both men were odd, didactic outsiders, and both were men of deep convictions.

Functionalism: August Comte

Sociology got a head start from the French Revolution. The brutal chaos of the Reign of Terror—typified by the theater of decapitation at the Place de la Concorde in Paris, one of many such venues contributing to a toll of over 1,300 beheadings in 1794—combined with decades of warfare

One. How to Explain Society

to decimate French manpower and drain the French economy. Those who lived through such times were left with an obsessive fear of mob rule and a compelling desire for order.

These sentiments are paramount in the work of August Comte. He was born in 1798, and as a child he experienced the social disruptions of the post-revolutionary period. Comte was greatly influenced by scholars who as mature men had lived through the revolution, but that influence was contradictory. On the one hand there was the thinking of revolutionary utopians, such as Henri de Saint-Simone, for whom he worked as a secretary, and on the other hand, there were those who hearkened back to the supposedly calm and orderly times of the monarchy.

Comte was brilliant, driven, sometimes unstable to the point of hospitalization, and comprehensive in his knowledge of the sciences; indeed he claimed to have mastered all the sciences. He regarded sociology (a term he coined from Latin, **socius**, and Greek, **logos**) to be at the pinnacle of the sciences. Furthermore, he saw society to be subject to laws in a manner identical to the natural sciences.

What can be mined from his major works, *Cours de Philosophie Positive*, a book of six volumes, and *System de Politique Positive*, a mere four volumes, is (1) the notion of intellectual progress through three stages, **theological**, **metaphysical**, and **positive**. Comte saw religious and mystical thinking as falling under the term theological; whereas abstract notions and speculation was classified as metaphysical. By **positive** Comte meant rational, scientific thinking. He saw social order and stability as a consequence of a rationally structured society, that is, a society organized on the basis of positivism. Within an orderly society, as Comte envisioned it, the various parts of society, its institutions, carry out their **functions** in support of all the other institutions. In short, the institutions of society are considered to be mutually supporting and to act in concert. Society, in Comte's understanding was closely analogous to an organism in which the various organs function together to sustain life. Society, in other words, is an organic whole. This perception of society is called **organicism**.

Increasingly Comte saw society in unconventional and mystical terms—"The Great Being"—and a suitable object of worship in the religion of the Great Being, of which Comte was the high priest. It did not long survive him. Its only lasting impact is found on the Brazilian flag: *Ordem e Progresso* (Order and Progress). In broad strokes, Comte argued that human society is a thing *sui generis*; that it is an organic whole consisting of mutually supporting social institutions that severally function to sustain the functions of all. By that means, human actors were, according to Comte, guided by the long "accumulation of culture." It is important to note that in his catalog of sciences Comte did not include psychology. There was no need for psychology: for Comte society, a thing *sui generis*, a consequence of natural law, solely guided the actions of men.

Comte presented society as being analyzable according to the functions of its major institutions: family, economic, political, religion, and education. If we talk of the mutual dependencies of different aspects of societies, institutions for example, a more useful image of society emerges. People depend on other people; groups of people depend on other groups of people; and institutions depend on other institutions to accomplish essential tasks of society. No one has ever doubted this and it is reasonable to talk about the **functions**—the utility, the benefits, the consequences—of the actions of institutions. What is the function of religion? How does it affect the economic system? These are useful questions, although the answer has varied from one sociologist to another. Comte never advanced the term **functionalism** but he would have been perfectly at ease with this perspective on society even as it developed greater sophistication.

Marx's Conflict Theory

Karl Marx, brilliant, sincere, and wrathful toward his enemies, died as he lived—angry. Born in Trier, Germany, in 1818, he was radicalized by the intellectual and political upheavals of the 1840s. The original student activist, he would have been at home among the Berkeley radicals of the 1960s. He is the great patriarch of a whole family of conflict theories.

Sociologists are inclined to pick the brains of dead men to get at what they "really meant" and so modernize their thought. The body of theoretical literature matures by this process. The works of past theoreticians are mined for what by contemporary standards is considered wise, while all the chauvinistic, racist, and otherwise harebrained things they wrote are ignored. This process has rightly diminished August Comte to the status of an intellectual pioneer. Not so Karl Marx. Pioneering? Certainly, but unalloyed Marxism, despite over a century of intellectual nitpicking, remains a very influential perspective on human society.

Marx's writings are voluminous and complex. Any Marxist scholar must master a menagerie of abstruse concepts and recondite language which to the uncommitted is akin to gibberish. Certainly Marx is not

One. How to Explain Society

the only scholar to couch his theory in difficult language. The celebrated French savant Lévi-Strauss comes to mind. Once this challenge is mastered, scholars are reluctant to abandon it, even though the objective facts are uncooperative. This is rather along the lines of the persistence of the old manual typewriter keyboard into the computer age. There is a better way of doing it but who wants to relearn to touch type? So it is with the persistence of theory. It is for this reason that science is said to advance one funeral at a time.

Due to a sad quirk of history, political idealists, practical revolutionaries, and violent crackpots of the late nineteenth and early twentieth century ascribed to the writings of Karl Marx a sort of Koranic infallibility. When in power they raised Marx to the level of near deification (scholars in the Soviet Union attempted to follow the Great Man's life minute by minute!) and ruthlessly applied his principles, often tendentiously, to retain power. Stripped of its subtleties, and its humanity, Marxism became a charter for tyranny to be rote-learned by hundreds of millions.

Most compellingly, Marxist theory is a very powerful analytical tool. It has given rise to a number of theories that emphasize the tension, competition, and conflict which takes place in all societies. These theories, which can vary substantially, are broadly categorized as **conflict theories**.

Comte, like Marx, saw a great deal of conflict in his life. To Comte this was an aberration, something to be controlled and ordered. But to Marx, conflict was a fundamental process, essential to life and the chief dynamic of society. Marx came to this viewpoint by academic training. He was at the inception of his schooling a typical German law student. He studied after a fashion, drank quantities of beer, and acquired the usual dueling scar. Then he was drawn to philosophy, becoming a committed student of Georg Hegel, who in life had been the academic darling of the Prussian monarchy and in death something of a cult figure. Hegel was heir to the early German Romantic movement; a diverse group of artists, writers, and philosophers who idealized nature—its enchantments, its "storm and strife"—to a degree that would make the contemporary American tree hugger seem a flinty realist. It's as though the artists of the Hudson River School painted only hurricanes and wildfires. The dynamics of nature, its destruction and rebirth, fascinated the German Romantics. Moreover, man's spirit, man's will, and thought mystically entered into this natural dynamic. In all of this, poetry, philosophy, and mysticism mingled freely.

An Introduction to Comparative Sociology

The Dialectic

Hegel's incredibly dense, abstract, and openly metaphysical works emphasize change. Human thought, human nature, and society progressed by a clash of opposites. This aspect of Hegel's philosophy will be familiar since many social thinkers have drawn upon it. Marx did so formally. As Hegel would have it, man's thought gives rise to an idea, a **thesis**, which must foster its opposite, the **antithesis**. Then a new plane of comprehension is reached through the reconciliation of these opposites. This is the **synthesis**. It is the tension, the dialectic, of the two opposites that drives this process toward the reconciling synthesis which becomes the new thesis, and so on through the dialectical process. This view was not new, and some philosophers have traced it back to Christian theology. Hegel simply put his stamp on it. Hegel was an **idealist** (this too was not new; it goes back to Plato) who believed that that all things, perhaps in nature but certainly in human society, flow from the realm of ideas and the dialectical process by which ideas evolve toward the "idea of the state."

Marx did not long remain an idealist—if he ever was one. Abandoning the entire apparatus of "idealist trammel," Marx nevertheless embraced the dialectical process. It is commonly said of Marx that he stood Hegel on his head: Marx became a thoroughgoing **materialist**, that is to say, the things in life, in nature, and in society are concrete processes. "No one drowns because of the *idea* of gravity," Marx once wrote. In human society the elemental things are the human dynamics of *material* things. He emphasized, in other words, the role of the necessities of life and the processes by which men produced them.

Because Marx held fast to dialectical process, his philosophy is called **dialectical materialism** or **historical materialism**. In order to live, men must enter into economic relationships. These economic relationships are not only cooperative, they are also, indeed must be in Marx's view, exploitative. The fundamental working out of economic relationships is the formation of opposing social classes, with opposing economic interests. These groups Marx identified with social classes. It is the tension between these opposing classes that drives the process of history through necessary stages: the master class that dominates slaves, on to feudalism in which lords dominated serfs, and then passing into capitalism in which the **bourgeoisie**, those who control the means of production—that is they control factories, energy, and money—dominate the **proletariat**, those

One. How to Explain Society

whose connection with the process of production is to contribute the only thing they have, their labor. The grand plan of dialectical materialism is the necessary working out of opposing social classes toward the final stage to come, which would be communism.

However this is too simplistic, and Marx's thinking is not simple. Marx was well aware that nineteenth-century industrial capitalism consisted of more than two classes; it also included the aristocracy and the underclass. Marx spent much of his life in London in close proximity to its ghastly slums, and he certainly knew of those at the bottom, those who had little stake in society—thieves, prostitutes, beggars, the starving poor. He referred to such people as the **Lumpenproletariat** whom he disregarded and disliked because in their desperation they could be readily manipulated by those in power. The aristocracy he regarded as frivolous, superfluous parasites.

It is necessary here to introduce Friedrich Engels, Marx's disciple, and primary economic support—Engels had money; Marx usually did not—and frequent collaborator. The son of a manufacturer, Engels was a thoroughgoing product of the bourgeoisie, except, that is, in matters of philosophy and sentiment. Engels was every bit as passionate about the condition of the industrial laborer as was Marx. Engels' best-known work, published in 1846 when Engels was 23, *The Condition of the Working Class in England*, documents a genuinely horrifying image of proletarian life in the factories and slums of Manchester, England. Others had preceded him, notably Thomas Carlyle who compared the life of a factory worker of the 1830s unfavorably to the life of a medieval serf. But even Carlyle's bitterly ironic prose cannot compete with Engels' harrowing documentation of pitiless exploitation.

A central assumption upon which Marx and Engels' theoretical edifice rests is that society, its culture, and institutions derive from economic relationships and the ownership of property. The elemental base of society is the economic relationships that men and women enter into. All else—institutions, values, beliefs, mythology—are a sort of fluff rather like the meringue on a lemon meringue pie. Not that the meringue isn't important; it is just that at the base of things it's lemons that make the pie. Marx certainly saw institutions like the law, religion, and politics to be important. Indeed, such institutions are particularly important as a means of keeping one class in the thrall of another. But to Marx such aspects of society, however important, are determined by economic organization. Marx doesn't call such institutions as law or religion fluff, of course; he calls them **superstructure**, an edifice constructed upon an economic base. This edifice serves the interests of the dominant class.

Why doesn't the proletariat revolt or at the very least withhold its labor to increase wages? For one thing, says Marx, the proletariat is guided by **false consciousness**: they don't see themselves or their place in society in a way that serves their own self-interest. In great measure this is because they have been gulled and deluded by religion, the "opium of the people." Furthermore they could not strike; or at least they could not strike without terrible cost because strikes were illegal and ruthlessly punished. Both religion and the law served the interests of the bourgeoisie.

Sociologists then and now have not been shy about pointing out that the facts are inconvenient to Marx's theory. The class system in an industrial society is much more complex than Marx asserts. Religion also exerts a profound influence on other social institutions, economics included. Roman law and common law have demonstrated great persistence despite vast economic change. These are incisive criticisms and only partially spring from the fact that Marxian theory was treated like a heretical religion during the cold war.

All the same, Marx's general perspective is powerful. Forget all the economic jargon and the dialectic, and what remains is an image of society as an arena for conflict, competition, and exploitation. To Marx, of course, this took place between opposing classes. But there is no need to make that assumption. For conflict theorists and that is what Marx's theoretical heirs call themselves, social conflict takes place at all levels. Individuals, groups, professions, institutions, bureaucracies, political parties, branches of the military—all of these overlapping social categories have self-serving and usually conflicting interests. Marx knew this, but he chose not to emphasize it, save only the conflict that takes place between socio-economic classes. Modern conflict theorists do emphasize these many realms of conflict and competition.

I have always thought the term conflict theory to be misleading, implying as it does that masses of people are out there every day attempting to bash in each other's heads. It is a matter of common experience that this does not happen on most days. Even in very violent cultures, such as the Yanomamo of South America, the Ifugao of the Philippines, or the antebellum South, interpersonal conflict is not an everyday occurrence, although it is certainly true that the men in these societies spent much of their time preparing for violence. It is perhaps the threat of violence that most strongly shapes these cultures. In modern industrial society there is

One. How to Explain Society

usually a veneer of civility. Bureaucrats exchange memos, people line up and wait, and then pay the stated price for commodities. They do not normally fall to blows. One theorist, **Paul Sites**, has chosen to call his brand of conflict theory **control theory**. He makes a good case for doing so.

Conflict develops over the control and distribution of scarce resources, although a problem arises when you attempt to define "scarce resource." Food and shelter surely, but in various societies great value has been assigned to feathers, shiny bits of compressed carbon, fast horses, inebriating chemicals, the gall bladders of bears, home entertainment centers, the bones of saints, deodorant, musk glands of smelly animals ... an incomplete list.

What we define as a scarce resource is under cultural and institutional control. You might doubt the essential nature of deodorant but chances are you spend a surprising amount of money for a commodity that people in other cultures find valueless. It is only "common sense" that diamonds are very scarce and hence valuable. At best this is only a half-truth. Diamonds are valuable but they are not scarce in nature. The scarcity resides in the marketplace because the mining, exchange, and sale of diamonds are under monopolistic control. Also, decades of advertising have installed diamonds as a paramount sign of male affection and as visible evidence of the value placed on past and future sexual exchange. A man must present an "engagement ring" in western society, or so Madison Avenue has told us. Money, a wholly abstract thing, is also a scarce resource, it is capital. Under very convoluted rules it can be bought and sold. Banks can charge usurious rates for the use of money. It is in their control. But should an individual strike out on his own and charge very a high interest for the loan of money and collect through the threat of violence, it is called loansharking and is a crime. The banking lobby is more powerful that the loan shark lobby. Marx would have characterized these examples as bourgeois manipulations to foster false consciousness among the proletariat. Al Capone, speaking from a less abstract plane, characterized such enterprises as the "legitimate Rackets." Both views have merit.

Power: Condign, Compensatory, Conditioned

There is a sense in which conflict theory can be regarded as the study of the legitimate rackets employed by the powerful. How, for instance, do brigands become kings? To single out one of many, William the Conqueror

An Introduction to Comparative Sociology

as a younger man was known as plain William the Bastard. His successful invasion of England and decade of unmitigated savagery, during which he destroyed most of the Anglo Saxon nobility, earned him the title of the Conqueror. Not long afterward, during a session of "deep speech" with his advisors, William ordered a census of all his lands and subjects, a project resulting in the *Domesday Book* (read doom, as in Judgment Day). By this detailed inventory taxes could be comprehensively leveed. As William undoubtedly knew, taxation was less fun than robbery but far more efficient in the long run.

William wasn't really a simple brigand when he invaded England; he was a duke. But his grandfather, Rollo the Viking, certainly was a brigand. He invaded what is now Normandy and, after conquering it, announced that he was a duke. In his new self-proclaimed status, Rollo had lands to bestow upon his followers, he had the legal right to judge and punish, and he had the means to courtly display in order to advertise his right to his ducal station.

There are three types of power according to John Kenneth Galbraith: **compensatory power**, by which Galbraith means the power to reward; **condign power**, to be in a position to punish; and **conditioned power**, to be able to shape a particular perception of the nature of society, as when citizens are condition to the majesty of the state and the just cause of its wars. Galbraith uses the long-term and "rightful" submission of women in western society as an example of the impact of conditioned power. More narrowly, and until recently, the supposed health-giving properties of a particular brand of cigarettes provides another application of conditioned power. The more totalitarian a state is, the more conjoined these types of power are.

It is certainly true, as Weber has written, that at the core of a nation-state there is a monopoly on the means to violence. But the use of naked power is inefficient. Mao Zedong was correct when he said that power flows from the barrel of a gun but he also knew the limits of ferocious application. He was careful not to exploit or directly intimidate the peasantry because he knew that he and his armies depended on them. Without peasant support he would not have long retained his guns or his head. To use a folksier example, we observe that the power of a man who robs a convenience store at gun point is fleeting. Power does flow from the barrel of a gun (and the torture chamber) but it more reliably flows from the judge's bench, bureaucratic memorandum, the lawyer's yellow legal pad, and the accountant's ballpoint pen as compensatory, condign, and conditioned power are legally dispensed.

If we look at the monarchy as a legitimate racket, its history is illuminating. In the early Middle Ages, kings (actually more like chieftains or war lords) were canny men of superior frightfulness. If they were not, someone who was more terrifying would take their job. In time the majesty of the man attached to his role in life, his office. "The king has two bodies" is the way medieval scholars expressed it. There was the actual man, the king who might or might not be a drunken lout, and then there was The King, the office, the social body of the king. This role, closely hedged about, has survived to this day. Long before newspapers, radio, television and the Internet (Queen Elizabeth II has a web page, by the way), there were "spin doctors." Perhaps none was more artful than Jean-Baptist Colbert, minister to Louis XIV and guardian of his public image. To this end Colbert founded a sort of "Department of Glory." Possibly the most public man in history, Louis XIV personified France in his dress, gestures, courtesies, and the grace of his dance (he founded the ballet). In his public deportment, and that of his court, Louis maintained what Clifford Geertz, a scholar of the ancient Balinese State, has called a **theater state**. He was always on display and in the most extravagant of settings, Versailles. If not personally on display, his image was always before the people of France: victorious, majestic as Apollo, and the Sun who shone upon his people. His statues, medallions, coins, and paintings were all scrutinized by Colbert. One drawing of Louis carries a scolding annotation to the effect that "it is necessary to show the King lifting his cane, instead of leaning on it."

The manufacture of the divine king is a glaring example of what sociologists call the **social construction of reality**. What we think will *not* alter the laws of physics. But much of what we socially define as real and of value is a social construction. In complex societies the social construction of reality is always up for grabs. Those groups with knowledge, resources, and the power to reward and punish, manipulate the definition of what is reasonable, virtuous, and right. The king after all rules by "divine right" and not by some quirk of history, which in actual fact is often the case. For royalty, aristocrats and legions of toadying courtiers and ministers, this image of reality was highly beneficial. And it was critical—indeed a matter of life or death—that the lower orders accept this construction of reality.

Functionalism vs. Conflict Theory

Functionalism assumes the social world to be organized along the lines of a complex organism in that society consists of interdependent parts which perform functions necessary to the whole. Individually and in combination the function of these parts is beneficial. Pathologies and disturbances tend to be eliminated. Equilibrium in society is desirable and a natural tendency. **Conflict theories**, in stark contrast, rest on the assumption that social life is dynamic and filled at all levels with conflict, that is to say, normal life generates conflict. This is so because necessary resources are scarce (or perceived to be scarce), and people individually or in groups act in their own self-interest to control such resources. Thus conflict and social change are inherent in society. However, as will be developed below, functionalism and conflict theory may be seen as operating on different levels of abstraction and on that basis should not be seen as fundamentally in opposition.

Émile Durkheim

Comte's successor and the man who saved his theory from being so much utopian balderdash was Émile Durkheim. Born in 1858, the year after Comte died, Durkheim became all that Comte wanted to be, a secure, highly esteemed academic. His influence on both anthropology and sociology was profound. He founded the journal *L'Année Sociologique* and then proceeded to write most of its articles. He also authored, among perennially influential texts, *The Rules of Sociological Method*; *Suicide*; and *The Elementary Forms of Religious Life*.

As a crusader for the discipline of sociology, Durkheim categorically denied reductionist explanations in his analysis of society. **Reductionism** is the tactic of reducing complex phenomena, human society for example, to a lower and more basic level of analysis, say psychology. But from the standpoint of psychological analysis, physiological chemistry beckons and from chemistry we pass on to physics. Such an exercise helps us little in explaining why there is a high level of violent crime in American cities or the fact that teenagers across this land routinely pay $200 for a pair of running shoes.

Society must come first: according to Durkheim, society is an entity *sui generis*, unique, a class alone. Society comes first and individuals respond to it. Society is there when the individual is born and will be there when he or she dies. One of Durkheim's most enduring insights is the concept of the **social fact**: those things of society—symbols and bundles of symbols, such as ritual and belief—that foster human behavior.

Social facts constrain the individual and guide action. The law is a social fact; people must conform to it. Even serial murderers conform to the law—most of the time. Society is, in a sense, a complex of social facts, and bring about conformity by exercising external constraint. They shape the propriety of the external world and foster a sense of moral obligation within the individual. It is perhaps in this latter sense, the inculcation of moral obligation to society, which Durkheim argued for the necessity of a **collective conscience** (*conscience collective*). There is some ambiguity as to what Durkheim meant by this term because conscience in French can be translated as either conscience or consciousness, as in the awareness of self and one's surroundings. Given Durkheim's interest in religion and the need for a moral community, he probably meant collective conscience as a set of moral understandings and associated sentiments, a sort of armature of moral order upon which society is constructed. Without a collective conscience, society must slide into a state of normlessness or **anomie** as Durkheim terms it.

In his book *Suicide* Durkheim demonstrated the influence of external institutions on even the most private of human acts, the taking of one's life. What intrigued Durkheim was the fact that the incidence of suicide—at least by official records—increases as one travels from southern to northern Europe. All sorts of reasons have been proffered, from the weather to geography. To Durkheim, the reason was social and he meticulously argued his thesis. Community cohesion, particularly as reflected in religion, decreases as you travel from the Roman Catholic south to the Protestant north. It is the diminished community support and heightened social isolation of northern regions that provokes the higher rates of suicide in northern Europe. Is it all that simple? Certainly not, but the influence of social structure does seem to be one factor, and that is a powerful fact to demonstrate.

Max Weber

Contemporary to the scholarship of Durkheim in France was the work of Max Weber in Germany. Weber is generally regarded as the most powerful intellect in sociology. He was middle class, protestant, conservative, and driven. He was an astonishing scholar whose career was characterized by periods when he could neither write nor teach. His interests were wide-ranging. He knew many languages, was an indefatigable researcher, and had periods of astonishing output. As something of a toss-off, Weber wrote a monograph on music that requires a degree in musicology to comprehend. He was a powerful theorist, comparative historian, and methodologist. It was Weber who most famously argued in *The Protestant Ethic and the Spirit of Capitalism* that religion can exert an influence over the course of economic development. Weber was arguing for detached, objective analysis at a time when some of his colleagues were relying on such nonsensical concepts as *Volksseele* (folk soul) and "racial memory." Weber was, among many other things, a masterful comparative historian. How do institutions change and develop within different societies at different times and what commonalities do they share? In this endeavor he often relied on a conceptual tool that he called the **ideal type**. The patterns of action, the concrete structure of social institutions and groups can vary but it is nevertheless possible to conceptualize an ideal pattern—an ideal type. Thus, we may conceive of an ideal type of bureaucracy. In this manner, Weber defined four types of social action: (1) **affective action**, in which emotion drives social action; (2) **traditional action**, in which action is channeled along the lines of tradition and ritual; (3) **wertrational**, in Weber's terminology denotes rational action that is value oriented, which I take to mean that individuals, groups, or nations may pursue an irrational goal by rational means, as often happens in modern society; and (4) **zweckrational**, is social action that pursues by rational means a rational goal. I'm far from sure that the distinction is so clear-cut in modern industrial society (who thinks their own goals are irrational?), but remember these are ideal types. Let us take a literary example. In *Moby Dick*, Starbuck tells us the purpose of the whale fishery: it is to equip and man ships to hunt sperm whales so as to light the lamps of the world. Starbuck also says that this task is "pleasing to God." Pleasing God and turning a buck at the same time is not irrational. This is a rational goal rationally pursued. But to hunt a single whale across the four several seas of the world out of a thirst for vengeance is an irrational goal rationally pursued. Captain Ahab's actions are wertrational. The past century produced many Ahabs; our present century will produce more.

However quirky, these early sociologists were gifted thinkers, and no one was more so than Max Weber. He certainly did not think that any individual or group was always rational, nor did he assume that any group of people are unfailingly irrational or given only to affective action or traditional action. The Khoisan hunters of Botswana track animals by means of the most incisive analysis of their tracks and their detailed knowledge of the animals they are pursuing. But they might well attribute their successful kill to rituals performed in advance of the hunt. Similarly in the industrial world, the discipline of economics—that most mathematical of all the social sciences—has for decades devoted itself to the periodically catastrophic delusion that the market system is "inherently rational" and self-correcting.

Unlike Comte, Weber was not a utopian thinker. Instead he saw that the dominant development in modern society was the rise of technocratic thought and rational-legal organization. He saw little that was good in this relentless shift to a world of contracts and bureaucracy and wrote of the "disenchantment of the modern world." He compared the new, rational-legal world to an "iron cage."

Weber was familiar with Marx's writing and respected it. He did not necessarily agree with it, as he certainly did not in the *Protestant Ethic and the Spirit of Capitalism.* His views on what constituted a social class and the primacy of power in human relations do shade toward those of Marx. He differed fundamentally with both Comte and Marx in his conception of historical process. Weber put absolutely no credence in the concept of "abstract history" (Comte's term). Weber did not think that the course of human history conformed to any necessary pattern. History is not fated. To Weber the course of history was entirely probabilistic. It was possible to find pattern in the course of history, but this pattern was not the result of any type of guiding dynamic. Borrowing a phrase from Stephen Jay Gould, a paleontologist and historian of science, the course of history is "massively contingent." A particular historical outcome hinges on previous outcomes. Some events may be regarded as more likely to occur than others, but highly improbable things do happen. In *The Economic Consequences of Peace,* John Maynard Keynes predicted with considerable specificity the catastrophic effects, both economic and social, of the Treaty of Versailles. Events transpired much as Keynes had predicted. However no one predicted, or could have predicted except on the basis of bizarre prophecy, that in the resulting chaos Germany would fall into the thrall of a ruthless, egomaniacal tyrant. Such things happen. By Marxist scholarship Hitler was entirely predictable. He was, it is said, a creature of the industrialists. But that was only one factor. Curious linkages and improbabilities abound in Hitler's rise to tyranny. It is impossible to imagine what the world would have looked like had Hitler not survived four years in the trenches.

An Introduction to Comparative Sociology

Conflict Theory vs. Functionalism: Redux

The problems associated with the strict organic analogy—the argument that each part of society directly influences and sustains the other parts, and that these parts necessarily evolve in such a way as to bring balance to society—contains an escape clause: raise the level of abstraction even higher. The heirs of functionalism now regard themselves as **systems theorists**. The language of systems theory and its insights, which may be applied to everything from the solar system to microbiology, provides an effective means of analyzing the workings of society. It is entirely reasonable to conceptualize society as a **loosely coupled system**, meaning that the linkages between subsystems are nowhere near as direct as is found in an organism. Society is a network of interdependencies but these interdependencies, these connections, are uneven and lopsided. The distribution of systemic power is not balanced—nor is it fair.

Power is a property of the social system in the sense that conflict and the consequent application of power can take place only within a social system. A common and doubtless ancient response to social conflict is to abandon the social system in which that conflict is taking place. Stated more directly, people pick up and move. This is a common reaction on the part of the San ("bushman") of southern Africa to quarrels between families or with a difficult, violent person. Villages of the Yanomamo typically fission when conflict reaches a certain level, with the two factions, usually consisting of brothers and their families, going their separate ways. One Inuit family quarreled with another and put more than one hundred miles between themselves and the offending group. The Cheyenne Dog Soldiers chose to camp apart when their policies were at odds with the rest of the tribe. The Puritans sailed for New England.

The rise of complex society is closely related to the inability of people to exercise the option of disgruntled flight. Absent that choice, they suffer exploitation—they must produce for the benefit of others. From a particular vantage point, according to Peter Brown, the history of Rome is the history of how 10 percent of the people lived comfortably off the toil of everyone else. The Roman Empire fell in the West when it could no longer protect, control, or tax its rural populations.

American Sociology

After such an extended discussion of the intellectual development of European sociology it may come as a surprise that the first department of sociology anywhere was established in 1882 in Chicago. In hindsight this is not really so surprising; there has always been a certain Midwestern, fix-it mentality to American sociology. There was much to fix in Chicago. Happily, it was wealthy and so was its university. Its newly minted professors often hailed from the Midwest. They were born into the middle class and grew up in small towns. The nation's "social problems," which were then regarded as urban problems, interested and concerned them. (Note the term: **social problem**. Problems have solutions; they can be fixed.)

The Chicago School

It was chiefly at the University of Chicago that these practical concerns mated with a home-grown philosophy, American pragmatism, to produce what is known as the Chicago School of Sociology. From the very beginning the city of Chicago was used as a laboratory. There are now monographs on Chicago's slums, its hobos, its street gangs, its immigrants, its dance halls, its ethnic groups, and its neighborhoods.

In discussing the Chicago School it is necessary to cast a wide net to include, among others, **Charles Horton Cooley** of the University of Michigan. Drawing upon the writing of William James and John Dewey, Cooley was to lay the groundwork for a different conception of society. Cooley placed society in the individual. To be sure, this is a somewhat puzzling statement at first glance. But given some reflection it isn't. To Durkheim the collective conscience is somehow "out there," external to the individual, but he must allow that it is also internalized. How else would people know about it?

But Cooley goes much further than that: society is in the mind. "The imaginations people have of one another are the solid facts of society," says Cooley. He begins by elaborating a concept of William James, who very likely got it from Adam Smith, for it is mentioned in *The Wealth of Nations*. James called it the **social self**. Cooley called it the **looking glass self**. Cooley meant by this term that our appreciation of ourselves depends on our perception of how others see us. We use those around us as a sort of mirror. This process would now be called the **reflexive self**.

Self-awareness is a consequence of society. People become self-aware as a result of life experience and especially as that social experience takes place in small intimate groups. Cooley called such groups **primary groups**. In primary groups individuals acquire an understanding of the ideals and expectations of larger society and how one's own self should feel about that understanding and adjust to it. Accordingly, Cooley referred to primary groups, as the "cradle of socialization." This is the basis for the view of society as an ongoing process that is built up and constantly revived by social interaction. In its fullest elaboration, this view of society is called **symbolic interactionism**. This powerful perspective is best approached through a discussion of socialization.

Becoming Human

The term sociologists use to describe the process by which the individual becomes socially competent is **socialization**. Humans when they are born have a great deal of maturing to do because of one of our peculiar adaptive strategies. We are bipedal; we walk about on our hind legs. Instead of having a rather square pelvis with a large birth canal such as quadrupeds, humans have this bowl-shaped skeletal structure with a very narrow birth canal. It is a consequence of bipedalism and has been a central part of the human family's biological history for a very long time. As humans developed larger and larger brains a problem developed in parallel: how to get a large-brained fetus out through a relatively small birth canal? The solution to this seeming impasse is easily stated but the biological and social implications are vast. The solution is early birth. The human species is **altricial**. Human infants are extraordinarily immature at birth. They are as helpless as the hatchlings of a robin. They see little, cannot raise their heads and it is many months before they can walk and years before they can feed themselves. In short, the human infant *must mature outside of the womb* and in a social environment. It is a safe assumption that a woman and infant alone could not have long survived during the Pleistocene—or now for that matter. The social support system for an isolated woman and infant in an early industrial city was probably far less than what was available during most of human existence. In such circumstance the routine solution was infanticide.

Isolates

The starkest, and most heart-wrenching, illustration of the importance of socialization is provided by cases where the infant has not been

One. How to Explain Society

socialized—or only minimally so. There are well documented cases of terribly neglected children who have been raised in near isolation. Such children are called isolates or, more informally, "closet children." How many such cases go undiscovered is an unanswerable question, but from time to time such children are rescued. Kingsley Davis wrote about two cases in the 1930s. It is not easy to get reliable information from people who have neglected a child, but in bare outline Anna's story seems to have been that she was the second illegitimate child of a rural Pennsylvania farm girl. When only a few days old, Anna was given up for adoption but after a few months the child was returned to her mother by the adopting family. From that point on, Anna was placed in the attic of her grandfather's house where her mother lived. There Anna stayed for six years when she was finally discovered in 1938.

It was thought at the time of her discovery that she was both deaf and blind. She responded to no stimuli. Anna, a diminutive child, was so lacking in muscle tone that when flat on her back the soles of her feet would touch the mattress. She may have been tied up at one point. She seems to have had no contact with other humans apart from being fed and occasionally cleaned, after a fashion. The immediate reaction of the authorities was to place her in the county home for the indigent elderly, the "old folk's home." Such a facility can hardly be described as a therapeutic environment, but it was vastly more stimulating than her previous situation. There was noise, speech, light; the staff fussed over her. Anna loved to have her hair combed. Grooming is a basic mammalian behavior, but it had been denied to Anna. Kingsley Davis, having learned of Anna in the newspaper, saw her 11 days later. By this time it was obvious that she could see and she could hear; she responded to and obviously delighted in such stimuli. Within weeks Anna was adopted by a local family who cared for her tenderly. Anna never learned to speak, however she could understand simple instructions. She could not walk unaided because of the effects of her incarceration. She was responsive and evidently happy; her greatest joy came on her weekly visits by car to a local clinic for a checkup. She died at the age of 11.

It is astonishing that Anna survived at all. A prominent institution in the nineteenth and early twentieth centuries was the foundling home. These institutions were established in Europe and the United States to care for orphaned or, more often, abandoned children given up by desperate young women who could not care for their infants. Left anonymously, the infant would be found—hence foundling—by the staff. The stark choice faced by these women was the foundling home or infanticide. In fact the choice was largely cosmetic: nearly all the infants given up to the care of a foundling home died—usually within the first year. So remorseless was this attrition that by the end of the nineteenth-century doctors coined a term for it, marasmus. In 1915 a report by Dr. Henry Chapin on such institutions in 10 American cities revealed that in only one of these institutions did any of the infants survive to see their second birthday. Marasmus means wasting away, and it defined a condition for which there was a number of underlying causes. Some doctors had a good idea of what the leading cause of marasmus was because by the 1920s many institutions had adopted a policy of "mothering." Institutional mothering is not complicated: every baby is picked up and cuddled several times a day "whether it needs it or not." When this practice was introduced into the pediatric wards of Bellevue Hospital in New York City the mortality rates dropped from 55 to 10 percent. That was in the 1930s.

In a classic study by Rene Spitz the impact of mothering in combination with a more stimulating environment is more sharply drawn. Spitz compared two separate institutions for the care of infants. Both institutions were clean and provided solid nutrition and medical care. Beyond that, there were dramatic differences. One environment was found in an institution for delinquent girls with infants. The children were in the care of their mothers or another young woman. They had toys and could watch the hustle and bustle of nurses and young mothers. Older children were present. The young women frequently held their infants and chatted with one another. The nursery was a busy, interesting, comfortable place. The other institution was a foundling home. There, after three months of age, the infants were moved to single cubicles in a large ward. There were relatively few nurses. Spitz describes the foundling home as bleak and quiet, except at feeding time. There were few toys. In order to control the transmission of germs, sheets were put over the side railings and feet of the cribs; this also kept the children quiet.

Children in the foundling home seemed to regress when moved to the larger (and unstimulating) ward. Marasmus appeared. None of these conditions was found in the prison nursery. A final comparison: out of 91 infants observed in the foundling home, 34 had died by the end of the second year. In the nursery, of the 186 children observed for a period of greater than six months, only two children died. Spitz neatly describes the primary cause of this grim disparity. Mothering was strongly present in the nursery and largely absent in the foundling home. When mothering

One. How to Explain Society

was introduced into the foundling home's regimen of care, infant mortality dropped sharply.

Isabelle is the second case reported by Kingsley Davis, although it is not really a case of isolation at all. Isabelle was the illegitimate child of a young girl who was a deaf mute. Her family locked her and her infant in a darkened room where they remained *together* for six years until 1938. Isabelle's mother cared for her child as well as circumstances could have allowed. Although it was never described in detail, mother and child seemed to have worked out their own sign language. When discovered, Isabelle reacted to the outside world and her rescuers with croaks of terror. She was promptly hospitalized and her severe rickets surgically corrected. She was then placed in a foster home where she blossomed. She soon acquired the rudiments of spoken language—as if she had only been waiting for the right setting. Her understanding of society and her ability to get along in it astounded all those who knew her, Davis included. Not long after sent to public school, Isabelle swiftly caught up with her age mates. Davis last saw Isabelle at the age of 14 at which time she impressed him as a perfectly normal young woman—as evidently she was.

Why were the life histories of Anna and Isabelle so different? The paramount difference, the thing that varied so greatly in the course of their early lives, was that Anna was raised in near total isolation whereas Isabelle was raised with her mother. Isabelle was denied the full experience of society but she was not isolated. Another likely difference is that Isabelle evidently had some contact with language—sign language.

Isabelle's pell-mell acquisition of language and social competence seems to have been enabled by the close, all but constant interaction with her mother, and because mother and daughter created their own sign language. Unfortunately no one bothered to record their language but it may not have been so rudimentary. Groups of deaf children if left to their own devices will develop a full-fledged sign language. But Anna suffered profound isolation for six years and this lack of any but the most fleeting contact with human society was destructive of her human potential.

The case that has been most closely studied and is best known to psychology students is that of Genie, who was discovered in a suburb of Los Angeles in 1970. She had been confined to her bedroom by an abusive father. The room was spare and there was little noise. If Genie tried to attract attention by making noise she was beaten. Her mother, who was nearly blind and entirely dominated by her husband, cared and fed Genie to the best of her abilities. But it seems that she was allowed only brief

An Introduction to Comparative Sociology

periods with her daughter. Finally, her mother, with Genie in tow, haltingly made her way to the local welfare office. Social workers were stunned by the tiny, stooped, vacant-eyed child who they thought was about seven years old. In fact Genie was 13. She was immediately hospitalized for malnutrition. She salivated constantly, was incontinent, and was unable to eat solid food. She could not focus her eyes on anything over 12 feet away, never cried, and walked in a cautious shuffling gait.

Genie somehow endured the stampede of psychologists, linguists, and social scientists who wanted to study her. Their sterile attentions seem to have done Genie little good, but the nursing staff, by contrast, cared for her with concern and tenderness. Within a year Genie achieved the linguistic level of an 18-month-old child but thereafter her speech improved very little. She also began to differentiate between people and objects. Her mental capacities seem to be a curious patchwork. She had good spatial sense and could draw. She had an uncanny ability to convey her wants by means of body language. For a while Genie was farmed out to foster homes—some abusive. Factions developed between scientists and caregivers which led to court battles. As of 1987 Genie was in the legal custody of her mother and resided in a home for developmentally limited adults. It is not known where she is at present. Genie seems to have suffered not only because of her abusive isolation but also from the length of her incarceration. Despite her amazing resilience to survive in an environment that was both abusive and isolated, the time for the full development of social and linguistic skill may have simply passed her by.

By all evidence the isolation of Anna was the most profound. When discovered, Anna manifested *no behavior at all*. According to her rescuers she responded to nothing—not noise, not light. It is inescapable that the notion of an isolated child somehow manifesting an original state of nature is completely wrong. There is no such thing. Human beings are creatures of society, or they are simply empty vessels.

In greater or lesser degree, all mammals are dependent on socialization. This is especially true of all higher primates. There are few introductory psychology students who have not seen the picture of the sad, isolated baby macaque clinging tightly to a wire cylinder wrapped in terry cloth. Inside is a light bulb that provides warmth—the original warm fuzzy. Only when driven by hunger will the infant leave its surrogate mother to feed. Infant macaques raised in isolation never adjust to primate society. They are wholly deficient psychologically and socially. Infant macaques raised with a mother, but otherwise in isolation, do far better.

But what about normal human children raised in a normal social environment? By what process does a helpless and unformed infant become a competent adult able to understand and participate in society? And how might this process be usefully conceptualized if we are to understand how human society works?

George Herbert Mead

Mead was by training essentially a philosopher and brought that training to the question of cognitive development. His views are really a philosophy of cognitive development which he then expanded to a theory of the *process* of society. It should be noted that there are two types of social psychology. Sociologists work in one academic realm and psychologists work in another. They don't talk to one another very much. Sociologists emphasize the concept of the **self** and particularly the discussion of the self and the nature of consciousness as found in the works of George Herbert Mead. Psychology, which is a highly experimental discipline, pays little attention to a concept of the self. It is hard to construct experiments on "the self" that are trustworthy and convincing. Text books on social psychology written by psychologists make only passing reference to Mead's work.

Sociologists, however, find it difficult to proceed with a discussion of society in the absence of a self-conscious and socially astute actor. It is for that reason that sociologists have emphasized the philosophy of Mead and the sociological perspective that has grown out of it. This is now known as **symbolic interactionism**, a term coined by **Herbert Blumer**, a close student of Mead's.

Born in 1864, Mead led a varied and somewhat adventurous life that included studying in Germany under the pioneering psychologist Wilhelm Wundt and surveying in the American West. A short stint at the University of Michigan at Ann Arbor, which seems to have been something of a way station to Chicago, brought him into close and congenial contact with John Dewey and Charles Horton Cooley. Mead and Dewey soon decamped to the University of Chicago; Cooley a retiring man, who would not have gone anywhere near Chicago, remained at the then bucolic setting of Ann Arbor.

Mead taught philosophy and social psychology for many years until his death. His course on social psychology became a magnet for students

An Introduction to Comparative Sociology

from a variety of disciplines and most particularly sociology students. It was in this class that Mead's theory on the self and society was honed. Mead was a brilliant lecturer. His major work, *Mind, Self and Society*, is in fact a compilation of stenographic records of his lectures and student notes. Naturally this circumstance has given rise to a festival of hairsplitting, much of which can be safely ignored. The basic outline is clear and compelling, and has given rise to a sort of inside-out view of society.

Mead expands on Cooley's notion of the looking-glass self and put it on a solid conceptual basis. Mead posits the origin of the self in social interaction. The self is not there to begin with; it is not merely a consequence of the development of the biological capacity for cognition. (The sad cases of Anna and Genie argue that this is so.) Instead, the self is forged in the process of social interaction and by perceptible stages.

Mead compares *nonsignificant* gestures and *significant* gestures (terminology that in part derives from Wundt). According to Mead, a growling, teeth-bearing dog is displaying a nonsignificant gesture. It will invoke an identical response from any other dog it is directed against. This is a visceral, emotive—instinctive, if you will—response characteristic of dogdom. It will not change. In sharp contrast, the relations of self-aware humans take place on the basis of significant gestures—symbols. This requires a common understanding of the meaning in both actor and the person toward whom the action is directed. That is, the actor can place herself cognitively in the position—the role—of the person she is acting toward. For example, among humans of a certain culture a proffered handshake is usually greeted by a similar gesture and so the two people "shake hands." But consider the possible common meanings this ritualistic gesture may take. Two people may be meeting for the first time and so shake hands in the prospect of future friendship. They may be sealing a business contract in which case the handshake is a pledge to honor an agreement. They may—and this is suggested as the origin of the handshake—greet each other with an open hand symbolizing that they are not going to slaughter one another. A handshake may mark a last sad parting. Shaking hands may take on all of these mutually understood symbolic meanings.

Significant gestures, to stick with Mead's terminology for the moment, are essential to society. Consider what your reaction would be if your offer to shake hands was greeted by blows and shrieks of outrage, or merely by puzzled confusion. You would act perhaps with outrage, or anger, or fear. You might take insult, or you might consider the behavior as a sign of insanity. Kurt Vonnegut writes of a space alien who was the product of a society that communicates by farting and tap dancing. Upon entering an American household and attempting to render greetings in the usual manner, the friendly space alien is brained with a nine iron by a frightened citizen of the Heartland. As Herbert Blumer would have it, **lines of action**—a common set of symbolic meanings—had not be been established.

Very young children, says Mead, often play like puppies. But soon the young child, who has long been immersed in an ongoing web of language and social interaction, begins to acquire the glimmerings of a vantage point that is external to herself. In this process language and play are essential. The child takes on the ability to play at being another person, at being a **particular other**. Children play at being in another social role, one that is known to them if only in limited form, such as mother, big sister. A social role is necessarily a relationship tied to another social role: one may not be "big sister" in the absence of siblings, unless, of course, you imagine them. Thus to **take the role** of someone else requires a certain comprehension of yourself in the role that you have just vacated. I am now my big sister, acting toward me. The child who is socially cognizant of another social role must necessarily imagine herself from the perspective of that played-at role. She can, posits Mead, take herself as an object. That degree of reflexivity, seeing yourself as others see you, taking yourself as an object, is a very great skill, but one that is, like language, readily achieved by a child. The **play stage**, in Mead's scheme, is characterized by the ability to take the role of a **particular other**.

The next stage is often called the **game stage** because it relies on the model that Mead used, a complex multi-role game such as baseball. As the child grows in comprehension and subtlety of knowledge regarding the workings of society, she can understand in similar fashion the workings of team games, games that have a variety of interacting roles. This understanding is acquired by practice and play, by failure and renewed effort, by, in other words, complex social interaction.

In the game stage, the child comprehends not only her role but also the role to be played by all others in the game. You cannot play baseball unless you understand the requirements of your position (role) but also the requirements of all the other positions in any number of situations. Not only that, you must also see yourself from the vantage of all of those separate roles and you must be able to do that in all sorts of plays that the game might offer. You must also anticipate what other players will do. The child first understands the roles of the people immediately around her and

An Introduction to Comparative Sociology

then, in time, achieves an understanding of the roles of those who interact with her important others, and so on to broader and more abstract understandings of the web of roles in society. This level of social comprehension including especially your place within that understanding of society, is what Mead called the **generalized other**.

A team sport among very young children provides an example. William Kornblum has called attention to a phenomenon that he calls "beehive soccer." In our culture, very young boys and girls are encouraged to play team sports often well before they can understand the rules and the several roles that the rules determine. The generalized other is not yet present among any of the players, and no amount of coaching is going to bring conformity to roles that require a sophisticated understanding of one's self in those roles. Take the example of soccer: the children are coached carefully in the several positions (wing, striker, goalie, etc.); the children are positioned on the field; they are walked through what to do in various situations. The ball, at long last, is put into play. And what happens? Everyone, goalie included, goes after the ball at the same time. From a distance it looks like the ball is surrounded by a swarm of bees. Hence, "beehive soccer." This is not correctable except through social interaction and maturation.

The generalized other is often described as a durable, external vantage point on one's self. It is that built-in understanding of society by which you evaluate yourself. One need not be in society to be social if one is possessed, so to speak, of a generalized other. Like the solitary Englishman in colonial Africa, his culture is always with him, and so he always dresses for dinner even if there is no one to see him.

Mead used the term generalized other as the ability to see yourself from the vantage point of society. He did indeed use baseball as an example and a model. And if we stick to baseball it can lead us concretely to broader and more complex realms of social interaction. There are manifold roles that connect the players to larger society. People watch as others play. Children may wish others to support them—mother, father, sister. There may be fears of injury or torn clothing as the child is perfectly capable of taking the attitude of mother should these eventualities occur. As the game becomes more formal—as in Little League—other more formal roles attach. There are coaches. There are sponsors who donate the cost of uniforms. There are umpires. There are moms and dads who conform—usually—to the expected role of spectator.

Does the individual player have to be cognizant of the great web of roles in order to have a developed generalized other? Certainly not. People do not ordinarily worry about all the roles all the time. In baseball, the batter bunts the ball and runs. He does not concern himself with the actions of the left fielder. The fan obtains a hotdog and settles in to watch. She is not concerned with the general manager's preoccupation with player salaries. She does not know about the groundskeeper's worries about replacing the turf. She does not concern herself with the role of network executives. It does not bother her, as it does them, that baseball lends itself to boring stretches of near inaction during which broadcasters may not "break away" for commercials to sell beer and tires. There is no requirement for comprehensive knowledge of this unbounded web of roles, yet the complex interconnection of social roles across society proceeds and in the process creates society.

Mead surely realized that this picture presents society as somewhat stiff and unyielding. If everyone had only an identical understanding of society's roles and played them out with minimal deviation and ingenuity, it is difficult to see how society would change, except on the basis of catastrophic events. Social roles are seldom as tightly scripted as they are in a play (from which the term role is derived). To be sure, some roles are closely hedged about by laws and principles that may go back hundreds of years. But even here there is latitude. Judges have inclinations; they have a style and a reputation. Good defense attorneys do all they can to avoid having their client's case tried in a certain judge's court. People bridle at the confinements of social roles; people try to change the expectations of others; people break the rules. Such actions, as Durkheim noted, change society.

Mead also realized that there is more to conscious behavior than the requirements of the generalized other. People are not automata; they have selves. It is this understanding that Mead's concept of the **self as a social process** is important. There is, as Mead puts it, a subjective aspect of the self. The self and self-consciousness does not arise solely as a result of a learned capacity to see oneself from the vantage point of other social roles, to maintain a sort of "inner dramatization" of the expectations of others. There is also an aspect of self that is impulsive, spontaneous, and subjective. There is the I. It is the I that is mediated and translated into conscious thought and appropriate social action by the social comprehension of the **Me**. The self develops as a result of a sort of inner dialogue between the I and the Me.

Perhaps this somewhat cryptic discussion can be clarified if it is pointed out that the I may be consciously experienced only in retrospect. By the time it has passed into the realm of conscious experience it has been transformed into the Me of social awareness. This process is wholly internal and may be thought of as a mediation of impulse to responsibility, the I being spontaneous, subjective, and visceral and the Me being the situational working out of the conscious expectations of the generalized other. I have always seen the I and the Me along these lines. Anyhow it suits our purposes. Above all it must be emphasized that in Mead's thinking, and in all species of symbolic interactionism, the I and the Me are entirely conceptual entities. There is no I part of the brain nor is there a Me part of the brain.

Esteemed by colleges of education, the work of the Swiss biologist **Jean Piaget** contributes to the knowledge of the moral and intellectual development of children. By means of hundreds of carefully designed experiments he assessed the mental capacity of children of different ages. On the basis of this work, spanning decades, Piaget argued for "universal stages" of cognitive development.

Piaget's most celebrated experiment deals with the concept of "conservation." How does a child deal with abstract notions like mass and volume. The child is presented with two identical beakers half-filled with an interesting fluid such as chocolate milk. One beaker is then poured into another beaker that is taller and thinner. This is directly observed by the child. Query: which beaker now contains the most milk? The usual answer for a young child Swiss child is to say that the taller beaker contains the most milk. When an older child is presented with the same manipulation, her invariable reaction is to gaze upon the experimenter as a fool for asking such an obvious question. For a time there was consternation because Piaget's universal stages don't hold up very well cross-culturally. Clearly children from other cultures don't develop the same cognitive skills as the same time as Swiss children. In fact cognitive development is situational. It has been known that children and adults who do not live in a "carpentered world," who haven't been reared in an environment of straight lines and angles, do poorly on problems dealing with perspective. One variation of the conservation experiment uses clay. The clay is molded into round balls, one of which is then rolled into a cylindrical shape. Has the amount of clay been altered? Children raised in a Mexican village that specializes in the hand manufacture of pottery do well. Children in other villages where pottery is not made do not do as well.

Piaget, like Mead, emphasizes the importance of interaction, language and games in the development of a child's cognitive skills. Young children, Piaget notes, frequently have difficulty describing simple tasks such as turning on a faucet. This is not, argues Piaget, because they do not understand the task; rather they do not appreciate what the other does not know because they cannot effectively imagine themselves as the other. This is not true of older children.

In another experiment a three dimensional topographic map is presented to a child. The map has prominent hills and valleys and the view from one side of the map is very different from that of the opposite side. The child is allowed to view the map from all vantage points. The question that is presented to the child, who now stands on one side of the map, is "What does it look like from the opposite side?" Again, younger children have trouble and tend to describe what they see. Older children, *who can take the role of the other*, can describe with some degree of accuracy what another person would see from the opposite side of the map. I am slipping into Meadian terminology here but that is the point. The larger point is that again and again the highly empirical work of Piaget and his school lends considerable support to Mead's philosophically based social psychology.

Certain aspects of Sigmund Freud's voluminous work have been compared to Mead's orientation. No academic of Mead's time could have been unfamiliar with Freud's theory but it does not seem to have significantly influenced Mead's perspective. It is important to establish that Mead's theory is philosophical; it is not a biological theory, nor is it deterministic. Freud's training was not philosophical nor, except for brief interludes, psychological. Freud's interest in neurosis and its treatment was galvanized by a brief period of study under Jean-Martin Charcot, the P. T. Barnum of French hysterics. However much that experience redirected Freud's interests, the biological roots of Freudian psychology cannot be overlooked. Freud's cogitations on the organization of the personality make this clear. The Freudian **id**, **ego**, and **super-ego** are "mental organs"—and Freud meant that in surprisingly literal form—constituting an "anatomy of the mind." Maturation is a consequence of passing through psychosexual stages of growth. Because certain thoughts are inappropriate, the mature individual expends energy in repressing such thoughts so that they do not become conscious. They repose in the unconscious. From Freud's perspective the wellspring of human behavior ultimately derives from the unconscious, a sort of biological inner darkness of the mind. Mead postulates no such mental realm. Freudian psychology centers on the process of maturation and the organization of the personality. It does not (and was not intended to) explain the workings of society.

There have been comparisons of the I and the Me with the Freudian id, ego, and super-ego. But in Freud's thinking the relationship of the id, ego and super-ego is emphatically one of containment and conflict, "like a horse and rider" is the analogy used by Freud. It is the unconscious id—this atavistic little worm inside us—that gives rise to all sorts of unacceptable desires and thoughts, particularly in sexual and excretory matters. It is the ego and super-ego that contain this unconscious tendency toward dark mischief. The comparison with Mead's theory is only superficial. The I is not like the id. The I is only impulse. And the super-ego is more often compared to one's moral compass, one's conscience. The super-ego begins and ends with the concept of personality and cannot be compared to the generalized other except in the most limited way.

Neither Piaget's empirically based stages of maturation nor can Freud's psychological insights be expanded to provide an understanding of the collective workings of society. The great feat of Meadian social psychology is that it is provides us with an understanding of the complexity of social process. The conception of the generalized other is applicable to the process of both cultural and historical awareness. It is in this context that one aspect of the work of **C. Wright Mills** may be examined.

The Sociological Imagination

What C. Wright Mills means by the sociological imagination is the ability to perceive yourself as partly a product of the larger social forces that influence your life and not just the immediate circle of social roles around you. The sociological imagination is the acquired social skill that enables you to understand the history and circumstances that shape society and how that impacts your life. In the *Sociological Imagination* Mills writes that the "sociological imagination enables us to grasp history and biography and the relations between the two within society." On a more personal level it involves the ability to see yourself in society with some objectivity. It involves the understanding that your achievements and position in society are not entirely your own doing. Likewise, it involves the understanding that hardships and lack of achievement do not necessarily arise from personal failings. On this Mills, who came of age during the Great Depression, was keen. It is easy, and reasonable, to see the sociological imagination as a logical expansion of the individual's grasp of the generalized other. But one must have knowledge of history and economics and politics. Lacking access to such knowledge, one's sociological imagination is subject to manipulation by the elite who are experts in the artful use of conditioned power and the manufacture of "false consciousness."

Institutions

"Institution" is one of those terms in sociology that denotes a variety of social processes. In one use, an institution is simply an area of analysis such as the economic institution or the religious institution. This is useful but arbitrary. Churches own property and engage in economic transactions. At what point does a particular set of activities cease being religious and become economic? Another view of a social institution holds that any regular pattern of behavior that is reinforced by social sanction is an institution. To use the example provided by Robert Bierstedt, a handshake is a custom, whereas a military salute is an institution. Failure to salute will be sanctioned. A failure to shake hands carries no formal sanction. There is merely the risk of being considered an oaf.

A more encompassing definition would hold that an institution is a purposeful constellation of social roles. An institution is purposeful, or dedicated, in that it is possible to define with some specificity the purpose for which many social roles act in concert. To Mills the stable configuration of social roles within an institution is disciplined and structured by an authority which has the right and duty to employ sanctions; to chastise infractions such as when a soldier fails to salute, or a king causes the murder of a "turbulent priest," or the manager of a store sells running shoes at too low a price.

An important subset of this notion of an institution is **Erving Goffman's** concept of a **total institution**. By this term Goffman denotes institutions such as military academies, mental institutions, prisons, seminaries, and convents, wherein the roles are closely drawn, encompassing, and strongly (often violently) sanctioned. Such institutions are places of intense socialization, or resocialization.

In industrial societies there is little that is not institutionalized, and therefore constrained in some degree by authoritarian sanctions that produce easily recognized regularity in social roles and patterns of interaction. These regularities, these patterns, may be called social structure. But, it is fundamental to understand that to call these patterns **social structure** is to invoke metaphor. But the regularities in society are not comprised of some crystalline matrix, there is no scaffolding, no supporting framework; we only find it tempting to imagine it so. Society hangs together only because of repetitive social interactions. Such acts are significant, and have consequences. They lead to other social acts which may be rather unique or they may be, more often, ordinary and routine. These common, often repeated patterns of social action are reified and regarded as "things." We talk easily about the structure, the team, the aristocracy, the middle class, and the college. These are "things" in the grammatical sense, but their fundamental existence in society takes the form of the repetitive processes that underlie our human tendency to lend concreteness to abstractions and patterns of social interaction, to, in other words, reify.

Two

Reliable Knowledge

Perhaps one of the difficulties in understanding human society is that we are trying to study it with the same tool that has created it—the human mind. We tend to impose patterns where none really exists. Sociology's entire armamentium of theory construction, scientific method and statistical procedures is designed to avoid this pitfall. Equally, there are patterns that we don't recognize. And perhaps there are long-term processes we just don't see, particularly with sociology's fascination with the here and now.

The problems associated with doing research in sociology stems from the fact that sociologists deal with people, which is trouble enough, but they also deal with people in groups, large and small. Producing reliable knowledge, which is the goal of science, is a difficult task. Broadly put, sociologists use two different approaches to the study of human society and culture: **qualitative research** and **quantitative research**.

One type of qualitative research is called **participant observation**, meaning that the sociologists participates and observes the actions of particular groups and subcultures. This approach is essentially ethnographic and differs little from cultural anthropology. The Chicago School in its heyday produced many fine studies of Chicago subcultures, groups and enterprises. Such studies require time and disciplined work. **W. I. Thomas**'s study of *The Unadjusted Girl* involved some 3,000 interviews. Such sociological work provides insights into how things really are, and, importantly, that things are not always as they seem. Other qualitative approaches might involve the study of letters, as in Thomas's study of the immigrant Polish peasant, or other sorts of published material, including "Internet culture." Comparative sociology, which might combine both qualitative and quantitative research, relies on historical and cross-cultural studies. A comparative sociologist might undertake a study of witchcraft panics— those times when more than the usual number of local witches were executed—and compare them to other twentieth-century panics and purges.

An Introduction to Comparative Sociology

Max Weber's magisterial histories of the major religions are classic examples of comparative sociology.

A variable is easily defined, it is something that varies. Quantitative studies involve the comparison of variables by way of tabulating them mathematically. Survey research makes use of various types of questionnaires to determine people's conditions or attitudes. Because you cannot survey everyone, those chosen for the survey, the **sample**, are chosen **randomly**. This simply means that everyone chosen to be interviewed has an equal chance of being selected. It would be pointless to try to determine American attitudes on nudism if you only interviewed people in nudist camps. If the sample is not randomly chosen, the study, no matter how large or well-funded, is worthless.

Other research derives from carefully constructed experiments which test theories about the relationships between social phenomena. Theories are carefully constructed sets of logically related propositions. Ideally, theories may be tested mathematically. Theories must be carefully drawn and the terms employed precisely constructed. The philosopher of science Karl Popper has forcefully argued that a theory is not actually a theory unless it is open to **falsification**, i.e., you can prove it wrong. Theories make predictions: apes and humans have a common ancestor; light will be visibly bent by the sun's gravitational field; all swans are white (falsified by the discovery of black swans in Australia).

Émile Durkheim's brilliant work *Suicide*, which established that the support of family and group is an important variable in the frequency of suicide, provides instance after instance of what a suicide is, or is not. He carefully defines just what constitutes a suicide. There can be no ambiguity. This carefully drawn definition is the **operational indicator**. It is what you predict will occur according to the theory. If not found, the theory is falsified.

In the construction of an experiment, variables are carefully defined as the **independent variable**, what is being manipulated in the experiment, and the **dependent variable** (sometimes called the outcome variable). This is an application of John Stuart Mill's **method of difference**. If condition A is present, and condition a is also present, one would be reluctant to conclude simply on that basis that A is causing a. But if then A is not present and a is likewise not present, barring coincidence, you would conclude that A is causing a. So what is A in an experiment? It is the experimental group which is the **independent variable**. And what is "not A"? It is the **control group**.

Two. Reliable Knowledge

Testing things in this manner is important because so many things are not common sense. The Scared Straight Program was an optimistic and generously funded program to control delinquency. In this program groups of "predelinquents"—meaning troubled teenagers who had not engaged in major crimes—were sent to tour Rahway State Prison in New Jersey to experience what maximum security prison is like. The common-sense assumption was that any rational being would alter their behavior in order to avoid being sent to such a place. The program was alleged to work miracles and was enthusiastically pursued for years. When at long last the program was studied by James Finckenhauer the results were counterintuitive. Finckenhauer broke the predelinquents into a control group and an experimental group. The independent variable here is the prison visit. The experimental group went to the prison and saw what it was like. The control group did not. This was repeated numerous times. It was revealed that the Scared Straight Program had a counterintuitive effect. The operational indicator here was a determination as to whether or not the predelinquents had been arrested in the following six months. On this basis it was discovered that substantially more of the predelinquents in the experimental group has been arrested than those in the control group. Maybe the control group predelinquents were more savvy delinquents and didn't get caught? But the disparity in numbers, *which is statistically unlikely*, suggests otherwise. In short the Scared Straight Program was counterproductive: it increased delinquent behavior.

Other fundamental concerns center on **reliability** and **validity**. Reliability, simply stated, resides in the question of whether or not a phenomenon can be defined and recognized with any degree of accuracy. Is it reliable? And does the method employed actually measure the phenomenon accurately? Are the measurements actually measuring what is supposed to be measured? The matter of validity is straightforward: is it real?

Here are the two research pitfalls: (1) are you actually measuring what you want to measure? And (2) does what you are trying to measure actually exist? Is it **valid**? Psychiatric diagnoses are notoriously unreliable, with one physician proposing one diagnosis and another physician proposing a different diagnosis for the same patient. The pattern of diagnoses can vary substantially from one country to another; one being more likely to diagnose schizophrenia and another more inclined toward depression. This is likely the result of different training, but the diagnoses of flu or appendicitis does not suffer from inconsistency.

Validity is also a vexing matter in psychiatry. Some types of mental illness do not seem to be mental illnesses. The American Psychiatric Association used to regard homosexuality as a mental illness and, for the psychiatrist, a very profitable one. A committee vote among the elders of this learned institution has now formalized the view that homosexuality is not a mental illness after all. Normally diseases cannot be voted out of existence; except that is when they totally lack content validity. Anyhow, the "disease" of homosexuality has gone the way of drapetomania, bicycle face, and wandering womb.

Junk science is a quasi-legal term that denotes slipshod, bad, or distorted science that is presented to support one side in a legal dispute. More broadly, it is a pack of lies, as when "experts" hired by the tobacco companies hatched studies that supposedly undermined the link between smoking and lung cancer. This went on for years. The term is also applied to bad or silly cogitations that are used to support a particular species of pseudoscience. This brand of junk science is primarily sustained by an overweening desire to believe which rests on political advantage and/or money. The profitability of "treating" young men for homosexuality may be mentioned in this regard.

Bad science as expressed in engineering or medicine has done and will do significant harm: drugs have side effects, bridges fall down. Bad social science can be enormously and enduringly destructive. Racism was (and is) an utterly groundless notion supported by unfounded assertions—some genuinely bizarre—and self-serving beliefs. The Third Reich represents a catastrophic triumph of junk science. With this and other tragedies in mind, the historian **William McNeill** has stated that whenever you have an ideology that purports to explain everything and solve all problems—and both Fascism and Communism did—the world takes a blood bath.

On the other hand, solid, tough-minded social science can be beneficial. The Coleman Report was mandated by Congress to inform the Supreme Court decision *Brown v. Board of Education*. The Coleman Report provided extensive and careful analysis that demonstrated that the policy of segregation was inherently damaging. **Kai Erikson**'s study of the aftermath of the Buffalo Creek Disaster, *Everything in Its Path*, brilliantly discusses the loss of community endured by those who suffered as a result of the collapse of a dam owned by a major coal company. **William Chambliss** recorded the differing treatment accorded upper and lower class boys in their encounters with the police. There are many such studies.

One reason that sociological studies often appear to be so stodgy and

Two. Reliable Knowledge

jargon ridden is the intractable nature of what sociologists study: human beings in complex groups. Sociologists go to great lengths to carefully structure their studies and carefully formulate their concepts and hypotheses because of what they study. A classic example, conducted by a whole gang of social scientists, is the **Hawthorne Study**, named after the plant in which the study was conducted. It is frequently examined in Business schools. In one series of observations, the lighting was manipulated in a room where complex electrical appliances were being assembled. First the lighting was increased in the not unreasonable assumption that workers would perform better if they could see what they were doing. Production increased. When the lighting was enhanced yet again production increased even more. No one was surprised by this. Then, not knowing what else to do, the experimenters reduced the lighting in regular increments. Production still went up! In fact production only went down after the lighting was reduced to the level of moonlight and the workers could not see what they were doing. The conclusion was that the experimenters overlooked an important variable: themselves. In the normal work environment officious young men were not prowling about the workplace taking notes. It was concluded that the female workers wanted to please the male experimenters. Maybe. Anyhow, the additional variable of the experimenter's presence is called the **Hawthorne effect**. It is also worth noting another important variable. These studies took place from 1927 to 1932, well into the Depression so it probably wasn't just some simple-hearted desire to please the experimenters, the workers were terrified of losing their jobs and assumed that they had to respond positively to any and all adjustments.

At their core, the social sciences and especially sociology are hard work. Literature must be arduously reviewed, data collected, entered and analyzed, subjects reviewed. Social experiments cost money and take time. This is equally true of surveys and participant observation. But the outcome can and often is beneficial to society. It is true that sociological investigations in comparison to other disciplines can appear ragged and poorly controlled. Finckenhaur's study of the Scared Straight Program is far from a perfect model. Samples varied, control groups and experimental groups were of different sizes, and just what is a predeliquent? No one knew this better than the investigator. But what was being studied was real life, with all of life's eventualities and clumsiness. And, by the way, Finckenhaur's study resulted in dramatic changes in the Scared Straight Program making it genuinely effective.

An Introduction to Comparative Sociology

All scholars fervently say that their discipline is really at the core of things; their discipline is at the center and all other disciplines merely support it. Sociology says that too. At the heart of sociology is the hard edge of driven curiosity about how society really works and the strong desire to make society less cruel.

Three

Culture

Let us begin with the definition of culture provided by Edward B. Tylor in his classic work *Primitive Culture*. "Culture ... is that complex whole which includes knowledge, belief, art, morals, law, custom and any other capabilities and habits acquired by man as a member of society." This elegant turn of phrase ably describes the scope of culture, but it does not reveal anything about the processes by which this complex whole is accomplished.

Culture is not exclusive to *Homo sapiens*. In rudimentary form some monkeys and all chimpanzees have learned to fashion tools. They trim small twigs to poke into termite nests. Upon withdrawing the twig, the annoyed termites may be licked off. This is a significant source of protein for some groups. They use stones to crack nuts. In some regions, chimpanzees have been observed using branches fashioned into crude spears to kill bush babies. Unquestionably these and other behaviors are learned.

Human culture in all its tremendous variety is learned. Human beings are altricial; their babies are born as helpless as the nestlings of a robin. From that point forward, the infant's brain, upon which so much energy and blood flow has been invested, begins to absorb and organize information about the world around it. An anthropologist would refer to this process as **enculturation**; a sociologist would call it **socialization**. These terms may be regarded as roughly coterminous.

How does the swiftly enlarging brain of a young human "pack in," all the information it receives? What the young human packs in are symbols. *Culture is symbolic.* It is an organization of symbols. A symbol, quite simply, is something that stands for something else. The Stars and Stripes symbolize America; blood symbolizes life; a heart symbolizes love, and so on.

Language, at the level that humans employ, is unique. Language creates and organizes symbols into meaningful discourse with others and, as symbolic interaction tells us, with one's self. The philosophical linguist

An Introduction to Comparative Sociology

Noam Chomsky argues that the greatest intellectual achievement that any of us will ever accomplish is the acquisition of language. Children everywhere do this at a remarkably early age. Chomsky explains this astonishing capability as the consequence of a sort of primal, underlying grammar. This universal mental capacity is usually called "deep structure." It is a compelling concept, and in times past it has led people to find deep structure at the base of many things. What Chomsky meant by deep structure was in fact highly technical and not everything can be supposed to have a deep structure.

It is incontrovertible that a child's ability to learn language is astonishing, and inexplicable on the basis of operant conditioning. Moreover, a young child will routinely make what Chomsky calls "errors of consistency" and say, for instance, "ranned" instead of run. They have learned the grammar but not all the irregularities found in the spoken language. A child raised in a bilingual household will with little difficulty become fluent in two languages, or three languages in a trilingual environment. Pidgin languages are simple in structure and limited in vocabulary. Such languages facilitate communication across different cultures—usually one is dominant—and enable trade, or obedience. Teach a pidgin language to a group of children, and they will develop a true language in less than a generation. Deaf children, in isolated groups and without the benefit of instruction in sign language, have created their own language.

The language that you speak is a fundamental part of your culture, and it influences your perception of how the world works. Just how strong this influence is remains a matter of controversy. An early and influential theory was developed by Benjamin Lee Whorf who worked, oddly enough, in the insurance industry. He was impressed by the fact people were blowing up their property with "empty" (but full of fumes) gas cans. His view of language was bolstered by Edward Sapir, a linguist, and they are jointly credited with the **Sapir-Whorf Hypothesis** which holds that language dramatically structures the nature of reality. This is also called **linguistic determinism**. Their argument is tendentious, and relies on very literal translations. It greatly overstates the case. The influence of language may be more profound in the underlying process by which language is constructed. To this end some basic linguistics is necessary.

Since the time of Panini, the fourth-century BC Indian scholar of Sanskrit and evidently the first person to realize that language had parts, linguists have studied the organization and processes of language. The smallest unit of sound that we can hear—in computer lingo something like bit of information—is called a **phoneme**. Given our anatomical equipment, humans can theoretically utter around 135 different phonemes. No language requires you to use all of these phonemes. Far from it. English employs some 35 (or so) phonemes allowing a vast number of permutations. English is not going to run out of sounds to make up English words. Combinations of phonemes make up morphemes which carry meaning. Words are **morphemes**.

The rules governing the formation of morphemes is called phonology. Phonology is central to the study of linguistics but it falls far short of explaining language process. The rules of phonology allow only for the production of "word salad," random strings of words conveying no meaning. This runs deep. You have to grit your teeth and concentrate to deliberately produce word salad; and if you start speaking word salad routinely, you *really* need to see a physician.

Syntax, derived from the Greek word for coordination, denotes the rules by which words are ordered so as to convey meaning, so that it "makes sense." Specifically syntax establishes the correct word sequence. "Jon loves Mary" does not, in English, mean the same thing as "Mary loves Jon." In the classic nonsense sentence coined by Chomsky, "Colorless green ideas sleep furiously," we are nagged by the sense that it should mean something. Perhaps this might have some private poetical meaning to a very few, but in the ordinary course of social communication it is entirely without meaning. It is nonsense. But it nags at you because that sentence is syntactically correct. It is not easy, by the way, to make up such sentences. Try it. There are several models of how syntax generates meaning; all are in the heady realm of philosophical linguistics.

Semantics is the branch of linguistics dealing with the meaning of words. How is it that a particular word denotes a particular thing, or things, or state or abstract idea? As always, what seems straightforward on the face of it is to a linguist a highly abstract issue.

These complex linguistic processes—phonology, syntax, and semantics—taken in combination constitute **grammar**. The native speaker at a very early age employs this sophisticated ability quite effortlessly. Every day everyone conjures up completely unique sentences, never uttered before and perhaps never used again.

The degree to which culture spins off from this cognitive ability is unknown, but it seems likely that culture and language at the level of deep structure are strongly linked. Culture, in sum, should be thought of as having a measure of grammaticality. Culture, in its "complex whole," has

An Introduction to Comparative Sociology

a certain underlying orderliness about it; its parts hang together in meaningful ways. Culture as it fosters the social construction of reality makes sense of obdurate reality and, likewise, it makes sense of social relations. It allows you to control things and people and to make predictions. This is not to say that at the surface culture provides perfect harmony. Aspects of culture may vary, and this is surely so for individuals within a culture who often hold inconsistent and contrary views about the nature of things. But at the deeper level, culture rests upon root metaphors and unquestioned understandings about the nature of reality that are consistent and orderly. More fundamentally, culture is set to rules and is in some measure grammatical.

Chomsky never speculates about how this inherent grammatical sense came about. He just says it's there. The paleoanthropologist Richard Klein argues on the basis of the early appearance 50,000 or 60,000 years ago of highly efficient tools in parts of Africa, and especially artifacts of symbolic importance (hxaro), that human culture as we know it evolved rather suddenly. This probably happened in small outlying groups, as a result of several key mutations. All humans alive today—seven billion plus—share these selfsame mutations and are remarkably similar genetically. Modern cultural and linguistic ability rests upon this legacy.

In the classical sociological formulation, behavior consists of norms— what is normally expected of a culturally astute actor. An early breakdown of norms into subcategories was introduced, at least in germinal form, by William Graham Sumner in *Folkways*, which describes virtually every behavior to have seen the sun. Not even the most anal of graduate students has read this tome in its entirety. A subsequent and widely read text by Robert Biersted sorted norms into **folkways, mores, and laws**.

Folkways are simply customs; the habits of speech, belief and action that are characteristic of a group or region. In parts of the Midwest the strip of land between the sidewalk and the street is called "the devil's strip." Folkways carry little or no sanction. If you don't use the term devil's strip you will not be formally punished or rebuked; and if you do use the term devil's strip in a region where it is not in use, you will only be greeted by blank stares or at worst be thought a bit odd. However widespread, the practice of sending greeting cards is merely a folkway and the only sanction for not reciprocating is that you may not receive a card in future. And so on to innumerable customs.

Mores (L. *more*, singular *mos*) are consistent, widely held, and deeply rooted conceptions of morality which, if violated, will bring upon the

Three. Culture

violator the social condemnation of disgust and the mark of evil (remember Hester Prynne and the bad rap she got). Mores are strongly sanctioned, and these sanctions are consistently upheld within society. Jeffrey Dahmer, to site a clear example, was in violation of a number of mores of which two may be mentioned: he was a serial murderer, and he ate his victims. He was sent to prison amid general sadness that the death penalty could not be invoked. There he was considered unwelcome and was swiftly murdered.

Laws are codified. Laws are written down, and published with explicit punishments. The symbol of Roman authority, the *fasces*, was an axe bundled around by sticks. It was carried before Roman magistrates and represented to all but the slowest of citizens the nature of Roman condign punishment. Malefactors were beaten with sticks or suffered capital punishment by having their heads chopped off by an axe. Even without the benefit of the *fasces* we all have general knowledge of the law and the punishments associated. A violation of a more is often, but not always, punished by law.

It is not only state level societies that have law. Laws are not written down but are nevertheless understood by all. And there are well defined sanctions. Among the Cheyenne the tribal buffalo hunt immediately followed the Sun Dance. Should anyone hunt in advance of that ceremony, that person ran the risk of being badly beaten and having his property destroyed.

Culture and the Social Construction of Reality

The classic dictum of W. I. Thomas holds that "if men define situations as real, they are real in their consequences." Witchcraft provides a clear and consequential instance of this. As witchcraft was defined in Europe, it was quite impossible to be a witch. No one then or now can do what a witch was supposed to do. That objective fact did not prevent the execution, often by fire, of conservatively 50,000 people, mostly women who were thought to be much more open to the blandishments of the Devil.

Society, through the agency of culture, constructs our understanding of reality. Culture establishes what is real. This process runs deep into history and to the fundamentals of how we symbolically organize and give meaning to reality. Historical linguistics has opened a window on this process. In the late eighteenth century William Jones, a Welsh jurist and linguist, was assigned to the Supreme Court of Bengal. Both dutiful and intellectually curious, Jones began to study Sanskrit, the language in which Indian law was written. Jones was the ideal man for this task as he was fluent in a number of languages including Welsh, his first language, as well as English and Persian. What soon struck him were the many similarities between Sanskrit and other languages, including, as it happened, Welsh, English, Persian and the majority of European languages. He lumped these widely distributed languages into what he called Indo-European. It had been long known that German and English were related and that the Romance languages derived from Latin, but the distribution and evident antiquity of Indo-European came as a revelation.

It is possible to reconstruct the lexicon and grammar of the earliest form of Indo-European: proto–Indo-European. According to David Anthony, in *The Horse, the Wheel and Language*, we share some of the selfsame grammatical guidelines to the nature of reality as did the ancient speakers of proto–Indo-European several thousand years ago on the Eurasian plain. Because we speak an Indo-European language, we must employ tense and number. We must specify if an event is in the past, present, or future and we must indicate that an action has been accomplished by one actor or by multiple actors (things and actors are singular or plural). Anthony states that "it is impossible to use an Indo-European verb without deciding on these categories." And, mercifully not true of English, most Indo-European languages assign gender to things. At the deepest level such constraints frame our construction of reality.

Different cultures "see" things differently. For Australian Aborigines, Dreamtime was a time when Dreamtime ancestors roamed the landscape and it was a time when Dreamtime ancestors became part of the terrain. The Australian Aborigines are related to the landscape—to sacred features. Dreamtime may be entered in the present through the portal of ceremony; one may ceremonially embody Dreamtime ancestors during ritual. Dreamtime exists in the future. Dreamtime is a time that surrounds ordinary time. It is the myths, legends, and ancestors that inhabit the perceptions of social reality for those raised in the culture of Dreamtime. When an Aborigine looks upon the land, what he sees is described as the Totemistic Landscape alive with Dreamtime ancestors, myths, and the sacred grounds that are passages into Dreamtime. All this is invisible to a white Australian from an urban environment, a speaker of an Indo-European language.

Three. Culture

Culture in the Longue Durée

In his seminal work, *The Mediterranean and the Mediterranean World in the Age of Philip II*, **Fernand Braudel** introduced the concept of the *longue durée* into the Annales School of social history. Braudel's study of the geography, ecology, and the social and political history of the Mediterranean world revealed the long persistence of some social behaviors. A case in point is the migration patterns of the sixteenth-century Spanish transhumant herders who drove their herds of cattle and sheep from winter pastures in the lowlands to high pastures in the summer. Such migratory patterns are very ancient and likely follow routes taken by game animals in the Paleolithic. These patterns have persisted over the long cast of history and remain in use today, although often the animals are transported along these routes by truck.

Patterns of culture and society do not change at a uniform rate. Persistent structures, behaviors, and beliefs—patterns of the longue duree—are common, so ordinary that we do not often think of them. Place names are remarkably enduring. Given a map showing only Native American place names in Algonkian or Muskogean, most of us could do a fair job of navigating east of the Mississippi.

In *Metaphors We Live By*, the cognitive linguist George Lakoff discusses how fundamental (and common) such metaphors are: we say we are "attacking" someone's argument. Or we say that we are "losing time." It is quite impossible to think of time as a commodity in other, non–Indo-European languages. Even metaphors such as "in my mind's eye" are so commonplace that we forget its Shakespearean birth. Here is the point of origin of so much of what we "see" in English. Shakespeare has provided us with dozens of such metaphors we live by and hundreds of neologisms: clangor, radiance, sportive.

Edward Hall a student of how different societies organize space—especially personal space—and time in ways that are culturally acceptable. There are vast differences. Americans and especially New Englanders are regarded in other cultures as standoffish. Our personal space extends out about a foot and a half; we are uneasy when that envelope is intruded upon by others. We are "late," depending on the occasion, if we are more than 20 minutes late. And to arrive "late" requires a mumbled explanation—even if it is a bald faced lie. Other cultures are not so strict. A South American may arrive at a dinner date 45 minutes late blissfully unaware of giving offence. Among South African Bushmen, it is probably not possible

An Introduction to Comparative Sociology

to be late. Hall's books used to be assigned reading for American diplomats. It would be wrong of a diplomat to construe a calculated insult on the basis of a late arrival when none was intended. On the other hand, not to take insult out of ignorance when an insult was intended would also be a mistake.

Many basic things are cultural, such as how we categorize (or "see") colors. We see many different colors. Women, as a rule, see more colors than men. Other cultures lump together colors, orange and red for example, that we see as quite distinct. Some cultures have had a vigesimal numbering system. The base is not 10 but 20. We would find this cumbersome but the Maya were able to use such a system to generate complex (and accurate) calendrical calculations. Other cultures have only the numbers one, two and three, and "more than three." They don't need more. Some, such as the ancient Sumerians, used 60 as a base for some calculations. This might seem odd until you look at a clock (not a digital clock please).

It has been said that habit is the flywheel of society. We often do things or think things because we have done so before. We do this as individuals and as a culture. There are many "taken-for-granted things" in our world. One way of illuminating these taken-for-granted aspects of culture is to use **ethnomethodology**, which deliberately sets out to "break the cultural grammar." Easily done. Students are encouraged to insist that they don't know what "everyone knows." "What's a flat tire?" insists the ethnomethodologist. Or students are sent home to pretend that they are guests in their own home. This produces puzzlement, frustration and annoyance among the unwary parents—and likely some reflection on the cost of tuition at Berkley where this tactic originated. Ethnomethodology examines how people draw upon their experience and larger culture to make sense of events. Drinking out of the glass of the person seated beside you at a formal dinner party is an interesting thing to do. It will produce uncertainty and ill-concealed irritability. Often the response to such tears in the fabric of culture is to "gloss." The behavior is studiously ignored. We do not do not drink out of another's glass in bars.

One such effort that I participated in involved sauntering into a high-class restaurant, sitting down as a group, and then one of us ostentatiously entered into the "drama" of rolling a "joint" containing, to my certain knowledge, pipe tobacco. Immediately there were furtive looks and alarmed conversation from nearby tables occupied by elderly patrons. The "joint" was lit and smoked with a casual air (in those ancient days, you could smoke in restaurants). It appeared to be obvious to all, *and despite the strong smell of aromatic pipe tobacco*, that a group of hippies—that was not how we were dressed—were partaking of a dangerous and illegal substance *right in the open*! The alarm was palpable in that room. It was then that our professor, who was observing from another table, was himself captured by his own experimental drama. "Hey," he hissed, "those guys are smoking real dope. They're screwing things up. We're gonna get arrested." He waved the experiment to a close and we all left in a hurry. In retrospect, this experiment was not a good idea. The police are not ethnomethodologists and take a dim view of such antics. There was perhaps the small added risk of having marijuana magically appear on our persons.

Culture Is a Layered Process

On the surface of things, at the level of day-to-day behavior, culture varies according to individual experience and by subculture—as among the Amish, for example—but as we probe deeper into the process of culture we see that society is encompassed by shared language, root metaphors, such as " blood," and the rituals, ceremonies, and the inherited world views of ancient peoples and cultures. The fundamental, or, if you will "deeper," aspects of culture are more broadly shared than the idiosyncrasies of local folkways and individual behavior.

The Characteristics of Culture

If you ask a sociologist or an anthropologist during a candid and relaxed moment just what culture is they are likely to say something along the lines of "I'm not quite sure." On a more formal and guarded occasion they may make reference to one of the dozens of definitions of culture presently in service. There are a very great many definitions to choose from. More than 50 years ago two doyens of anthropology, A. L. Kroeber and Clyde Kluckhohn, wrote an exhaustive review of the concept and definitions of culture. The number of definitions collected during this enterprise ran to over 140 (by my count). Some are impressively opaque. Moreover, they don't all agree, not by a long shot. What they do agree on are the characteristics of culture.

Culture is learned. This is true by definition. Those genetic predispositions that all humans share, such as the eminently practical fear of snakes, cannot be regarded as cultural. Culture is learned and passed across generations by the process of enculturation (or socialization). As one generation is enculturated and matures, the culture they have learned is passed on to the newer generation and so on over many millennia. *Homo sapiens* are (and were) the only Hominids to have grandparents. Anciently, to have elders in the band (and later tribe) in whom reposes the collective store of knowledge—often retained by myth, ritual and song—was immensely valuable. It was a matter of survival. This is sometimes and not unreasonably called the "granny factor."

Culture is symbolic. Culture is created by symbols. It is an **organization of symbols** the meaning of which is shared by members of a particular culture.

Culture is shared. The nature of this sharing is comprehensive when it comes to the core of a culture, its root metaphors and rituals. At the surface level of culture, at the level of individual experience, there is invariably some difference in the knowledge shared from one person to another. Similarly, cross-generational sharing is not perfect. The experiences of one generation are not identical to the succeeding generation. The experiences and attitudes of those who lived through the Great Depression are not the same as mine, and they are assuredly not the same as yours.

Culture is patterned. It is not simply willy-nilly, an accumulation of things. It is organized, integrated, and is, *sensu lato*, grammatical and therefore it is predicable. It makes "sense." This is true not only because language is a major part of culture, but also because of the overall pattern of a culture is shared and understood.

Culture is dynamic. Culture is a process; it is always changing. The pace of change can vary greatly. The rapidity of cultural change today, which we accept as normal, would have been quite inconceivable to the medieval mind. Useful things, such as stirrups, or annoying things, such as crossbows, cropped up at long intervals to spread across cultures and bring change. But there was nothing like the current transformations that can make one generation's culture markedly different from another. The average person in the Middle Ages might experience political or military change on a cyclical basis—rotten kings come and go—but transformational change they would not have experienced nor understood.

Culture is emergent. New cultural configurations emerge from antecedent configurations of symbols. The elements of culture shift into novel and more complex patterns, much as oxygen and hydrogen combine into something new and more complex. Indeed culture itself is an

Three. Culture

emergent phenomenon. At some point during the late Pleistocene of Africa a suite of genetic predispositions assembled in the human species, and consequently the ability to create, sustain and transmit the complex of symbols we call culture emerged. Population size may be related to innovation and the emergence of culture. This culture granted an extraordinary ability to humans to respond to the hazards of the environment and to, with increasing effectiveness, buffer its effects and to manipulate it to their advantage.

Culture is adaptive. *Homo sapiens,* now and anciently, configure their cultures to the ecology in which they live. Humans have adapted efficiently to an astonishing variety of challenging environments: desert, tropical forest and the arctic regions of the world have been adapted to. We have enlisted plants and animals into our service and shaped them to benefit us. If we take culture in the abstract as an *energy capturing system* then the entire history of *Homo sapiens* is the ever-increasing ability of our species to channel energy into our cultural systems.

Human culture is unique. It is important here to make a distinction between society and culture. Social, but not necessarily cultural, animals are more successful than solitary creatures. The biologist George Schaller has demonstrated that social carnivores such as lions and wild dogs make more frequent kills than solitary hunters, with wild dogs succeeding close to 100 percent of the time.

Social behavior in general is highly adaptive. The success of social insects—particularly ants, wasps, bees, and termites—is extraordinary, so much so that social insects make up a significant part of the biomass in the tropical forest. There are tens of thousands of species of social insects participating in complex adaptations. But in all of these insect societies there is not a single individual possessing an iota of cognition. It is all instinct. *Homo sapiens* is the only species to develop and adapt by means of culture. It must be emphasized that societies based on a structure of instincts are all but ubiquitous; but *culture at the human level* is entirely singular. Our adaptive niche is culture.

Four

Social Organization and Stratification

Human society is hierarchical. It is organized on a number of levels but kinship structures, even in complex societies, still provide the base. **Consanguineal** (literally: with blood) and **affinal** (related through marriage—your brother-in-law is an affine) relationships between people are fundamentally important to all human societies and have been for many thousands of years. Families in some form are found in all cultures. There appear to be no exceptions.

The most common type of family is the nuclear family which is the logical outgrowth of monogamy, consisting of mother, father, and descendent children. Of course there are single parent families and etc. Lévi-Strauss, the doyen of French structural anthropology, has stated that the nuclear family is the building block of larger kinship structures. **Extended** families simply refer to families that are related across generations, as in the typical farm family. Or the term extended family may refer to the larger web of kin outside the immediate family. **Polygamy** (Greek for multiple marriages) introduces a measure of complexity. By far the most common type of polygamous marriage is **polygyny** (multiple women) in which one man is married to a number of women at the same time. This is likely the most common type of marriage worldwide that is *legally* permitted. **Polyandry** denotes a multiple marriage in which a woman is married to a number of men at the same time (often these men are brothers). These arrangements can be visualized as a linking of nuclear families in which the man (polygynous marriage) or the woman (polyandrous marriage) has a duel role as spouse to more than one partner of the opposite sex. Most importantly, these various sorts of families do a good job of socializing children. The great majority of people are socialized within a family of some sort. Alternative institutions such as foundling homes and orphanages often do a poor job, however well intentioned. The track record of utopian societies is typically little better.

Four. Social Organization and Stratification

Kinship is the backbone of tribal societies: social roles, linkages, membership in larger groups, political power, all derive from kinship. Tribal societies are often based on descent groups, people descended from a common ancestor. These are called **lineages**. If that ancestor is male the descent group is called a **patrilineage**; if female, it is called a **matrilineage**. Groups of lineages that claim descent from a common (usually mythical) ancestor are called clans. Kinship is really based on two principles: alliance (marriage is an alliance) and descent. Such concerns are paramount in a tribal society. One common feature of tribal kinship is the distinction between cousins. There are **parallel cousins** (the offspring of mother's sister or father's brother) and there are **cross cousins** (the offspring of mother's brother or father's sister). We make no such distinction—cousins are just cousins. Parallel cousins are called either brother or sister. One can marry, and in many cultures should, marry one's cross cousin but one cannot marry your parallel cousin. This all seems rather arcane but in fact it is not. The effect of differentiating between parallel and cross cousins is to code alliances. To marry a parallel cousin is to marry within your lineage and some cultures do this—as in the Bible. To marry a cross cousin is to establish an alliance with another lineage. In the modern world, to suppose that tribal politics is not incumbent on the strong ties of kinship is to make a grave, and all too common, error.

Within all societies, whether relatively simple or highly structured, the importance of one's relatives is a matter of significance. In tribal societies it is paramount. For all practical purposes you cannot live outside of a family and the larger kin groups of which a tribe is constructed. We also rely heavily on our relatives within industrial society and probably more than we realize. Beyond emotional support there are frequent material acts of support which are informally reciprocated. Such acts of support are expected and often essential. Think of baby-sitting.

It is all too easy to turn sociology into "groupology," but the fact remains that the extra-kin associations within industrial society are legion and vary in size, form of organization, and purpose. A framework, a typology, is essential. One good way of breaking the various sorts of organizations down is on the basis of two criteria: on a continuum, groups can be said to vary (1) according to the degree of social interaction among members of the group and (2) on the basis of the size and level of organizational complexity. **Primary groups**, a term coined by Charles Horton Cooley, are small, face-to-face groups in which people interact frequently and informally. The attachments within a primary group are often intense.

Cooley referred to primary groups as the *cradle of socialization* because of the influence they have on their members. Families work well because they are primary groups. **Secondary groups** are set apart because such groups are more formal and can be much larger.

Voluntary associations are larger in size, with substantial personal interaction but also some degree of social complexity. They are formal groups because they have rules (often written), own property, have a leadership structure, and maintain sanctions—the usual sanction being expulsion from the group but it can be more severe, as in the mafia. In size and purpose voluntary associations vary greatly, from fan clubs, to garden clubs, to school boards, to social clubs, and on and on. The usual example provided is the volunteer fire department. There are thousands of these and what they do is essential. Such groups are fairly small, and I am reliably informed that on occasion interaction can be quite informal. At the same time formality is required because the equipment maintained is valuable, the training is demanding, and there is little tolerance for mistakes or indifferent commitment. Firefighting is too dangerous.

Bureaucracy

On the far end of the simple-to-complex continuum we have an organizational structure characterized by size, rigidly complex organizational rules, and relatively little face-to-face interaction. Since the mid-eighteenth century this type of organization has been called a **bureaucracy** (rule by desk), a term coined by a French official, Jean Gourney, who also complained of the malady "bureaumania." The classic formulation of bureaucracy, presented as an ideal-type, derives from the work of Max Weber. There are a number of renditions of this but essentially what Weber argued for as the ideal-typical Bureaucracy was an organization characterized by: (1) career lines, (2) being rule-bound, (3) being universalistic, and (4) having a rigidly hierarchical structure.

Career lines: those staffing a bureaucracy operate with some assurance that so long as they follow the rules their jobs are secure. They cannot be fired without significant cause (in theory) and they can expect with reasonable performance of duties to be advanced in responsibility and pay. This security not only attracts people to work in a bureaucracy, it protects the bureaucracy from the inroads of outside forces. Bureaucratic operatives at all levels are less subject to pressure from outside forces.

Four. Social Organization and Stratification

Rule-bound: The actions taken by officials within a bureaucracy are subject to detailed and stringent rules. Bureaucrats have little if any flexibility in decision making. They can breach the rules, which of course are published, only at their peril. Thus it is that bureaucracies can be inflexible and overprotective of position. These restrictions do not apply to those at the very top of the bureaucratic hierarchy.

Universalistic: In theory, the rules within a bureaucracy apply equally to all, without exception and evenhandedly. Only the most naive will suppose this is what actually happens all the time but, again, this is an ideal-type. This quality is designed to prevent outside influence and breaches of the rules by the powerful, well-placed, or wealthy—hence the Roman Catholic Church's concern with **nepotism** and **simony**. Nepotism is derived from the Italian word for nephew and reflects the practice of appointing singularly unqualified relatives to high offices within the Church; simony refers to selling offices.

Hierarchical: Bureaucratic structures are layered in responsibility and power. The separation between these layers is distinct and guarded by rules and ceremonial trappings. Every bureaucratic organization is presented by a carefully drawn table of organization which shows every position within this hierarchy of power and decision making from the very top—president, commanding general, Pope, king, grand exalted cyclops—down to those at the bottom of the hierarchy—workers, soldiers, clerks, devoted thugs. In theory, and often in practice, this arrangement allows for swift decision making and fast, effective action. Minimally it permits some kind of action. Weber's view was that in complex industrial society, bureaucratic structure takes on tasks that are otherwise impossible to accomplish. It is impossible to run an army in the absence of some hierarchical structure that is well established by sanctions against breaches of discipline and the trappings of rank symbolizing status and power. During a desperate period in the Second World War, the British, at great cost, were shipping critical supplies to the Soviet Union. At this juncture the Soviets requested quantities of gold braid. The British queried the necessity of this and were told that the Soviet Army had an imperative need to reestablish the status of military rank.

Weber, who was a very political animal, was perfectly aware that bureaucracies are never bureaucratized at the top. At the pinnacle of power, men (usually) operate quite informally and will do whatever they can get away with. This is a basic principle with few exceptions.

As anyone who has ever dealt with a bureaucracy knows they can be slow, erratic, stonily indifferent, and in general inefficient. Various reasons, usually subsumed under the term "bureaupathologies," have been adduced for this inefficiency and at times spectacularly inept performance. The sheer size of some bureaucracies renders them cumbersome. Toward the latter part of the Second World War, the U.S. Army ordered a command reveille for every single unit on the same day. Ideally, every single man was to be counted. The reason? The army did not know with a satisfactory degree of precision how many men were actually in the army. This was hardly surprising since the U.S. Army had grown from 200,000 men to more than eight million in only a few years.

Informal rules develop in any large organization. Often these rules enhance efficiency but often they do not. The security provided by bureaucratic positions can also mean that people are retained who are not effective in their job. It can come as no surprise that for those at the upper levels of a bureaucracy, their primary goal may not be the goals of the bureaucracy but rather the maintenance of the status quo which is beneficial to themselves. Bureaucracies for that reason and others can be slow to change and adapt. Paperwork, "red tape" which is so called because of the red ribbon that once bound government documents in England, can slow or entirely obstruct the workings of bureaucracy. Stalin often railed against "red tapists." The stately and eminently rule-bound Hapsburg bureaucracy sometimes required the submission of a "negative form." A negative form is a form stipulating that you do not need a form.

Bureaucracies develop their own traditions, which become familiar and are deeply valued. The structure of the Roman Catholic Church—the oldest bureaucracy in the world—is modeled after the administrative structures of Imperial Rome of late antiquity. Indeed the church administration existed for a time as a sort of doppelganger to the imperial administration and when the empire finally fell, the Church administration simply took over—at least at the local level. Bureaucracies are by definition rational structures but one can question the rationality of the goal. The Strategic Air Command was an intensely bureaucratic organization that sought to achieve Mutually Assured Destruction (MAD) which not all agreed was rational.

Social Stratification

Stratification is a geological term referring to the layering of rock strata. When set to the needs of sociology, it provides an analogy to the

Four. Social Organization and Stratification

distribution of human wealth, power and prestige. Social stratification is about **life chances**. It is about who gets more and who gets less. It is about who can shape the actions of others to their advantage. Allowing for a good deal of variation, there are three systems of social stratification: **caste, estate and class**.

Caste systems are about ritual purity. In the Indian caste system the several castes, more properly called **varnas**, are ranked from the most pure according to Hinduism to the least pure. By definition there is no individual mobility within a caste system and the varnas are entirely endogamous. You cannot marry outside your varna. The fact that one spouse would be polluting to the other renders exogamy (out-marriage) impossible.

Brahmins are, by virtue of their purity, at the top of the caste system and all other castes are polluting to them. Brahmins have a monopoly on sacred ritual. Even the most powerful in Indian society had to defer to religion and the ceremonial services of a Brahmin priest. Much of the life of a Brahmin male was devoted to the ritual preservation of this valuable commodity. All other castes were polluting in degree to the Brahmins.

Kshaytriya is the caste most closely associated with military and political power and it is the caste from which warriors, governors, and princes of the British Raj were drawn.

Vaisya is the caste of merchants and craftsmen. Much of the Indian economy derived from such people, some of whom achieved great wealth. But wealth did not bring any enhancement of status within a caste system which allowed no upward mobility.

Sudra caste members are chiefly peasant farmers and laborers and were the great majority of the Indian population.

De facto there is a fifth caste—that of the untouchables who are also known as **Harijans** or **Dalits**. Harijans, the term Gandhi used, were regarded as polluting in the extreme to all castes. Close proximity, much less the touch of a Harijan, was profoundly and dangerously polluting. Harijans performed the most polluting of tasks: they were tanners, emptied cesspools, cleaned the streets. The life of a Harijan was brutal and precarious. If she did not work, she did not eat, nor did her family. Demeaning and burdensome restrictions abounded. In some regions the shadow of a Harijan was polluting, and a Harijan could not enter public areas when the sun was low in the sky. One group of washer women was simply never to be seen. They had to do their work between midnight and dawn.

This simple taxonomy does not begin to unravel the complexity, past and present, of social stratification in India. In the first place, there are

An Introduction to Comparative Sociology

other religions in India besides Hinduism and all are allotted a position within the all-pervasive caste system. Just because you are Christian, it does not follow that you are not subject to the caste system. In point of fact, due to the Englishman's persnickety devotion to the niceties of social status, the advent of the British East India Company to Indian shores had the effect of enhancing the existing caste system, which was possibly the only facet of Indian society that they comprehended.

Additionally, each of the four varnas was broken down into sub-castes—better termed **jati**—which could be tribal groups but were usually occupational specialties. By traditional accounting there were once some 10,000 sub-castes found in India. The true number is unknown. Jati, as with varnas, are strictly endogamous and have been for a very long time. Hindu religious texts from the *Rig Vedas* (circa 1,200 BC) describe the caste system in detail; the veracity of this ancient description is supported by genetic studies. The work of David Reich and his laboratory, presented in Reich's *Who We Are and How We Got There* demonstrates that some jati have been endogamous for millennia.

A caste system is, nevertheless, not immutable. A change in caste position was possible *as a group*. **Sanskritization** is a tactic whereby a sub-caste would take on the rituals of a higher caste. Over time, this enhanced position would perhaps be accepted. It's not just about ritual purity; membership in a higher caste brings wealth, lands, and privilege. It has to be emphasized that the lines demarcating caste and sub-caste are patrolled by violence; beatings, murder and acid throwing are employed to keep out-of-status people "in their place." The stakes can be high. The use of a particular well by one group might, for example, render that well polluting to another group. It has proven impossible to maintain the status quo in an India that is urbanizing and industrializing. Harijans have successfully used the political system to enhance their status. Above all, the caste system is no longer legal, as would be expected in a country founded by Gandhi who loathed the caste system.

There are variations on the caste system. In particular many societies set apart some groups as outcast or pariah groups. The **Burkumin** in Japan were a group that was regarded as pariah because of its historical association with polluting occupations. Also referred to as Eta, they were set apart by settlement restrictions and sumptuary laws. Their touch was polluting. Such discriminations are no longer practiced; nevertheless, marriage to anyone whose ancestry lay in this group is thought to be undesirable.

Four. Social Organization and Stratification

Estate systems are a product of feudalism which organized society into three estates comprised of those who pray, those who fight, and those who labor. The first estate consisted of those who fight, the warriors. As with all things feudal, this was organized hierarchically. At the peak were the king and his warrior buddies at court. Arrayed beneath, according to title and land holdings, were dukes, barons, earls, and knights. Being a knight was only of middling aristocracy, men who frequently had only enough land and serfs to support a small entourage and a stable of highly trained and valuable horses. In French, Spanish and German the word for knight was horseman. Above the estates was God who reigned supreme in heaven over his celestial court. In theory this was a very orderly system but among these very acquisitive and bloodthirsty men the reality was violent and chaotic.

Those who prayed, the priesthood and Church hierarchy, ministered over all of this, clucked at the misbehavior of the king and nobles, and maintained the docility of those peasants who were insufficiently terrorized by the warrior aristocracy. As in India, the king depended on the Church for celestial approval. The Church attempted to mitigate the incessant violence in Europe by introducing the Truce of God and the Peace of God which institutionalized days when fighting was not permitted. The effect, if not the intention, of the Crusades was to siphon off large numbers of these violent men to places where, according to Church decree, they could kill people without the burden of sin.

Those who labored were by far the most numerous. Some were freemen but most were serfs who were tied to the land by law and who owed the lord of the manor free labor (corvee labor) to maintain his land and to harvest his crops. A serf was required to have his grain ground at the lord's mill—for a fee. A serf had to serve under the lord's banner when the king required the lord to join him in battle. Serfdom was not an enviable estate and it was bitterly resented. Peasant revolts were regarded by the aristocracy as teachable moments and were put down with memorable savagery.

The different estates were set apart by elaborate sumptuary laws. There were restrictions on fabrics, embroidery, precious metals, and weapons, including swords of "excessive length." The Tudors expressed particular concern that those of "mean estate" were displaying such excesses. It was important that the estates be set apart "by their apparel." In *The Court Society*, Norbert Elias discusses the incredibly refined etiquette and ceremony at the court of Louis XIV. It was utterly essential that the cosseted residents of Versailles master the manners of the court. Matters of dress and behavior were in Louis's view required to set apart the aristocracy from the baser orders of society. It was not just fashion; it was politics.

In no other system was proximity to power more important. One had to "court" the king's favor to succeed. One needed to "be seen" at court in the proper display of style and manners suitable to your rank—or the rank you wanted to gain. It wasn't mere dandyism that caused men to spend lavishly and sometimes go into debt to outshine their peers. In dazzling haberdashery men strutted about court like peacocks for quite rational reasons.

Estate systems did present some paths of mobility for the lower estate. Highly intelligent and literate peasants could rise within the Church hierarchy and serve in an administrative capacity at court. (Our word clerk derives from cleric.) And there were opportunities in the military for peasants who were adept at breaking heads. This avenue was characteristic of the curiously termed Bastard Feudalism in which the lord found it more expedient to hire trained mercenaries than endure the disruption of a feudal levy. Some mercenaries formed armies and got rich.

Any threat to the invulnerability of the armored knight was a threat to the entire feudal system. Crossbows, which could sometimes penetrate plate armor, were an annoyance but as early as the sixteenth-century guns were universally decried because even the dullest of peasants could be swiftly trained to shoot and kill a knight. This, plainly, was not part of God's plan. The Japanese dealt with this problem quite rationally by outlawing guns.

There were also merchants who lived in towns and cities. Their increasing numbers represented a budding middle class. Moreover, "city air" was free: if a serf could make his way to a city and reside there for a time, he was free, not a serf anymore.

Aspects of the estate system lingered for centuries. The landed aristocrat's right to the labor of *his* peasants was a despised feature of the *ancien régime* until the time of the French Revolution. There was also the entirely legal system of debt peonage in parts of South America. One way of reducing social stratification is to tax the movement of wealth across generations. On the other hand, one way of maintaining the social hierarchy is to transfer debt from one generation to the following generation. In parts of the Andes, if you lived on a hacienda and owed the land owner, the *hacendado,* money—and this was hard to avoid—you were tied to the land like a feudal serf. And like a feudal serf you owed the *hacendado* free labor. When you died, this debt and these obligations passed to your son. This practice persisted well into the twentieth century.

Class systems are characterized by social mobility—both up and down. The social classes may be thought of as loose groupings of people who stand in a similar relationship to power and wealth. Wealth enhances your "life chances." That is, wealth buys education, lawyers, access to powerful people, better medical care. Of course you can be born to great wealth and still be run over by a bus, but in the main, your path through life's chances will be eased by money. Then there are the good things that money can buy, the things that bring pleasure. I need not list them.

There is nothing more given to theoretical hair splitting than Marxist scholarship, but as a general statement Marx saw industrial society as consisting of four classes: the **aristocracy**, the **bourgeoisie**, the **proletariat**, and the *Lumpenproletariat*. Neither the aristocracy nor the *Lumpenproletariat* mattered in his scheme. The aristocracy, few in numbers, Marx dismissed as frivolous, parasitical, and incapable of anything useful to society. The *Lumpenproletariat* ("lumpen" meaning something like miscreant) was the down and out underclass, the dregs that could be easily manipulated.

The bourgeoisie were those who controlled the **means of production**, the sources of power (water and coal) and the factories that produced products. As a group, the bourgeoisie controlled the law and shaped it to their advantage. It is to the dynamic between the bourgeoisie and the proletariat that Marx's theory of economic determinism chiefly applies.

Those whose only resource was their capacity for labor comprised the proletariat. Their power to influence the political realm was nil because the law served only to keep them in their place within society. Even the prevailing economic theory of the time reinforced the inevitability of the laboring poor as revealed by the **Iron Law of Wages**. It was reasoned that if the working poor were to be paid better wages they would, as Malthus has told us, procreate to excess and the resulting increase in laborers would drive wages down to a bare subsistence level—or worse. There was a widespread and self-serving faith in the "Iron Law" justifying the great reservoir of half-starved laboring poor. In practice, the bourgeoisie and the landed gentry saw to it that the Iron Law held true. The poor laws established conditions so harrowing that only a person at death's door would willingly enter a work house. Such laws that were belatedly passed to control the conditions in factories offered little relief. And organized efforts to protest economic conditions were put down with much the same ferocity as the peasant revolts of centuries before.

An Introduction to Comparative Sociology

Roughly a generation after economists determined that the poor must always be with us, **Social Darwinists** revealed that it was the poor who were to be blamed for being poor. It was their fault. This revelation derived from a crude dumbing down of Darwin's theory of organic evolution, which prompted Marx to comment acidly on how accurately Darwin had applied the English social system to nature. Not long after the publication of *On the Origin of Species* in 1859 the Social Darwinists fastened onto the concept of "the survival of the fittest"—a phrase coined by a sociologist, Herbert Spencer—to declare that the best people in society by virtue of inheritance (their blood) would infallibly rise to the top of society. Such people were wise, moral, and industrious; whereas the poor were just the opposite by virtue of their inferior inheritance, otherwise they wouldn't be poor. The middle and upper classes embraced this crude pseudo-science and made best sellers of these racist tracts that popularized Social Darwinism. Alas and alack, they fretted, the "Great White Race" was being mongrelized. A highly influential book, *The Kallikak Family* (1912), purported to follow the ancestry from colonial times of a family that supposedly produced degenerate and feebleminded offspring generation after generation. Recent work has revealed this opus to be essentially a work of fiction.

Social Darwinism is a self-serving corruption of Darwin's theory. It totally ignores the constraints that society places on some and not others. How anyone could have failed to see that is hard to understand. Take the example of a child whose task was to lead the pit ponies that hauled coal from a mine. Such a child was wholly uneducated, ill nourished, and literally did not see the light of day for long periods. The Social Darwinists seem never to have asked a simple question: are we to blame that child for not somehow rising to be a captain of industry? This is not an extreme example. In England, the Mines and Collieries Act of 1842, initiated only after a mining accident drowned more than 20 children, documents the fact that this task was one of the least horrendous exploitations of children in the mining industry. The Horatio Alger stories of a "poor but honest boy" presented implausible plots of success to a believing upper and middle class (notice that a poor boy could not be assumed to be honest). The influence of social Darwinism is still very much with us today. It is soothing to those who have inherited great wealth, allowing them to look upon the poor with an air of superiority.

Toward the latter part of the nineteenth century, the assault on the poor became, by law, physical. This began with the work of Francis Galton, a

Four. Social Organization and Stratification

brilliant and somewhat loony cousin of Charles Darwin. A genuine polymath, Galton developed the regression line as a result of his studies of the leading families of England. He was discouraged by the fact that these great families "regressed toward mediocrity" after only a generation or so. Galton founded the study of **eugenics** (Greek for good stock), which argued that the "unfit" should be culled from the breeding population by means of sterilization. The disturbing consequence of the "eugenics mania," as Nancy Isenberg calls it in *White Trash*, is that a near majority of American states passed sterilization laws resulting in the sterilization of some 65,000 Americans. California sterilized the most, Virginia was second. The laws allowing this became the model for the racial laws of the Third Reich. This truly disturbing fact was unearthed by the defense counsel of various mass murderers and introduced as evidence at the Nuremberg trials.

The new "science" of intelligence testing sorted unfortunate people into the categories of imbecile and moron, providing the justification for many of these sterilizations. During the First World War, the military began widespread IQ testing and the results were not encouraging. The average (mean) soldier tested at the level of a moron. To many this was shocking. But to those who knew anything about the American education system in poor regions it was unsurprising. Many soldiers were illiterate. Some had never held a pencil before. Among other patterns, IQ testing also revealed that northern blacks did better, and a lot better, than southern whites. The obvious implications of this were largely ignored except by a few social scientists, among them Franz Boas, who flatly declared on this and other objective evidence that there was no difference in the intelligence of blacks and whites.

The English class system was characterized by sharp distinctions of dress, speech, education, and much else. Even physical appearance differed. Military records from the Victorian era indicate that the average height of an upper-class Englishman was over one inch taller than that of a lower-class Englishman. As all evidence would suggest that there was no absence of gene flow between the classes, the only reasonable explanation is nutrition. This would not have been the typical Victorian view. English eugenicists were chiefly concerned that the purity of the brave, intelligent, and highly moral upper class (a description never objectively assessed) was threatened by the base alloy of the lower classes.

In the United States the main concern was with race. Such concerns were widely popularized and widely accepted. Madison Grant's edifice to

An Introduction to Comparative Sociology

junk science, *The Passing of the Great Race* (1916), sent chills up the spine of "white Anglo-Saxon" America. Many states had laws prohibiting marriage between whites and blacks. Such laws were not declared unconstitutional until 1967 (*Loving v. Virginia*). Federal laws dramatically restricted immigration of "undesirable groups," which excluded whole categories of people by race and region.

The American class system was once laden with caste-like persecution of its black citizens. It is now hard to appreciate just how comprehensively blacks were once caged and denigrated by social restrictions. This happened more than once: During the Second World War a train carrying German prisoners was sidetracked to a southern town where the prisoners were fed at a local restaurant. The American soldiers guarding them were not fed, as they were black.

The persistence of the discriminatory system in southern states has long been a matter of legal design. Shortly after the Civil War, the **convict leasing system** passed into law throughout the South whereby those convicted of a crime could be leased out to a contractor to work in mines and plantations. Blacks convicted of petty crimes and vagrancy dominated this pool. This widespread and persistent practice was only cosmetically different from slave labor, which was its intent. The **Jim Crow laws**—named after a stage act played in blackface—placed all manner of restrictions on black life: voting rights were denied and black education crippled. The degree to which naked terror underwrote this system may be gauged by the fact that well over two thousand blacks were lynched between 1880 and 1960. The triviality of the purported offence for which the victims of lynching were murdered makes it clear that terrorization was the true purpose. Arthur Raper disclosed in the 1930s that there exists a strong inverse correlation between the frequency of lynching and the price of cotton. As cotton prices fell, the pace of lynching went up. It is not as simple as that. A much finer study (by county) demonstrates that in those counties dominated by cotton economics, lynching was most frequent just before the seasonal need for cheap labor.

Herbert Gans has written of the utility of poverty. He notes that it is the poor who do the dirty work in our society, the hard agricultural stoop work, and many other tasks for the barely survivable minimum wage. The poor he notes consume what others do not want and they buffer the cost of social change for the rest of us. The poor can be used as a scapegoat and they provide uplifting examples of deviance. They provide jobs for sociologists. It is an easy task for sociologists to elicit a litany of critical labels

Four. Social Organization and Stratification

for the lowest class, e.g., white trash. They are in some ways a commodity of disparagement. The poor will always be with us, it may be said, because we want them that way.

Individual status varies along a number of dimensions. Status—simply described as one's position in society—can be either **ascribed status** which is assigned by birth or **achieved status** which is earned. The Queen of England is an ascribed status. You may work as hard as you can and go to night school, but you are never going to be the Queen of England. An MD is earned; it is an achieved status. The Queen of England cannot be a physician unless she earns that degree. Class systems, in sharp contrast to caste systems, are weighted toward achieved status.

Wealth is always important. Great wealth brings power and influence but aside from that, it is the chief criterion to determine one's class. One can achieve great wealth but one may also be born to it. It is better to have "old money" than new money. Old money derives from wealth that has been in your family for generations. How your wealthy and beneficent ancestor acquired his money is unimportant (smuggling alcohol and selling opium have established many fortunes); it is only important that you have it. Status and the influence of others in the same position follow from this accident of birth. In *The Theory of the Leisure Class* (1899) Thorstein Veblen expanded on the fact that great wealth is displayed with an eye toward **conspicuous consumption** (a phrase usefully expanded to "the conspicuous consumption of fancy goods" by an archaeologist, Olaf Prufer). Fancy goods? A long list, but at a minimum we can include fine wines, horses (for among other things, fox hunting, an expensive sport), yachts, mansions, trophy wives of great beauty. There were also trophy husbands of aristocratic title but little money (Winston Churchill was the result of such an alliance). In China, a bride's status was enhanced by the allure of tiny feet, about which Chinese poets rhapsodized and for which generations of Chinese girls endured the cruelty of foot binding. The influence of Veblen's book was such that the very wealthy—with notable exceptions—became circumspect in their display of wealth. Indeed the wealthy are secretive as a group. They don't like prying eyes. We probably know more about tribes in the Amazon Basin than we do about the very wealthy.

Other displays of wealth and connection are more subtle: travel, languages, prestigious education at Ivy League universities or Oxbridge and their associated exclusive clubs. There are elite schools such as Eton and Harrow. These institutions provide an intensive boot camp for "young gentlemen." There one acquired on the basis of periodic beatings proficiency

An Introduction to Comparative Sociology

in both Greek and Latin. One also acquires "old school ties" (literally ties in one sense of that phrase) and knowledge of esoteric practices and games such as the Eton Wall Game that can be played only at a particular wall at Eton, which is the larger purpose of it. (The rules can be found on the internet; I defy you to understand them.) Mention of your prowess at the Eton Wall Game might serve you well in certain circles in England. And, of central importance, you make important connections with young men of your exclusive class when attending such exclusive (and expensive) schools.

Investigations of American communities have found general agreement as to what characteristics define social class. W. Lloyd Warner's study of "Yankee City" found that the community could be readily sorted by their informants into six classes: the upper upper class, the lower upper class, the upper middle class, the lower middle class, the upper lower class and, with a nod to Marx, the *Lumpenproletariat* of the lower lower class. Informants were quite vociferous in their denouncements of this latter group. Wealth and the source of wealth—whether, capital, salary, or wages—neighborhoods (including the location of your deceased ancestors in the local cemeteries), perceived morality, and that window into the soul of the American male, the condition of his lawn, were consistently factored into this assessment. These and other criteria are broadly applied, but Warner's system is probably too fine. More commonly the American class system is considered to consist of four classes: lower class, middle class, upper class and the elite who are possessed of great power and wealth.

Any social system, even the worker's paradise found in Marxist states, is maintained on the basis of structured inequality. The distribution of wealth in the United States provides an indication of the great disparity between who gets more and who gets less. There are various elaborations of this disparity, some even claiming precision. The trends and general pattern are plain. This country has always been enormously stratified. In the 1920s the bottom 90 percent controlled 20 percent of the wealth in this country. By the 1980s, with an assist from the New Deal, that percentage had risen to 30 percent. Today the top 1 percent controls a very large percentage of all the wealth in this country. Just how much wealth is hard to tabulate because of the ability of the very rich to hide their wealth. Beyond that, an accounting of dollars overlooks the great changes that have taken place. Due to the maldistribution of health care in this society, poverty puts you and your children at great hazard. During most of the

Four. Social Organization and Stratification

nineteenth century there was less disparity for the simple reason that, except for broken bones and gunshot wounds, American doctors often did more harm than good.

Presently the position of the middle class and the lower class is eroding due to automation, globalization, and corporate control over the legislative process. Additionally, because of the legalization of all but the most blatant levels of usury, student loan debt and credit card debt are burdensome to perhaps a majority of the young citizens of this country.

Globally, the structure of inequality presents an enormous, almost unfathomable, disparity. To be poor in a poor country is to live at the outer edge of starvation, to have no shelter—there are people who are born, live, and die on the streets of Indian cities—and to have no prospects of education for your children who will likely never throughout their lives see a physician. This is the condition of many people the worldwide.

Five

Economics: Symbolic Exchange, Technology, Wealth and Colonialism

We can for once resort to a dictionary definition: Webster's 2nd edition: "Economics ... a social science dealing with the production, distribution and consumption of commodities." Strictly true, but it has always been more than that.

In fact, it did not begin solely with commodities. It is useful to look deep into prehistory to examine the root behaviors of human society. Richard Klein writing in the *Dawn of Human Culture* discusses a discovery from 40,000 years ago in a cave located in Africa's Rift Valley. The cave, known as Enkapune Ya Muto (or Dawn Cave for those who do not speak Maasai), yielded hundreds of broken ostrich egg shells and 13 carefully fashioned egg shell beads about a quarter of an inch in diameter. Beads of similar antiquity are found at a number of sites along the South African coast and ivory beads are found at a number of sites in Europe. The burial site of Sungir, some 150 miles east of Moscow was found to contain upwards of 13,000 beads, probably strung in long strands, to decorate the clothing of the corpses of an adult male and two children. It too dates to this early period.

What is so important about this? What impressed Richard Klein is the fact that the shell beads found at Dawn Cave exactly resemble beads made by South African Bushmen of a type called **xharo**. This term refers to strings of shell beads and to the type of exchange by which xharo is given. Among contemporary Bushmen and especially in the recent past xharo exchanges were a means of obtaining long-term mutual support from the bands and families of xharo partners who, according to Polly Wiessner, "hold each other in their hearts." One's potential for support during hard times extends as far as one's xharo network which on average

Five. Economics

includes some 16 exchange partners. Some networks reach out to two hundred kilometers.

In the Trobriand Islands just off the east coast of New Guinea a pattern of interisland exchange between trading partners sends decorative armbands and necklaces from island to island along a ring of 18 small islands. Traveling in opposite directions these armbands and necklaces have been circling probably for centuries. This is famously called the **Kula Ring**; it was discovered when the ethnographer Bronislaw Malinowski was doing his field work a century ago and it is still circling today. These objects bring prestige to those who have them in their possession, but to retain such a prestigious object is to bring magical punishment. So it must soon be traded. It is the fear of malevolent magic that drives the Kula Ring. But it is important to understand that quite unmagical material goods of practical value also flow along the path taken by the Kula traders. So it is that useful commodities piggyback on the Kula Ring.

Among the Yanomamo, men from different villages exchange gifts at Feasts which are ostensibly to seal an alliance, but guests run the risk of a murderous ambush. On those occasions when the guests are left alive, useful commodities are traded, but men sometimes exchange identical things, such as a bow for a bow. The important thing is the pattern of reciprocity which links people together. Jumping into the supposedly rational modern world, I note that the Cleveland Indians once traded a third baseman for a third baseman. Perhaps it was considered important to maintain the strong trading relationship with the Texas Rangers. In short, economics is certainly about the production and exchange of commodities but it is about much more than that.

In a classic exercise in macrosociology, Gerhard Lenski has examined the impact of technology and economic systems on political structures and social stratification. Over the long sweep of history there have been four types of economies: **hunting and gathering, horticulture, agrarian**, and **industrial**. These selfsame economies may still be found today.

Among hunters and gatherers, who by definition produce no food (they do not farm or herd), there is little social stratification. Living in bands of 20 or 30 people small group dynamics prevail. People gain prestige and influence on the basis of prowess in hunting, trade, shamanism, and interpersonal skills. Disputes are often resolved by violence or by the simple device of moving away from disagreeable people.

Horticultural societies are based largely on food production by means of hoe agriculture to grow grains or root crops, thereby sustaining larger

An Introduction to Comparative Sociology

groups of people which we may, as a matter of convenience, call tribes. Farmers are sedentary but pastoralists are not. Tribes vary greatly in size but all are organized by kinship. Some lineages and clans have more status than others. Individual status and power largely derives from your kin group. Membership and control over societies and associations—such as the military societies of Plains Indians or, as among the Cheyenne, membership in a select civil organization, the Council of Forty-Four—bring prestige and power. Some men amass power by means of social connections deriving from the gifts they bestow upon others in the form of desirable goods such as shells, feathers and pigs. Such men who are experts at wielding compensatory power are called **Big Men** and are a common feature of tribal society in New Guinea. A limited degree of condign power is available to tribal leaders. And men with the capacity and inclination to violence gain respect, prestige, and status. This is conspicuous in violent societies. Land is held in **usufruct** which means that land is the property of the lineage or clan and *not* the individual. Under usufruct, land may not be alienated, a fact systematically ignored as the American frontier moved west.

Agrarian societies are based on plow agriculture and animal traction. Land holdings are owned by individuals and can be enormous, as in the plantation system of the American south or Roman *latifundia* a term meaning something like "great estate." Both systems relied heavily on the labor of slaves who were also property, **chattel**. Agrarian societies are highly organized and capable of producing vast surpluses. The profits in an agrarian society accrue partly to a still small middle class but in the main belong to the small upper class elite. Agrarian societies are enormously stratified and the elite have access to great power and vast wealth. Their status is protected by law, as is the case in all complex societies. Typically, the tiny aristocratic elite of such societies control over 50 percent of all wealth, goods and land: half of everything, or more. This was clearly the case within the *ancien régime* of France. Agrarian societies have a complex legal system, and punishment, often lethal, was the basis for stability. Wind and water power provided some of the energy in an agrarian system but the chief source of energy came from the labor of human beings (a quarter or more of the population of Rome may have been slaves) or draft animals. Trade and manufacturing by comparison to horticultural societies is greater by orders of magnitude. By any measure the least artistic Roman "monument," but one of the most telling, is Monte Testaccio which is an accumulation of broken amphorae, a remnant of the

Five. Economics

vast trade in olive oil required to sustain Rome during the period of the early Empire. Monte Testaccio is comprised entirely of pottery sherds, the remains of an estimated 80 million vessels. It is 120 feet high.

Industrial societies are much more complex and rely on fossil fuels as the principal source of energy. Because they are so productive, by orders of magnitude in comparison to agrarian societies, they are somewhat less stratified. This is so because the high productivity of industrial societies provides a much larger economic pie to be divided and because these complex economies required highly trained people with *skill monopolies* in order to function. This Marx did not foresee. His view of the proletariat derived from the horrifying and very dangerous working conditions endured by factory workers and miners in Britain during the early to mid-nineteenth century. While there is no evidence that Marx ever set foot inside a factory, his collaborator Friedrich Engels, certainly knew firsthand of the conditions in the factories of England. As a young man his father sent him on business to Manchester where it has been estimated that the average life span in the early nineteenth century was 17.

As productivity went up so, modestly, did wages. But it should not be supposed that the elite did not possess vast wealth. They did. One only has to think of the wealth (and power) of the menagerie of robber barons during the Gilded Age, as Mark Twain called it, or in the early twentieth century, or now. Nor must it be supposed that many people within industrial societies were not desperately poor. Some lived at a bare subsistence level. The gnawing photographs of New York City's underclass taken by Jacob Riis and published in *How the Other Half Lives* leave no doubt about the urban poor in industrial society.

Lenski's categories are not perfect. Some hunting and gathering societies live in an ecology so productive that they develop a high degree of social complexity. This is the case with the Indians who lived off the Northwest Coast fisheries. The Inca in South America did not have plow agriculture but their agricultural system was so well organized and so productive that it should be regarded as an agrarian society.

We now live in a postindustrial society wherein most people are paid for manipulating symbols during the course of research, communications, computers, and so forth. Manufacturing and primary production are more and more in the province of machinery.

Capitalism as we know it came about because of more efficient manufacturing, especially of cloth, increased trade, banking, and such financial esoterica as double-entry bookkeeping. Prior to rational accounting

An Introduction to Comparative Sociology

businessmen had only the crudest understanding of how much they were making—or losing—or where their money was going. Arabic numerals helped a lot; try balancing your checkbook with Roman numerals. Banking is vital to capitalism. The early Italian bankers did their business in the open on tables, *banca* in Italian. Such men pioneered the ability to guard, provide credit, and safely move money about. Curtail such activities and the economy will collapse, as it nearly did in 2008 when the deregulation bubble suddenly burst leaving the Secretary of Treasury literally on his knees before congressional leaders begging for federal loans (bailouts) to bolster failing businesses.

Capitalism is unquestionably the most effective of all economic systems with unrivaled ability to produce, distribute, and innovate. Its very success has imbued many a true believer's faith in its magical abilities. It is regarded as something *sui generis*; it is thought to be balanced, self-regulating, unerring, and infallible. Such is the cult-like reverence for capitalism that its regular and sometimes catastrophic failures are invariably ascribed by the faithful to "overregulation" or indeed to any regulation whatsoever. Efforts to curtail the accumulation of wealth, power and unbridled "animal spirits," in the words of the economist John Maynard Keynes, have been feeble and rare. Theodore Roosevelt broke up the monopolies when the entire U.S. economy was falling into the hands of only a few men. Franklin Roosevelt heretically pumped money into the economy and imposed regulations across the board after the Wall Street crash. Even today such cultists contend that had Roosevelt done nothing, the economy would have magically sprung back to prosperity in no time at all. Anyone who has a memory that goes back beyond 10 years knows that the virtues of deregulation are still with us. The economic institution has an impact on every aspect of society but it must be recognized that its investment in rationality is not as great as supposed.

Economic development entered firmly into the political and scholarly consciousness following World War II, especially as the post-colonial world approached. Why were poor "backward" nations not developing as they should? Why were they not like us? There were several explanations for why these undeveloped countries had not improved their economies. Daniel Chirot has characterized these get-well scenarios as the "liberal interpretation."

Economic development became a topic at major universities and a swift route to national prominence. A whiff of superior morality runs through these several perspectives which are generally similar in their

Five. Economics

view of development. Such "benighted" countries lacked a work ethic, an educated population, and the capital to invest. Democracy and stability were also part of the equation.

Those countries that had moved through the "stages" of development were supposedly rendered immune to the advertised utopias of communism. This naturally made such models politically attractive. That of Walt Rostow, an advisor to President Kennedy, was highly influential. It was in fact the economic strategy justifying our intervention in South Vietnam. As the United States government waited patiently for South Vietnam to pass through the expected stages, other models of economic development emerged. Dependency Theory and World System Theory explained under development very differently. Economic dependency and underdevelopment were seen as an *intended* part of colonial development.

World System Theory

In many respects the globalized world begins just after the end of the Middle Ages in 1452, the date of the fall of Constantinople to the Ottoman Empire. Immanuel Wallerstein in a massive multivolume historical study, *The Modern World System*, develops a model of the evolution of the global economy over the course of several centuries. It is complex and exceedingly detailed (if you are interested in seventeenth-century Polish grain prices, this is your book). But in bold outline the model is straightforward. Wallerstein discusses the emergence of three types of economies: **core states, peripheral states** and **semi-peripheral states**.

Core states developed huge manufacturing economies requiring ever increasing amounts of raw materials, which more and more had to be obtained from distant lands. The political and military elites of core nations began to acquire such distant lands by means of economic interpenetration or military conquest. As anciently, these conquests were motivated by a desire for loot in the form of precious metals and furs. Later, as colonial control was established such commodities as cotton and indigo were produced to feed England's weaving industry. There was also a thirst for other profitable commodities such as sugar, tea, coffee, and opium, none of which could be grown locally. Slaves can be added to this list of commodities as **chattel slavery** reduces human beings to the status of being just another form of commodity. In the antebellum South slaves were bought, sold, and used as collateral for loans. A source of great profit was the production of highly addicting substances such as tobacco and opium, which had the advantage of creating an ever-expanding market as addiction spread. The British fought two wars against the Chinese in order to expand the use of opium, which the British insisted was a healthful and efficacious substance. The opium trade was (and is) extraordinarily profitable.

The economy and infrastructure of colonized regions developed primarily to produce and ship raw materials to core countries, there to be transformed into manufactured goods and sold back to people in the colonized periphery. Colonies provided both raw materials and markets. For the colonized countries this lopsided arrangement was a distortion of what would be expected in the course of unfettered economic development. By design the economy of these colonies did not expand, innovate, or modernize. According to what is called **dependency theory**, such colonies were prevented from doing so. It should not be forgotten that the entire Indian subcontinent was at one time ruled either directly or indirectly by a British company: the East India Company.

Spain, unlike other core societies, stagnated. This resulted from a succession of feckless leaders, a series of hugely expensive wars, and the ossification of Spanish society at the hands of the Spanish Inquisition. An institution of inflexible piety and considerable lethality, the Spanish Inquisition pursued religious purity (*limpieza de sangre*) by guarding Spanish borders with hermeneutic vigilance—expelling Jews and Muslims who were consistently the most innovative and productive people in Spanish society. Predictably, Spain sank into the category of a semi-peripheral state. Other societies were to follow.

The British who were then the leading colonial power had colonies throughout the globe and it was said, quite accurately, that "the sun never set on the British Empire." By the end of the nineteenth century, Europeans of various nationalities had colonized Africa and nearly all of Asia. Those few countries that were not colonized lay between opposing empires, for example, Thailand and Persia. Every bit of the African continent was colonized, the majority of it during a stupendous multinational land grab in the latter part of the nineteenth century. Conditions were often indescribably brutal. Joseph Conrad's *Heart of Darkness* accurately portrays conditions in the Belgian Congo. Nevertheless there were a few critics of empire. Mark Twain was one. Another was John A. Hobson who as a reporter and economist was appalled by colonial aggression and the Boer War which he witnessed firsthand.

Five. Economics

Hobson became an incisive critic of colonialism. He saw imperialism as unalloyed economic exploitation justified by Social Darwinism and supposed moral superiority. The "white man's burden," as Kipling would have it, really consisted of weighty bags of gold. Hobson saw that any supposed advance of civilization brought about by colonialism was minimal, or nonexistent, and in all cases a delusional cover for economic aggression. In *Imperialism, A Study*, Hobson decried the rise of what he saw as **racial imperialism** by races of the highest "social efficiency" (a term much in vogue among Social Darwinists) against the so-called "lower races." Hobson understood, as few did at the time, that the social sciences were then fast in the grasp of that most catastrophic of all junk sciences: racism. He did not believe in "lower races." He believed that colonized peoples were being exploited.

Hobson regarded the driving force of imperial conquest to be the close cooperation of the military and industry or, more to the point, the elite who benefited from that alliance. He saw this world situation as dangerously volatile, a circumstance that would lead to a conflict between imperialistic powers.

Drawing upon Hobson, Vladimir Ilyich Lenin, writing two years into the First World War explained the cause of the conflict to be the rise of oligarchical finance and monopolistic capitalism within competing Imperial powers. So in part it may have been, but few things have been more closely examined by historians than the causes of the First World War. There were many contributing causes and all the usual suspects were in play: nationalistic hatreds and past grievances, stupidity on the part of military and political leaders, carefully nurtured jingoism, cowardly and indecisive leaders, and the moronic view that military struggle improved the "race."

Besides killing upward of 10 million people, World War I realigned the world dramatically. Czarist Russia was taken over by Bolshevism and the Austro-Hungarian Empire vanished leaving only the rump state of Austria. Germany was shorn of land and all of its colonies. Italy was dramatically weakened. From the standpoint of World System Theory it may be said that these weakened states had become part of the semi-periphery.

The economist John Maynard Keynes considered the Treaty of Versailles to be a catastrophe. In *The Economic Consequences of Peace*, written shortly after the signing of the treaty, Keynes explained in detail how the enormous reparations demanded would unravel the German economy and cause immense suffering. Nationalism in its most aggrieved form would rise and the potential for conflict would become overwhelming. It's all there: the course of events leading up to the Second World War.

"History doesn't repeat itself, but it does rhyme," said Mark Twain. I take this to mean that history unfolds along a broad channel set by social forces. There are, to be sure, outliers. Not even Keynes could have predicted that Germany would fall into the thrall of a delusional, egomaniacal mass murderer like Adolf Hitler.

It is interesting to impose the perspective of World System Theory on more recent events. The Second World War was, in addition to the Soviet Union, fought by core countries; the United States, Britain, France (the Allies), who fought against the Axis Powers, Germany, Japan, and Italy, countries that fit the category of semi-peripheral. On one matter at least we can take the word of the leaders of the Axis powers: they went to war over land and resources.

During the Second World War, the hobgoblins of nineteenth-century economic and racial imperialism emerged once again and with unimaginable virulence. In the *Taste of War* Lizzie Collingham describes the policy, officially titled the Hunger Plan, by which the Third Reich planned to starve to death 30 million people. It was only because the course of events on the Eastern Front did not go as expected that the Hunger Plan was not fully implemented. As it was, the Soviet Union suffered well over 25 million deaths from all causes. Resources and land were confiscated on a gigantic scale. Entire races were deemed by junk science, raised to the level of a national cult, to be inferior. Such people, deemed to be *Untermenschen* by the cult leaders of this junk science, were massacred on an industrial scale in factories designed to murder and cremate 10,000 people a day. China lost an estimated 27 million at the hands of the Japanese. Sixty million people died during the Second World War; the majority starved to death.

Six

Strategies of Political Control

Nation states maintain a monopoly on violence and therefore the means to violence are strictly controlled. The United States is unusual in that firearms are available to even its most demented citizens. But a citizen may not purchase a fully automatic weapon, except under strict license, and tanks, cannons, flamethrowers and other weapons are strictly forbidden. During calm times a state rests upon its authority to use condign punishment, as symbolized by the Roman *fasces*. This imposing symbol is now found behind the podium in the House of Representatives, among other places. But in times of unrest, violence will be met by the greater capacity of state violence. During the war in Vietnam two brigades of the 82nd Airborne—professional, enthusiastic and armed to the teeth—were maintained at home as a national constabulary. The National Guard in its historical role of strike breaking and controlling minority unrest was deemed too undisciplined and untrustworthy to be used in extremis.

The more threatened and inefficient a regime is, the more it will resort to naked violence. The USSR presented such a state, as did China. The contemporary world scene provides many more examples. Many regimes find it expedient to conjure up a threat as justification for unbridled state violence. In Africa, drought, famine, unrest, and state violence are closely linked; so much so that the Pentagon regards global warming as a major threat to security.

Politics is about forming coalitions and just who may, or may not, enter into a coalition. *Kratos* is the Greek word for power and has been compounded into terms denoting the extent of coalitional power: **monarchy, aristocracy, oligarchy, plutocracy,** and **democracy** (including parliamentary democracy with a constitutional monarch). With some archness **kleptocracy** has gained currency. **Dictator** is the Roman term for a man who was granted absolute power during a crisis. Now it refers to a man who arrogates onto himself absolute power without legal authority. In descending order: A monarch is concerned chiefly with his or her immediate family and those who provide him with military power and the means to enforce taxation. Septimus Severus, a second-century Roman emperor, advised his sons "to enrich the soldiers, and scorn all other men." Aristocracies depend on a wider coalitional power among nobles. Plutocrats, by virtue of wealth and position, retain a closed circle of coalitional power. Oligarchy means "rule by the few." Democracy affords the potential for most, but not all, citizens to support or enter into a political coalition.

C. Wright Mills wrote of the **power elite** by which he meant a coalition of business leaders, generals and admirals, leading politicians and the very wealthy who, in combination, have come to dominate American society. President Eisenhower's last speech warned about the power and cost of the **military-industrial complex**. Since in this country wealth buys power the ability of what amounts to an oligarchical coalition to shape domestic power is enormous. The ability to shape public perception by the powerful in any system should not be underestimated. It would be difficult to imagine a more drab, lackluster personality than that of Joseph Stalin, but within a few years of taking power in the Soviet Union his status has been described as "only technically short of deification." He had not changed; he was the same plodding cutthroat he had always been. The new, public Stalin—"Great Stalin" the "Engineer of the Locomotive of history"—had been created by the publicity organs of the USSR.

Wealth and Power

Money talks. That is, it buys communication; it teaches and spreads ideas; it elects malleable politicians; it ridicules and slanders people and ideas. In short, money greatly enables the application of conditioned power. This potential is magnified in societies characterized by an enormous disparity in wealth—such as ours. When the Supreme Court ruled in favor of the suit brought by *Citizens United v. FEC*, it abrogated at a stroke the limitations on campaign spending enforced by the FEC and released a geyser of money into American politics. By various avenues—direct contributions, Political Action Committees (PACS), and unsourced money ("dark money"), and a legion of well-funded lobbyists—corporate and individual wealth holds in its grasp the gift most desired by politicians, reelection.

Six. Strategies of Political Control

Retreat from Modernity

One of the consequences of modernization is that it leaves some people behind; it threatens to undercut their way of life and destroy what they hold dear. A common refrain in Third World countries is "things fall apart." The modern world disgusts and frightens them. One response is to hold the new world at bay, to retreat from it and cling to the fundamentals of an imagined, godlier world of the past. Often this world is revealed to the faithful by a literal interpretation of sacred texts.

Another response is to engage the modern world in order to shape the modern world according to the values of the faithful. This is a prominent feature of our national politics. Birth control, abortion, women's liberation are presented as threats to family values. As no rational politician would be against family values, it is an effective way of **framing** (the sociological term for "spin") the fundamentalists' political agenda. Secular humanism is regarded as a threat to Christianity and satanic in its origins. It is considered to be a separate religion that supposedly espouses everything they dislike and fear. Much of the fundamentalist agenda has been installed into law. Abortion is hard to obtain and dangerous to provide in many states. Birth control is likewise under constant attack. A signal success is the failed ratification of the equal rights amendment to the Constitution.

Fundamentalism is a global phenomenon. Religions have always engaged in violent clashes and the modern world continues this ruthless tradition. Ironically, the modern world provides the means of spreading the godly path of righteous fundamentalism. If the Protestant Reformation was spread by the printed word, the Internet is the chief means by which religious orthodoxy and political and military goals of a theocratic caliphate are furthered.

Racism, Ethnicity and Xenophobia

The genetic diversity found in the human species is remarkably small and most of this diversity is found within populations, not between them. That should have put the issue of racism to rest. But, of course, it has not. Racism is much too valuable politically and economically. Marvin Harris has noted that wherever you find mono-cropping—the growing of a single commercial crop, cotton for example—there you will find slavery. When slavery is profitable, or perceived to be, those groups enslaved are defined as biologically distinct, uncivilized, inferior, and at the mercy of animal passions. Such was the strength of this self-serving perception that there was widespread acceptance of a bizarre tidbit of medical folly which argued in clinical jargon that runaway slaves did so because of a disease, "drapetomania," that caused the sufferer to run away—to the North. This affliction magically disappeared after the Civil War. But, as noted, slavery was seamlessly replaced by the convict leasing program. Racism remains deep seated and politically useful. One little sidebar to Martin Luther King, Jr's march on Washington, and the occasion for his "I Have a Dream" speech, is that a great many whites fled that only recently desegregated city. "Not since the Battle of Bull Run have so many evacuated Washington," chortled one contemporary account. Lyndon Johnson, riding through Tennessee with the columnist Bill Moyer, passed a group of women holding up racist signs, prompting Johnson to quip, "I'll tell you what's at the bottom of it. If you can convince the lowest white man that he's better than the best colored man, he won't notice you're picking his pocket."

White supremacy is blossoming in cyberspace where it propagandizes for white supremacy and celebrates conspiracy theories. And, like ISIS, it recruits murderers. You need only browse a few of the many such sites to understand that what Lyndon Johnson said remains true today. It was certainly not lost on Richard Nixon when he embarked on his "southern strategy" which drew upon these sentiments. No one now says, "We must control minorities." What is said is "We must have law and order." "Dog whistle politics" nicely describes this well-funded tactic. Racism in combination with **xenophobia** (Greek for stranger fearing) in its most current form, **Islamophobia**, also attracts a large pool of voters.

Ethnicity

Ethnocentrism and the "us versus them" perspective of one's social surroundings is a fundamental part of the social world. Groups of like-mindedness develop; people of common background, whether real or imagined, group together as do those of similar language and culture. Some of these communities have ancient ties of religion and origin. Most are of recent origin. Ethnic groups have always been a major factor in politics. This is increasingly so in the modern world. Much of this is the result of the **mythogenesis** of national origins at the hands of nineteenth-century historians and linguists. This scholarship, which was either incompetent

Six. Strategies of Political Control

or tendentious, conflated race and ethnicity. Much of this folly can be laid at the feet of physical anthropology during its romantic head-measuring phase. Churchill referred more than once to the "American race." Who knows what he meant by that phrase? The French aristocrats of the *ancien régime* were pleased to claim descent from the Frankish kings of the early Middle Ages but, by contrast, the peasants they lorded over were regarded as the descendants of unwashed, pig farming Gauls who were conquered by Caesar.

According to Patrick Geary in his *Myth of Nations*, historians worked hand in glove with politicians, linguists, and archaeologists in the manufacture of "imagined communities." *Germania*, written by the first-century AD Roman historian Cornelius Tacitus, who never got near what is now Germany, has exerted a great influence on German nationalism. Any connection between modern Germans and the people that Tacitus wrote about is impossibly remote.

Improbable heroes are celebrated as paragons of budding nationalities. Arminius, a strongman who massacred three Roman legions in the Teutoburg Forest of northern Germany in 9 CE, was a great favorite of the German Kaiser. He erected a 110-foot-tall statue of Arminius ("Herman" to the Kaiser) who now waves a 21-foot-long sword at France. Napoleon III placed a statue of the Gallic chief Vercingetorix on the site of an ancient battlefield. Vercingetorix, a great favorite of "Celtomaniacs," is revered in film, novels, and even in the comic "*Astorix*," which, by the way, may be read in Gaelic. On a plane of genuine depravity, Horst Wessel, a notorious SA (storm trooper), thug and petty criminal was raised to glorious martyrdom by Joseph Goebbels, the Nazi minister of propaganda. Horst Wessel was shot and killed during a brawl and a bloodstained Nazi flag found in the aftermath became a relic, sacred to the party. "The Horst Wessel Lied" (song) became a Nazi anthem and was obligatorily sung at party gatherings.

Somewhere stashed away in many history departments are large maps, dusty and forgotten, showing with sweeping arrows the routes supposedly taken by the "tribes" of the Invasion Period of the late Roman Empire and early Middle Ages. These arrows are variously labeled: Goths, Vandals, Alemanni, Germanni, Franks, Celts, Huns, and Avars, without in any way exhausting the list of "barbaric tribes." These "tribes" are said to have wandered for centuries unchanged in social organization and with innate cultural characteristics romantically described as a "folk soul" (*Volksseele* in German). The Goths were believed to have arisen in Scandinavia, wandered about, culturally and linguistically unaltered, only to have crossed the Danube into the Roman Empire centuries later. This is not history; it is ethnic taxidermy. Ethnic groups are quite fluid and transitory. They always change. It is the unbridled romanticism of nineteenth-century historians that led them to depict these ancient groups as culturally immutable, to live on, unchanging, like so many stuffed squirrels. No one today has any objective idea of what a Folk Soul could possibly be apart from an expression of mystical properties. This did not prevent the Nazis from making good use of racially charged junk science upon which the regime was founded.

Geary emphasizes that modern historians see the genesis of these "wandering tribes" as analogous to the rise of the Zulu, who were also depicted by missionary historians as wandering in the wilderness much after the manner of the biblical Exodus. A closer reading of Zulu history argues that they developed from indigenous groups, as in all probability did the "tribes" of ancient Europe. These "tribes" are better thought of as opportunistic warbands. They often had a kin-based core, but these warbands were host to all sorts of rootless clans and individuals who glommed on in droves to the warband in hopes of a more secure life. Motivation for gate-crashing the Roman Empire was two-fold: they wanted to get a piece of the Roman good life, and because they were being chased by people more horrible than they were.

In the nineteenth century such groups were used as the basis for **charter myths** by the emerging nations of Europe. These nationalistic enterprises forcefully promoted a standard national language at the expense of local dialects and languages—e.g., Gaelic, Basque, Catalan, Sioux—and, as Antonio Gramsci has told us, with the intention of swamping minority identities. Graham Robb's *The Discovery of France* reveals just how partitioned France was by dialect and minority and how little nationalized much of France was well into the nineteenth century, if not the early twentieth century. It was no different in other regions and nations. Children were schooled in the mystical qualities of the charter tribes and folk heroes. Geary regards this tactic as not only a product of junk science but as politically "toxic." During the nineteenth and twentieth centuries the already blurred line between ethnicity and race was eradicated by political leaders in wars of conquest by one pseudo-race of mystically superior qualities against other pseudo-races of diminished qualities—as in "untermenschen." Thus did "toxic" junk science enable the death of many millions during the Second World War.

Six. Strategies of Political Control

It would be foolish and dangerous to believe that we have left all this behind. A conservative and floridly nationalistic politician, Jean Marie Le Pen has harkened back to the Franks and called from the hustings to "the French people born with the baptism of Clovis in 498, who have carried the inextinguishable flame, which is the soul of the people, for almost one thousand five hundred years." This is only one such recent manipulation of imaginary mystical charters and xenophobia.

In this century ethnic minorities are asserting their rights to recognition and political control. Calls for independence, or a degree of independence, come from Scotland, Brittany, the Basque Pyrenees, Catalonia, and Wales. Ancient traditions are clung to and disappearing languages are being revived in schools and broadcast over the airways. Taking one example, Scotland has always invested emotionally in the novels of Sir Walter Scott (as did the gallants of the Confederacy) and the national costume of kilt, sporran, bonnet, and clan tartan. Symbols are important. The Stone of Scone (also called the Stone of Destiny), a symbol of Scottish Identity was stolen from the Scots by Edward I in 1296 and incorporated into the Coronation Chair in Westminster Abbey. There it graced the bottoms of six centuries of English monarchs. In 1996 Scotland demanded its return and with great ceremony it was transported to Edinburgh. Amazingly, the film *Brave Heart* had a galvanizing effect on the cause of Scottish nationalism. In an action that calls to mind the classic headline in the London *Times*, "Fog Isolates Continent," the English have voted to separate from the European Union and its annoying foreigners. This crass manipulation of xenophobia may be costly. The Scots, soon to be separated from trading partners, are now contemplating leaving the English. Just how fragmented the map of Europe will become and how violently achieved is anybody's guess.

It is quite correct to view politics as the rational pursuit of self-interest through the formation of coalitions. This is how power is parceled out in the nation-state. It may be narrowly constrained and held by only a few, or it may be open to the majority who call themselves citizens. This is the rational-legal world that Max Weber envisioned, a world sadly scrubbed by modernity of its enchantments. But there is the other deep-seated part of politics that is mystical and magical in its nature and in the control of those who shape those myths. Weber did not like the **iron cage** of the rational-legal world but the student of sociology must wonder what Weber's thoughts would be if he knew just how dangerously enchanted the world has become.

Seven

Demography

Demography (*demo*s, Greek for "people") is the study of population. Doubtless the first demographers were ancient kings. Their interest in their subjects was not scholarly; they wanted to tax them and conscript them into the army. Such concerns have persisted to the present day. The Romans had a particular magistrate, the censor, charged with collecting data on the population within the Empire—the census. After a decade or so of pillage, William the Conqueror, directed his agents to determine what was left. This work resulted, as noted, in the *Domesday Book*. Additional manuscripts contain some of the raw data upon which the *Domesday Book* was based, providing evidence of just how thorough William the Conqueror's agents were.

The modern science of demography begins with the work of John Graunt who studied the Bills of Mortality, a record of deaths in each of London's parishes. These provided a revealing look at the health of an urban population in the mid-seventeenth century. London of that time is a fascinating subject to read about but you would not have wanted to live there. People died from all sorts of diseases and they usually died young.

A major concern of these parish tabulations was the onset of bubonic plague which would have initiated certain preventative measures, none of which worked, save flight. But Graunt's interests went far beyond that. He recorded all manner of facts about London's population: age of death, the mortality of men versus women, and so forth. His data on the mortality rates at different ages, when graphed out by later scholars into survivorship curves, trace a U-shaped pattern. Very high mortality rates for infants and young children are succeeded by a reduction of mortality for young adults and then the mortality rate climbs dramatically. Few Londoners lived out their biblical three score and 10. In a pioneering speculation about the potential for population growth Graunt suggested that if the population of the earth had doubled every 64 years since Adam and Eve there would be "far more people that are now in it." Not being familiar

Seven. Demography

with exponential numbers, Graunt would have been surprised. It is something like 2 to the 87th power.

Thomas Malthus, an Anglican minister, explored the forces shaping population growth in his *An Essay of the Principle of Population* (1798) in which he argued that population potentially increases "geometrically" (exponentially), whereas the resources to sustain life increase only arithmetically. Accordingly, population outgrows its subsistence base, bringing on the Four Horsemen of the Apocalypse: famine, disease, war and death. The horsemen fell most heavily on the poor. In a world where famine, plague, and warfare were regular occurrences this was nothing new. But Malthus's work put this global process into a clear model that was highly influential. It was a corner stone of Darwin's theory of evolution.

Malthus was a trained theologian and in holy orders, so it should not surprise us that a whiff of morality runs through his writing. He saw the enthusiastic fertility of the poor as a prime cause of the Malthusian trap. He recommended celibacy and late marriage. (After the horrendous experience of the Irish Potato Famine the surviving countrymen did in fact turn to primogeniture and late marriage. Or they went to America.) Nor did Malthus approve of birth control which was strongly associated with the French. His other recommendations such as improved agricultural practices did not involve improbable levels of self-control.

Malthus's image of the unfailing presence of the starving poor influenced the leading economist of the nineteenth century, David Ricardo, whose notions earned for economics the tag of the "dismal science." Ricardo's Iron Law of Wages also rests upon the Malthusian model.

Demography provides an objective view of the condition of society, showing as it does mortality, migration, health and social stratification. Sometimes this clear-eyed view is not welcome. Not long after the Soviet Union had endured the devastations of collectivization, famine in the Ukraine, and the purges, Stalin, the architect of these upheavals, ordered a census. A thoroughly professional study exposed the fact that the population of the Soviet Union had dropped by several million. Stalin, against all logic, had expected a healthy increase in population. The chief demographer was promptly shot and a wiser demographer appointed. The missing millions were soon found.

Better data on population, and more importantly long-term data, have modified the views of demographers and fostered controversy. There are the New Malthusians and the Anti-Malthusians. The New Malthusians look at the pace of population increases—seven billion and counting—and see the prospect of a calamitous collapse. Their views should not be cavalierly dismissed. The history of this and past centuries shows that famines are a regular occurrence. But these disasters are localized. And they are always, to some degree, man-made. The Irish Potato Famine followed the destruction of that blighted crop but it would have been greatly mitigated had not the British stood by with folded arms. Inaction by the British and the diversion of wartime shipping exacerbated the Bengal famine of 1943. It was, as noted, the express German policy to starve to death 30 million people on the Eastern Front by means of the aptly named Hunger Plan which calculated nutritional needs down to the last calorie and gram of fat. It was only because the fortunes of the Third Reich did not go as expected that the Hunger Plan was not fully implemented. Laying siege to a city is an age-old practice and during the Middle Ages was subject to formal rules. Starvation has long been a weapon of war and until the development of nuclear weapons, by far the deadliest. The New Malthusians see population growth as driving much of this and project even greater famines—man-made or "natural"—in the future.

The Anti-Malthusians also have data on their side. On the basis of a study of long-term population patterns in Europe, pioneered by Warren Thompson in 1929, the Anti-Malthusians have emphasized a future in which a **demographic transition** is in play. Graphing the balance of fertility rates and mortality rates plots a path wherein the slow pace of population growth was dramatically accelerated during industrialization. Toward the middle part of the twentieth century population stabilized—in Europe at least.

In other words a period of high birth rates and high mortality rates (i.e., a lot of people die young) is followed by a period when the birth rate remains high but the mortality rate declines due to relatively effective medical care. Population therefore rises dramatically. Toward the middle of the twentieth century urbanization and widespread birth control brought about a leveling off of population growth, albeit at a much higher plateau. In some countries there was a slight drop in population. Consequently, in those countries that have gone through the demographic transition, low birth rates are balanced by low mortality rates.

The assumption here is that the demands and complexities of urban, industrialized society encourage couples to use birth control to limit the size of families. The problem is that gathering information on such private matters is not easy. All the same, a study of family fertility in the city of Bueno Aires conducted by Aaron Cicourel has demonstrated that

Seven. Demography

Argentine families, *regardless of social class*, were knowledgeable about contraception techniques and made use of them to limit the size of their families. This was despite their frequent insistence that they did not use contraception. The demands of urban life and the expense of children were frequently cited as the reason for limiting the number of children.

Just how these conflicting views of the New Malthusians and the Anti-Malthusians will play out in the long term cannot be known. We'll have to wait. The speedy pace of population growth does seem to be slowing worldwide, not only because of the demographic transition but also because of the increasing use of birth control in poor nations. This is linked to the education of women. However, for many people large families are an asset because children are a source of labor and security. At present there are many countries where the average age is under 18. And, of course, many people do not support birth control on religious grounds.

And there are pro-natal programs. In times past and present, cannon fodder is regarded as coin of the military realm. Following the First World War, after France had lost well more than a million men and the French population was falling below that of Germany, the French government initiated a pro-natal policy. By means of bill boards, public announcements, and financial inducement, Frenchmen were encouraged to do their patriotic duty and rectify the shortfall. Hitler, concerned that there were too few "Aryans," also encouraged patriotic reproduction. Romania, under the dictator Ceaușescu, once pursued an appalling pro-natal policy. Presumably this was to enhance the pool of conscripts. By official mandate all women of childbearing age had to undergo a periodic gynecological examination and, if found to be pregnant, subsequent proof either of miscarriage or childbirth had to be provided. This remarkably intrusive policy ended with the death of Mr. Ceaușescu, which graced the fall of communism in Romania. Tradition and state policy sometimes combine to bring unforeseen results. When the population pressure threatened to literally eat up whatever progress China had made, Chinese authorities implemented and stringently enforced a policy of limiting couples to one child only. Boys are esteemed in China, girls are not. Sonograms revealing the sex of the fetus to be female often brought an abortion. As in India, the abortion clinic might be conveniently located next door. Little girls are frequently put up for adoption to foreign couples. In time, predictably, the sex ratio in China tilted such that there are now many more males than females: 121 males to 100 females, a ratio that compares with some tribal societies practicing female infanticide. The increase in the number

An Introduction to Comparative Sociology

of young unmarried males—unavoidable because of the paucity of young women—has led to a large number of Chinese men who are unhappy with their lot in life. This unhappiness is often expressed in ways that are troublesome to Chinese authorities.

Population pyramids are expressive of the shape of society. They are essentially bar graphs laid on their side and stacked up vertically to show the frequency of ages, wealth, education, and so on within a population. As an extreme example, the population pyramid of the *ancien régime* of France looks fittingly rather like the Eifel Tower. Upon a broad base representing the overwhelmingly numerous poor we see above them the relatively sparse number in the middle class, and way up at the tippy top there is the .25 percent of the French population who were aristocrats. This group owned more than half of France and paid no taxes. Had such a population pyramid been available in the mid-eighteenth century, our hypothetical proto-sociologist need not have ruminated long to decipher what lay in the future.

An **age cohort**, a group of people born during the same relatively narrow span of time, provides an incisive way of looking at the impact of social forces on the individuals within that group. Peter Lowenberg examined a cohort of men born in Germany between 1900 and 1915, men who would have been too young to have served in World War I but would have suffered the privations brought about by the war. For a child, wartime conditions were brutal; there was protracted and severe famine, and the absence of a father who, if he survived to return, was often shattered by his experiences. After the war Germany underwent hyperinflation which bankrupted millions and effected the disorderliness of Weimar Germany. Many missed the monarchy—if not the Kaiser. Lowenberg found that the SA (the storm troopers), the SS, and Hitler Youth attracted large numbers of the men in this cohort. By the prescience of a sociologist, Theodore Abel, Lowenberg had another body of evidence to analyze. Abel offered a cash prize for the best autobiographical essay from a member of the Hitler movement. By l934 hundreds had responded. The great majority wrote of starvation, the absence of a father and the bitterness of defeat. With few exceptions Hitler was clearly a father figure. It places a heavy burden on collective psychology to say that this was the only reason for Hitler's rise to power but it does seem to have played a part in that tragedy.

Demography is a highly mathematical discipline but the basic calculations are straightforward: the crude birth rate is the number of live births per thousand; the crude death rate is the number of deaths per thousand;

Seven. Demography

rate of natural increase is derived by subtracting the crude death rate from the crude birth rate. The rate of natural increase can be a negative number, another unwelcome truth. Nations spend lavishly on the task of amassing and analyzing demographic data because it reveals the condition of society and allows leaders to anticipate problems.

Eight

Urbanism

In *Urbanism as a Way of Life* Louis Wirth defined a city as a "relatively large, dense, and permanent settlement of heterogeneous individuals." Such large, dense, and heterogeneous settlements are the products of the post-glacial world. Just what prompted this fundamental change in the way human beings live is unclear but the beginnings of food production, particularly domesticated grains, was a contributing factor. Modest population growth is likely another.

The first urban settlement, Çatal Höyük, is found on the Plain of Konya in Turkey. Çatal Höyük appears abruptly on the archaeological horizon as early as 7,500 BC and was inhabited for over two millennia. According to Ian Hodder, the chief archaeologist for this World Heritage site, Çatal Höyük was founded when separate bands joined in a common settlement. Many cities began this way. The ancient Greeks referred to this process as *synoikismoi*, meaning "a gathering together." The Athenians remembered their city as having this origin.

Çatal Höyük was a dense cluster of mud brick buildings, constructed cheek to jowl. In its heyday Çatal Höyük may have had a population of several thousand and likely resembled a Hopi pueblo; people entered their houses through the roof. It was assuredly large and dense but, it does not seem to have been very heterogeneous; nor is there evidence of a central ceremonial center dominated by an elite. Perhaps there was no elite. This is unlike later cities which are typically clustered close about the architecture of power displayed in political and religious centers. As with all cities, Çatal Höyük exerted its influence over the surrounding countryside and maintained extensive trade connections. Genetics and the evidence of pottery show that Çatal Höyük hived off of its excess population into southeastern Europe. The new arrivals interacted with the local hunters and gatherers. Farming, and in time urban centers, came with these migrants.

They likely brought new diseases. In *Plagues and Peoples* William

Eight. Urbanism

McNeill discusses the role of cities as forcing beds of disease. Urban dwellers fell victim to disease at a high rate. Those fortunate survivors developed immunities that were lacking among hunters and gatherers who were mobile and more isolated. Such populations suffered by contact. The effect can be imagined to be rather like what happens when penicillin is introduced into a petri dish covered with a bloom of bacteria. Around the penicillin is a circular swath of dead bacteria. This image does not fall far short of actual impact on human populations. The arrival of new diseases in North and South America was catastrophic. Nearly everyone alive today has the advantage of immunities acquired by our urban ancestors of long ago.

Geographers like to joke about the bishop who marveled that "God in his wisdom situated all cities on a navigable river or a natural harbor." There are exceptions of course but generally cities are so placed. (Paul Wheatley in his magisterial *Pivot of the Four Quarters* has shown that capital cities in Asia and elsewhere are sometimes situated for religious reasons in auspicious and sacred locations.) Cities buy, sell, manufacture, and ship commodities. It is only since the development of the railroad that commodities could be profitably transported overland for any distance. There was one notable exception. Precious metals, jewels, spices, and silk were carried for thousands of miles on the Silk Road that spanned Asia.

Rome was founded near a ford over the Tiber River, close to a source of salt, and on defensible hills. By Iron Age standards it was prime real estate. The legendary date of 753 BC is likely close to the actual beginning of Rome. Seven centuries later Rome had a population approaching a million. That figure is probably the largest number of people that could be sustained by classical shipping. It is of passing interest to know that the oldest working municipal construction is the *Cloaca Maxima*, the Great Sewer of Rome. Not until the industrial revolution did cities grow any larger. It is uncertain what the upper limit is for an urban center. There are now several cities with a population of more than 30 million, and counting.

Cities are characterized by high **functional density**. Goods, services, and manufactures are in close proximity. Cities are thus more efficient, even in sprawling Los Angeles. Cities also educate and innovate. They always have. It should be no surprise that philosophy began in an ancient city, the port city of Miletus. Located on the Turkish coast, Miletus was a trading emporium and in contact with other cities around the Mediterranean Sea. It was the seventh- century BC home of Thales who is usually credited with being the world's first philosopher on the strength of the fact that he explained the world on the basis of natural forces instead of the whims of gods. He was the founder of the Milesian school of Pre-Socratics. Herodotus, a fifth-century BC gadabout, traveled through the Mediterranean, visiting its cities, interacting with local people, interviewing, collecting stories, observing, and recording everywhere he went. He wrote the first book of history (derived from the Greek for "inquiry").

When sociologists think of a preindustrial city they often have in mind the scholarship of Gideon Sjoberg and his model of the medieval European city. Set within the violent world of the Middle Ages, European cities were walled and almost tiny by comparison to Classical Mediterranean cities. They centered on sacred space—a church or cathedral (the seat of a bishop). They were ghettoized—the word derives from the word for the Jewish ghetto in Venice—and different communities and trades within the city were set apart and even walled. Medieval cities were very dangerous, especially at night after curfew (cover fire) when it was frequently worth your life to venture out alone. Densely populated, these cities were unimaginably filthy and very unhealthy, so much so that cities relied on a steady stream of migrants from the countryside to replenish the population. The rural migrants were drawn to the city for the age-old reasons. Hope springs eternal, after all, and you might do far better than if you remained in the countryside. You might even get rich. And in the city there is more to do; the ritual life and the social life are much richer. These calculations have not changed.

Squatter Settlements

Squatter settlements go by a variety of names worldwide—*favelas, villas miserias, bidonvilles, pueblos jovens*. Such terms describe the way many millions of people live. The general term "squatter settlement" is used to describe the sprawling settlements that typically ring Third World cities. They are illegal because the residents are living on land they do not own or rent—they are squatters. During the Great Depression as much as half of Central Park in New York City was covered with jury-rigged shacks. The residents called it "Hooverville" in honor of President Herbert Hoover. Such settlements were common during the 1930s. New York City's housing problem and the nation's came to notoriety when the *New York Times* reported that a family was living in a shallow cave in Central Park.

Eight. Urbanism

Squatter settlements are a consequence of the fact that rural areas can sustain only a limited number of people; the rest head to the city and very often to the settlements on the city's outskirts or to the city's dump where they live by recycling anything salable. Once they were regarded as chaotic places, filled with the anomic and the indolent, until scholars belatedly began to investigate. What they found was contrary to expectations. In many squatter settlements there is substantial organization. In some cases the squatters arrive as an organized group to set up an encampment overnight. Generally the residents are law abiding, industrious, and ambitious. It would be misleading to suggest that these places are not squalid and sometimes dangerous. All the same, squatter settlements have advantages: you don't have to pay rent; you do have access to urban advantages as the city is only a bus ride away. And the settlement provides a haven (of sorts) for the rural poor who are learning the ins and outs of urban life. The residents of squatter settlements are ambitious, especially for their children; if a school is not provided, they will organize one. Such settlements are hotbeds of penny capitalism. The houses often have a little store in front selling food, trinkets, clothing, and in one case known to me, monkeys. Cottage industries produce pottery and leatherwork among other things. Those who live in these settlements are politically savvy and only the foolish politician will ignore them.

The Urban Elite

In some respects the automobile has turned the settlement plan of the pre-industrial city inside out. There are, as before, some wealthy and powerful people who choose to live in glittering splendor in the inner city. They can afford the hundreds of thousands of dollars for rent, and the thousands to park their cars. Cab fare presents only the most trivial inconvenience. But often the elite moved out of the center city to exclusive neighborhoods—exclusive by wealth and, until recently, by race. Zones near the center deteriorated into slums and existing slums expanded. The elite tended to regard the city as theirs and they exerted a strong direction on how the city would develop. Not as a rule directly, politics was beneath them (Theodore Roosevelt was a significant exception), but through the influence that comes from wealth and position.

A fundamental enemy of an orderly city is rapid growth. Chicago grew from an intermittently occupied mudflat covered with wild onions (supposedly that is what Chicago means in Algonkian) to, in 1833 an incorporated village of two hundred souls. Then it exploded into a city of hundreds of thousands within decades. Chicago's infrastructure and city services could not keep up. The great laboratory for the Chicago School, the city had the unhappy legacy of this explosive growth which may be seen in pervasive and flamboyant crime and violence and unique municipal concepts such as "honest graft."

Gentrification is presently having a substantial effect on the urban environment. Poor neighborhoods in the inner city are refurbished at great expense and then rented to the upper middle class. This widespread practice has "revitalized" parts of the city. It has also displaced the previous residents who can no longer afford to live there. This continues a long-standing tradition. Urban renewal, which destroyed old neighborhoods and displaced its residents who often had lived there all their lives, has been informally called "Negro Removal." That may have been one unacknowledged intention.

In the 1950s and 1960s the reciprocal of urban renewal was low-income housing. This often took the form of huge complexes of high-rise apartment buildings (the "projects") designed to contain and control the urban poor. These enterprises did nothing very well. The most dramatic failure was the 47-acre complex of high-rises in St. Louis: the notorious Pruitt-Igoe Housing Project. Poorly designed, poorly constructed, poorly maintained, and poorly policed, Pruitt-Ignore became essentially uninhabitable within a decade. The city fathers mulled over this abject failure for some years. Finally the Pruitt-Igoe complex was given over to demolition. It was blown up. Today the site is a great expanse of brick-strewn rubble covered by brambles and saplings. It is surrounded by barbed wire and is said by urban mythology to be the lair of feral dogs.

Herbert Gans has written about "Urban Villagers," those who inhabit close-knit neighborhoods within a major city. Such neighborhoods provide much the same support of kinship and neighborliness that is found in a rural setting. But other, and more common, urban settings leave people and especially children isolated and without support save such as may be provided by poorly paid and understaffed social services. The "projects" have not filled this gap with sufficient humanity.

The Urban Underclass

Karl Marx referred to the underclass as the *Lumpenproletariat*. Marx was not a kindly or sympathetic man, except, perhaps, in the abstract.

Eight. Urbanism

He described rural life as idiocy and he harbored a special dislike for the *Lumpenproletariat*, the underclass, the criminals, the prostitutes, the impoverished homeless. They were, in Marx's view, unduly liable to manipulation. Runaways head for the city where they fall prey to drugs and crime. This is a global problem. A child or young adult who has been surviving on the street should not be expected to be a model citizen. Prostitution, petty crime, and drug use are perennial problems. In some countries paramilitary groups have dealt with this troublesome presence by murdering the homeless of all ages.

The number of homeless children in some cities is large but usually overestimated for political purposes. It is possible to accurately census homeless, at least in some cities, because such "street children" make a practice of sleeping in fairly open areas out of the fear of attack in more out of the way places not under public or police vigilance. Additionally such children are known in many cases to social workers. In the upshot, the number of homeless children is much smaller than the prevailing urban legend which had them running about in locust-like swarms. Nonetheless the numbers are far higher than a civilized world should permit. Why don't they go home? Many simply have no home, and for others conditions at home are worse.

Primate Cities

Many countries are dominated by primate (meaning first-rank) cities such as Sao Paulo, Brazil, London, Istanbul, Turkey, Mexico City, Seoul, South Korea, and Buenos Aires, Argentina. Primate cities, which are often the capitals, are the home of a significant portion of the population, perhaps as much as 10 percent. They are in a word, huge. Some primate cities really don't know how large their population is and, in any case the pace of in-migration is so rapid that any figures arrived at are swiftly out of date. Primate cities are dominant politically, commercially, and financially; they are also the principal transportation hub of the nation. They are centers of education and set cultural trends in fashion, art and technology. Primate cities are a powerful magnet for rural populations and for the populations of smaller cities, which some migrants regard as mere way stations to the bright lights of the capital. Country people often follow the path of vanguard relatives who are already established in the city or, quite often, in the squatter settlement nearby.

An Introduction to Comparative Sociology

Large, Dense and Heterogeneous

The pace of urbanization is staggering. The current term for regional urbanization, and this would apply to many countries, is Megalopolis, a vast region of conjoined urban complexes. Simply stated, finding places to put people is now a major problem. There are many countries where well over half the population is urban. Moreover the world is now nearing a time when half of all people worldwide will be living in an urban environment. We are left with a question that has been hanging fire. Cities are about communication. The primary attribute of a city is functional density; that is services, manufactures, and innovations are in close communication by virtue of sheer proximity. This no longer need be the case. The ability to communicate instantly with people across the nation and around the globe is an established fact. Making an international phone call, after all, is only a matter of dialing a few extra digits. To most of you it is a long established fact, taken for granted, as are social media and Skype. Are these electronic webs comparable to a city?

Nine

The Sociology of Religion

Émile Durkheim, who always viewed society in functional terms, held that the way to understand the central function of religion was to examine the role of religion in a "primitive" society. There were then few suitable ethnographies to choose from and Durkheim drew upon the work of Baldwin Spencer and F. J. Gillen who studied the Aboriginal groups of Australia, especially the Arunta. The result was Durkheim's classic *Elementary Forms of Religious Life* in which he saw religion to be at the core of Arunta society, its moral and societal center. This is how he defined religion, by its function. Stated more directly, it can be said that if you strip society down to its core, to the thing that holds it together, you will be left with religion. This is how he saw Arunta society and this is how the Aborigines see their religion.

So far from being primitive, Aboriginal religion—usually called **Dreamtime**—is subtle, exceedingly complicated, and virtually impossible for anyone not raised in such a society to understand. And it is undoubtedly essential to the integrity and viability of Aboriginal society. Robert Tonkinson in his *The Jigalong Mob* quotes an Aboriginal elder as declaring flatly that "without the LAW [meaning Dreamtime] we would be dead." It is Dreamtime, in Tonkinson's view, that buffers Aboriginal society from what may be mordantly described as the "blessings of civilization." Whether in very large and complex societies or in very small communities, religion is a system of sacred beliefs and rituals that are the foundation for a moral community.

Organizational Structures, Beliefs and Ideal-Types

The terms **sect** and **church** have been around for a very long time. Weber made a distinction between the two. **Ernst Troeltsch**, a philosopher of religion, expanded upon sect and church as ideal types. Over time sociologists of religion have come to distinguish four types of religious organizational structures: Cult, Sect, Church (or denomination) and Ecclesia. This is a typology of how religious structures are *organized* and not about what the members of a particular religion believe.

Cults are defined as a relatively small group of minimal organization that is led and inspired by a *charismatic leader*. Charismatic leaders are described by Weber as having special grace and powers of inspiration. Such people have magnetism and draw members into the sanctity of their belief system. Cults are transitory. Either they die with the death—or in some cases the hurried departure—of the cult leader or they grow and organize into a more durable structure.

Sects are groups whose membership has chosen a separate path from the main body of the larger church organization, a path of truly righteous belief. Such communities of the "really holy" may cut themselves off from the ungodly world. Once again, such organizations are transitory. They either fade away or prosper into a larger and more stable organization. In order for a sect to survive in the long term it must establish specific religious and administrative roles. It must formalize dogma and a moral code, maintain property, socialize children and new members, and enact rites of passage and religious ceremony. If all this is done successfully the sect has become a church.

Churches or denominations are larger and far more stable organizations. Churches hold to formal dogmas and codes of behavior. These are derived from the written word as found in the Torah, the Septuagint (Old Testament), and the New Testament, the Quran, the Book of Mormon, the Rig Vedas, and the Upanishads underlying the Hindu religion. Denominations can be very large, some having a membership of hundreds of millions. They are enduring. The oldest formal organization in the world is the Roman Catholic Church, which began as a small Middle Eastern cult, became a sect spread by missionaries, grew to become a church based on the recorded sayings of its charismatic leader—the Christ, the Anointed One. In three centuries it grew to achieve religious dominance and finally to adopt the administrative structure of the late Roman Empire, much of which it still retains.

Ecclesia (derived from the Greek word for assembly) is an encompassing religion that dominates a particular society or nation-state. Christendom in the Middle Ages may be so described. It was entirely dominated by Christianity, which under the medieval popes took on state-like characteristics and was intolerant of heresy, although in some places, Judaism was tolerated because its members could be conveniently robbed. In an ecclesia religious leaders and secular leaders are commingled, and the religion approaches a theocracy. Shia Islam has assumed that position in contemporary Iran. Howard P. Becker has suggested that the Mormon Church approached that status in nineteenth-century Utah.

Belief Systems

Keeping the categories of religious orthodoxy distinct among the wide variations in types of religious beliefs is not an easy task. There are, nonetheless, a number of agreed-upon categories of belief systems.

Animism derives from a worldview that nature is animated by numerous spirits which are found in natural objects. This is a nineteenth-century notion leading—it has been claimed—early anthropologists to ask informants, "Do you talk to rocks and trees?" The belief systems of band and tribal societies are very sophisticated. Australian Dreamtime, as noted, is wonderfully so. Anthropologists who have studied under the tutelage of aboriginal elders have found the symbolism and mythology of Dreamtime hard going, and in some instances students have been informed that they have reached their intellectual depth and that it was pointless to continue. Dreamtime is probably classifiable as animism but it goes far beyond talking to rocks and trees.

Animatism, or **mana** as it is called in Polynesian societies, is a belief in an impersonal force—not a spirit or an anthropomorphized god—that controls fate and personal success. Polynesian chiefs have large amounts of mana. Kamehameha I, who unified the Hawaiian Islands, is said to have defeated an enemy force by having a lava flow engulf them. Social scientists have long suspected that George Lucas suffered through a sociology class which seeded his idea of The Force.

High church is a term used by Anglicans to denote the ceremonies of the Church of England. Here it is used as a general term to denote the highly complex, and often abstract, expressions of liturgy, cosmology and ritual of the major religions—Buddhism, Judaism, Hinduism, Islam and Christianity. These religions are highly literate (Jews, Christians, and Muslims are described as the People of the Book) and rely on formally trained sacerdotal leadership to educate and guide their members in matters of morality, cosmology, and the ceremonies celebrating the truth of their religion. High church religions may be monotheistic (Islam and

An Introduction to Comparative Sociology

Judaism are strictly so) or polytheistic. Hinduism has numerous gods, with some such as Krishna spanning the whole of Hinduism while others are of local renown. The teachings of Buddha provide a foundation text linking together a variety of related belief systems. There are other ancient and established religions, Jainism for instance.

Millenarianism is a belief in the impending transformation of the world; a world that is free of the corrupt, profane, and threatening present. The members of a millenarian religion have an expectation, a promise, that they will be redeemed from the bondage of a profane world. Norm Cohn has described this seeking in *The Pursuit of the Millennium.*

Cargo cults in Melanesia are a conspicuous variant. In the nineteenth century and early twentieth century much of this region was subject to slave raids, known by the inelegant term "blackbirding." Modernization in combination with such rapacious practices brought about terrifying changes. By means of sympathetic magic and other ceremonies, cargo cults promise to bring back the older and better world of the recent past. They promise to bring back good things as defined by the pidgin word "cargo." The natives of New Guinea saw the sudden arrival of strange people, some violent and some profligate with "cargo" of all types: metal tools, clothing, and spam. Then virtually overnight these strange people disappeared by ship and plane, taking their cargo with them. Cargo cults come in many variations. Some have constructed fake airfields stocked with dummy planes in order to attract real planes bearing cargo on the principle of sympathetic magic that like forms attract like forms. One such cargo cult is the John Frum cult—now a well-established Christian sect—said to have been established by a black American sailor, John from America. There are other origin myths.

In North America the Ghost Dance of the Plains Indians falls into the category of a world redeeming religion. After a series of disastrous wars followed by punishing life on reservations, it is not hard to fathom why the Plains Indians would seek a new world, one repopulated by the buffalo and free of white men. The cult leader Handsome Lake led the rejuvenation of his tribe, the Seneca, from a state of collapse following the American Revolution. How Handsome Lake and the new values embodied in the Handsome Lake Religion brought this about is described by A. F. C. Wallace in his *Death and Rebirth of the Seneca.* Such religions may seem exotic, such as the cargo cult that deified Lyndon Johnson, but they are a predictable response to social disintegration. The Handsome Lake Religion can still be found, little changed, in upstate New York. The Lyndon Johnson Cult's

Nine. The Sociology of Religion

offer of $20,000 to purchase Lyndon Johnson was refused and cult members have since moved on.

Shamanism is a set of practices emphasizing ecstatic or hypnotic states allowing its practitioners, who are called shaman, to enter the spirit world in order to heal or alleviate misfortune. These deep trances, which are the shaman's stock-in-trade, are achieved by varying techniques such as drumming, controlled breathing, isolation, and the ingestion of psychoactive (and dangerous) substances. It is a very commonly held set of beliefs and practices found throughout the world in both tribal societies and in modern urban settings. Sometimes defined as religious entrepreneurs, shaman in the contemporary world may be found practicing before large audiences and on television. Those who resort to their services see no contradiction between shamanistic beliefs and healing ceremonies and membership in a major religion. Shamanism constitutes a very ancient suite of practices and beliefs that probably dates back to Paleolithic times.

These ideal-types are heuristically useful but, in fact, religion is an enormously complex philosophical problem: what is the nature of god(s) and what are the forces of nature? Why is there evil in the world? And, indeed, what is a religion? Some branches of Buddhism barely qualify as religion, even by broad definition. From the perspective of sociology it must be recognized that religions do not fall exactly into types. Far from it. Aspects of animism, mana, theism, and magic can be found in most religions. Few religions, unlike Islam, are entirely monotheistic. Christianity has one god with three avatars (Father, Son, and Holy Ghost) and angels and saints in close attendance. Christianity began as a Jewish sect and includes the Torah within its Bible. To Muslims, Jesus is a revered prophet. And as Weber has told us, strict Calvinism was debased such that God became a bestower of riches upon the hard-working and the frugal. Perhaps we can think of this as an early version of prosperity Christianity. In *Burmese Supernaturalism* Melford Spiro discusses the role of spirits called Nats in the practice of Buddhism. Nats are often feared and are embodied by shamans when in a trance state. Japanese Shinto evolved from the animistic religion of the prehistoric inhabitants of Japan. Shinto centers on the spirits (*kami*) worshipped in a multitude of local shrines. Along the way Shinto has incorporated aspects of Buddhism and Confucianism. No religion is so isolated that it is not influenced, to some degree, by other religions.

Émile Durkheim and his successors would have little difficulty agreeing on the functions of religion. Religion establishes a moral community of believers, it provides moral guidelines, and is a source of meaning and purpose in the lives of its adherents. All societies have "theories of misfortune" and religion provides this (as does witchcraft according to Favret-Saada). Religion can also be an agent of social rejuvenation. With a modest amount of reflection, it is easy to come up with additional functions.

The conflict perspective sheds light on the manifestations of religion that are beneficial to the few as is embodied in Marx's well-known aphorism "Religion is the opium of the people." Others have said much the same thing. Religion may soften the blows of existence but it also gulls people into acting against their self-interest. Perhaps Joe Hill said it better in the IWW *Little Red Songbook*: "Work and pray and live on hay / and you'll get pie in the sky by and by."

Religion has costs. It can, and often is, manipulated in the interest of the powerful. In *Mill Hands and Preachers*, Liston Pope examined the influence that mill owners exercised over the local churches in the mill town of Gastonia, North Carolina. This took several forms: Some of Gastonia's many churches were often owned by the mill owners. The content of sermons was scrutinized lest the mill hands get "stirred up" over living conditions and become susceptible to union organizers. Those few preachers with the courage to investigate Gastonia's appalling social conditions were effectively driven out of the ministry and out of town. Those who occupied the mill owner's pulpit were expected to maintain "labor discipline" through moral suasion. Mill owners discouraged churches whose congregations could be plumbed by labor organizers. Communists were regarded as akin to the Anti-Christ and were swiftly driven out of town. Perhaps some of this can, with charity, be ascribed to the traditional paternalism characteristic of what the journalist H. L. Menken has identified as "the hookworm and pellagra belt." However, Pope is clear that in ministering to the docility of the workforce, the churches acted as "an arm of the employer."

The Confederacy provides an unusually sinister instance of the manipulation of religion. During the Civil War the Confederate States, or more accurately, the slave-owning elite, wrapped themselves Christian pieties and trumpeted passages from the Bible that supposedly revealed the just and godly nature of slavery. Owning slaves was revealed as a task of particular moral rectitude. In the ante-bellum South at least a hundred books honed this remarkably crass and self-serving version of Christianity.

When frustrated by the Pope in his desire to remarry, Henry the

Nine. The Sociology of Religion

Eighth placed himself at the head of a new church whose bishops agreed that remarriage was Henry's Christian duty. Additionally, it was discovered that in God's opinion all the lands and property of the monasteries now belonged to the Crown.

In Polynesian religions, the taboo system, which renders certain practices at certain times, dangerously magical, was used to manage the agricultural cycle and marine resources. And in a nifty bit of ecological control, the Pope initiated meatless Fridays just when meat proteins were scarce and the availability of salted cod had dramatically increased.

After the Meiji Restoration (1868), which marks the birth of modern Japan, the ancient animistic religion of Shinto—which pays homage to hundreds of regional deities called *kami*—was placed under the control of the Japanese state's Ministry of Rites. The cult of the goddess of the sun, *Amaterasu* (a direct ancestor of the emperor) and its principal shrine, Ise, was raised to dominance among the multitude of *kami* shrines. To worship at these regional shrines, to which the local population was symbolically linked, and most especially to worship at the ancient shrine of Ise, was to worship the Japanese state. Equally, to worship at the shrine of *Yasukuni*, established by the first Meiji emperor, is to worship, by design, the state and the war dead who are enshrined there as *kami*. (*Kamikaze* would express the belief that they would "meet again at *Yasukuni*.") Shinto was considered by the state to embody the "rites and creed" of the Japanese. Some regard Shinto as a national religion. Not all experts would go that far, but all would agree that Shinto empowered the throne and the government until the end of the Second World War.

Civil Religion

Civil religion is an old idea but interest in it was revived by the scholarship of Robert Bellah. Focusing on the United States, Bellah reviewed the symbols and ceremonies regarded as sacred to American sensibilities. Within our culture the mantle of sacredness covers political ritual, oaths, monuments, documents, the flag, historical figures, battlefields, and burial grounds. Americans can name the identities of these with little disagreement. We are one nation "under God," a phrase added to the Pledge of Allegiance in the 1950s. Our coins insist that "in God we trust." All of this hallowed apparatus, sometimes archly called American Shinto, is fundamental to American life. We do not question it.

An Introduction to Comparative Sociology

To a greater or lesser degree this backcross of religion and ideology is found in all nations and is often crassly, and all too successfully, manipulated by political leaders. The Third Reich's civil religion—or "national religion" as historians would have it—was grounded upon a bizarre pseudo-paganism (loyal citizens hung swastikas on Christmas trees) and the crackpot faith in the superiority of "Aryan blood." According to one Nazi savant this had been "formed in ice." A fetish was made of torchlight parades and vast, paramilitary gatherings before the Fuehrer, as at Nuremberg, which were later celebrated in film throughout Germany. Symbols of sacrifice for the Fatherland, such as the Horst Wessel's "Blood Banner," were treated exactly like a holy relic of the first degree, which by its touch could confer sanctity upon other flags. Hitler accomplished this magical transfer on numerous occasions.

Soviet civil religion was orchestrated by state agencies in a manner that is reminiscent of the tactics of the Japanese state following the Meiji Restoration. The ritual life of the Soviet Union had the express intention of establishing the state as an object of veneration. Soviet civil religion was comprehensive and intrusive. The stages in the life cycle of the citizen—birth, coming of age, marriage, death—were all marked by government issue rites of passage. Entrance into the military, youth groups, and school was similarly demarcated by rites of passage. The calendric cycle was set by the state and included massive displays of patriotic fervor. And, as is well known, Lenin reposes as an icon in his tomb in Red Square. In chambers beneath his tomb is the elaborate apparatus required to keep his corpse in presentable condition for the public. On important state occasions, such as May Day, Stalin, along with surviving members of the party hierarchy, would be standing atop Lenin's Tomb from which "Great Stalin" would give his grandfatherly wave to the masses below. Apart from being taken below for sprucing up, Lenin's corpse has left his tomb only once. During the Second World War the icon Lenin and his entire entourage of morticians and guards was transported by secret train beyond the Urals in order to safeguard it from the Germans.

The cult of personality requires sanctity. So it has been with Mao Zedong. Even his *Little Red Book* possessed magical powers. The "great Helmsman" now lies within his mausoleum in Tiananmen Square. Ho Chi Minh, benefiting from Soviet expertise, lies within his mausoleum in Hanoi. This has become the norm in totalitarian states. It has been said, not entirely without reason, that the most powerful religion of the past two centuries is nationalism.

Nine. The Sociology of Religion

It must be clear that religion and religious conflict continue to dramatically influence our daily lives and the world at large. Unquestionably this will continue. It is clear as well that the rational-legal world, a world scrubbed of enchantments as Weber has put it, has not materialized. The modern industrial world is no more free of magical enchantments or the influence of sacred worldviews than tribal societies. Some national leaders seem to know this intuitively. When Napoleon introduced ribbons and medals into the Grand Army of France to reward exceptional courage, his marshals were incredulous: "No one is going to risk his life for a bit of ribbon." Napoleon responded by saying, "Men are ruled by bits of ribbon."

Ten

How to Manufacture Deviance

Deviance is about social control. It is about the boundaries of acceptable behavior and who defines and patrols those boundaries. Early scholars relied on the hedonistic calculus, arguing that crimes will be committed when the gains outweigh the risk of suffering the cost. The problem with this perspective is that criminals are not necessarily rational thinkers. Pioneering criminologists such as **Cesare Baccaria** did suggest some improvements in the area of deterrence: the punishments meted out should be proportional and swift, rather than merely horrible. Public executions continued apace, albeit with diminished ghastliness, well into the nineteenth century. There are still some nations that hold fast to public execution because of its supposed advantages. It is cheap (incarceration is not), it is thought to be exemplary, and it is reliably entertaining.

A remarkably influential school of thought may be considered an adjunct to Social Darwinism. It can be found in *The Criminal Man* (*L'Uomo Delinquente*). The author, Cesare Lombroso, was an Italian physician in the employ of the military. His early interests ran to recording prison tattoos. Inspiration closely followed the widely published discovery of the Neanderthal man in 1856. Lombroso was performing an autopsy on a local brigand when, by his recollection, the scales fell from his eyes and he realized that this man resembled a Neanderthal, at least as Lombroso imagined them to be. Aha! violent criminals are atavistic throwbacks to the Neanderthals. This is not genetically possible and for all we know Neanderthals may have been quite nice. That may have been their problem.

The result of Lombroso's subsequent cogitations was *The Criminal Man* which is a rogue's gallery of mug shots accompanied by commentary on the "primitive" aspects of their appearance. Although couched in clinical jargon, it is simply a list of facial features that were not pleasing to Dr. Lombroso. *The Criminal Woman* soon followed. Despite the oddity of

Ten. How to Manufacture Deviance

Lombroso's thought, in the context of Social Darwinism and racism it was accepted as valid. Even today there is a hint of the notion of a "criminal type" in the features logged by the police in some countries. Needless to say, in the United States skin color betrayed a criminal type.

Not all views of criminal behavior in the nineteenth century were so misguided. To Marx and his students criminality was an artifact of the social system and the oppression of the bourgeoisie's legal system. Émile Durkheim examined deviance (and not just criminality) from a purely functionalist perspective and argued that deviance functions to the betterment of society. This was so because deviant behavior and its punishment advertised the latitude of acceptable behaviors and thus bolstered the norms of society. Too much deviance, however, is **dysfunctional** and brings on a state of normlessness, **anomie**. Just precisely how these norms, considered uniformly benefiting to all regardless of station, came about Durkheim does not say.

In keeping with Lombroso's ideas, many students of deviant behavior argued that the cause of deviance resided in the individual. Deviants were depraved, insane, lacking in discipline, morally bankrupt, and, as noted, throwback Neanderthals. In short, these were all "**defective people theories**." One critic of this general approach stated that the sociology of deviance should move beyond the study of "nuts, sluts, and perverts."

A sharp break with this myopic view came in an article published by Robert Merton in 1938, "Social Structure and Anomie." This was only a few years after the FBI began publishing its national crime statistics which revealed, in keeping with the prevailing orthodoxy, that most crime was located in the wicked, disorganized city. Merton's theory is usually called **strain theory**. Merton reasoned that (1) there are approved cultural goals, and (2) there are approved means by which a member of society can obtain those goals. If, said Merton, you have both the approved goals and access to the means to obtain those goals, you are *conforming*. If, on the other hand, you are desirous of obtaining the culturally approved goals but, lacking the approved means, you may choose to take advantage of illicit measures to obtain those goals. If so, you are *innovating*. Bank robbery is an example of an innovative strategy. Admittedly, a man who has inherited many millions is unlikely to rob a bank at gunpoint. He will use other methods.

There are other categories in Merton's scheme which are usually mentioned. If you have the means but are indifferent to the goals you are *ritualizing*; and if you don't care about either the goals or the means you are *retreating*. Frankly these latter categories are of little interest. The importance of Merton's work lies in the contrast between conformity and innovation because the clear implication is that a *normal* person, and not a *"defective person,"* under some circumstances will commit a crime. In this Merton was hewing close the Marxian view. At the time few understood what he was talking about and failed to see the Marxian connection. Some did understand the implications of Merton's article. The real contribution of Merton's article is that it got sociologists to start thinking like sociologists. What are the *social* reasons for deviant behavior?

One such social theory, **differential association**, was developed by **Edwin Sutherland**. As an explanation for criminal behavior differential association is deceptively simple and derives from the observation that criminal behavior is learned. It is learned as a result of associating with those who have the skills, self-justifications, and inclination to crime. Sutherland went far beyond this simple assertion, and structured his theory into deductive propositions. Differential association is that rare thing in sociology; it is a **falsifiable theory**. And, it is predictive. Of course there are some crimes that are not learned. Axe murderers have learned the skill to use an axe but otherwise have achieved their status untutored and alone. Embezzlement is a solitary crime but somehow along the way embezzlers have acquired the standard excuse: "I'm only borrowing the money." But very often, it is the association with criminals that explains criminality.

Conflict theories of deviant behavior examine the ability of different interest groups to shape opinion and the law to their advantage. If Marx saw only one overweening interest group, the bourgeoisie, contemporary versions of conflict theory see many interest groups competing to influence the law to their advantage. The reason that the law is, at times, so convoluted is that the law reflects the influence of various contesting interest groups on the legislature. The laws surrounding the sale of alcohol can be unusually bizarre.

Labeling theory, more properly called the **interactionist perspective**, draws upon the scholarship of Edwin Lemert in his misleadingly titled *Social Pathology*. Lemert argued that society can attach a label to an individual because of real or perceived behavior and that such labels may seep into an individual's self-definition. "I really am an X sort of person." Labels can be very damaging, particularly to an adolescent, but labeling can be misunderstood. If someone mistakenly or maliciously labels you a bank robber, you are not compelled to lead a life of crime. Whether or not

Ten. How to Manufacture Deviance

a label "sticks" has to do with a variety of factors: Is the behavior public? How powerful is the audience? How powerful is the labeled person?

It is vital to appreciate the distinction that Lemert makes between **primary deviance** and **secondary deviance**. Primary deviance simply refers to the initial acts of deviant behavior. Secondary deviance refers to those deviant acts that are public, labeled, and accepted as part of the actor's self-image. The interactionist perspective pays **no** attention to the origin of primary acts of deviance. It ignores the matter of what caused the primary deviance, as the reasons why an act of primary deviance occurred may vary greatly; they are, in Lemert's words, "polygenetic." The focus is entirely on the process of secondary deviance. The importance of the labeling process is spotlighted by the numerous self-report studies in which people with no criminal record are asked to check off which of a list of felonies they have committed. Such studies indicate that (1) there is more deviance out there than there are deviants by official records to account for it and (2) the respondents, who have never been labeled, do not regard themselves as deviant. Indeed, in the absence of a label, they are not deviant. Furthermore, it is possible to have secondary deviance without any primary deviance. Charges of witchcraft have taken the lives of some 50,000 people in Europe, most of them women. It is simply not possible to be a witch nor, as a rule, were these women under the delusion that they were witches. They had been tortured into a confession. The statistics from the early modern period do not permit a finely scaled reckoning but it seems likely that the frequency of witch executions is directly correlative with the permissibility of torture.

Individuals and groups engage in "stigma contests" (from the *stigmata*) in an attempt to demonize, or label, an opponent as wicked and dangerous to society. Calling your troublesome neighbor a witch was an excellent tactic and in some parts of the world remains so. Large organizations with vastly greater resources are more efficient at stigmatizing individuals and groups with opposing economic, ideological, and religious interests. Modern political campaigns are essentially stigma contests.

The processes associated with the manufacture of deviance are employed by the state to protect its position and further its interests against the designs of evil-doers. Typically internal nests of supposed deviant actors, "wreckers" in the official parlance of the Soviet Union, exist in vast numbers. In the case of the McCarthy Era it was claimed that communists and "fellow travelers" of various stripes lurked among us by the hundreds of thousands—this on the authority of J. Edger Hoover. In the

Soviet Union, untold numbers of "wreckers," which means something like a destructive insect, had "bored into" Soviet society. This assertion came on the authority of Stalin and the NKVD.

The threat posed by these internal enemies is either enormously exaggerated or wholly chimerical, a state-manufactured fraud justifying a massive mobilization of the apparatus of social control. The Holocaust, the Great Purge in Stalinist Russia, the McCarthy Era in the United States, the Dirty War in Argentina are examples of internal crusades marshaled against grossly exaggerated or simply fake menaces. In these conjuring acts by the power elite of the nation-state, the metaphors of disease and vermin, occasionally supplemented by the antichrist, dominate the political discourse. The internal enemy is a cancer. Like rats and insects, "they bore from within."

Highly skilled and successful practitioners of the art of defining deviance are called **moral entrepreneurs**. Howard Becker documents the career of one such entrepreneur, Harry Anslinger, the head of the Federal Bureau of Narcotics (FBN) who, possibly out of zeal and probably out of a desire to increase the size of his bureau, lobbied for the passage of the Marihuana Tax Act which was passed by an enthusiastic Congress in 1937. An extensive campaign of salting popular magazines with horror stories of crazed, murderous marijuana "addicts," posters warning of the "devil's weed," and the film *Reefer Madness* alarmed citizens and Congress. The repeal of prohibition seems to have inspired this campaign which resulted in a dramatic increase in the size of the FBN. Prohibition agents were a notoriously corrupt crew; it would be interesting to know how many of this breed sought employment enforcing the Marihuana Tax Act in the burgeoning FBN.

The sociology of deviance traditionally examines relatively small-scale events, deviant lifestyles, enforcement policies, the harassment of homosexuals, attitudes against same sex marriage, the socialization of criminals, and gang dynamics. These are important things to understand. But deviance theory also has much to say about the designs of nation-states to cow, manipulate, and gull their populations with the threat of manufactured deviance. These campaigns proceed on a vast scale. The Great Purge in the Soviet Union, for instance, is only one of several enormous, state-manufactured horrors.

The Mass Production of Deviance

The sociology of deviance examines one of the most scale-invariant processes in society; that is, the theories and notions applied by sociologists

Ten. How to Manufacture Deviance

to explain small group behavior are equally applicable to the behavior of nation-states. Until recently, the focus in sociology has been on relatively small-scale events—events that are brief and involve small numbers of people—leaving large-scale events, such as the Cultural Revolution in China, to historians.

The term mass production of deviance is entirely apposite. The nation-state has repeatedly generated huge numbers of deviants by means that fully merit the image of the assembly line. This image is not exaggerated. William Preston, in *Aliens and Dissenters*, describes the deportation of immigrants during Palmer Raids of 1919 and 1920, which deported hundreds of aliens said to be communists: "Like a pig in a Chicago packing plant, the immigrant would be caught in a moving assembly line, stripped of all his rights, and packaged for shipment overseas"—all in one efficient and uninterrupted operation. Vastly more harrowing, the death camps of the Third Reich were in every way factories to produce the death and disposal of millions. It must be acknowledged that such mass productions of deviance have shaped the twentieth century and it would be both idle and Pollyannaish to suppose that the present century will be any different. It is vital to study such events, not only from a historical perspective but also from a sociological standpoint.

The ability of the nation-state to generate deviance is virtually without limits. Only the constraint of circumstance—such as losing a war—or the rise of countervailing power limits this process. The bureaucratic, industrial, and educational resources (propaganda) available to the nation-state provide enormous potential for the application of, in Galbraith's terms, compensatory, conditioned, and condign power. In dictatorial regimes this resort to power is all but unfettered in the production deviants.

The concept of a **moral panic** introduced by Stanley Cohen in *Folk Devils and Moral Panics* (1972) stemmed from his investigation of a series of (so-called) riots that erupted at seaside resorts in Britain from 1964 to 1966. These outbursts followed confrontations between two quirks of English popular culture: the Mods and the Rockers. Rockers were a leather-wearing species of Marlon Brando wannabes who rode motorcycles. The Mods dressed in "Modish" fashion in sports jacket and tie and rode scooters. Both groups were combative and would meet on the weekends to engage in fisticuffs, smash beach furniture, and break shop windows. There were few serious injuries and no deaths. In perhaps a too candid moment, an eminent criminologist, Jock Young, who seems to have had some direct knowledge of these events, said that "they got together at the beach for a terrific punch up and had a great time."

An Introduction to Comparative Sociology

It is important to bear in mind that these were not major riots, but they were invariably described as such in the press, which inflated these confrontations into dangerous breaches of the moral order. Headlines such as "Day of Terror by Scooter Group" and "Youngsters Beat Up Town" spread the unsettling news across Britain. Press copy referred to "invasions" and, more inventively, to an "orgy of destruction." The criminality of these "**folk devils**," to use Cohen's term, was presented in terms of an unraveling of society. In the House of Commons, alarmist speeches trumpeted this national menace. As is typical of moral panics, the beach "invasions" were transitory.

Moral panics are fostered by exaggerated and inflammatory reporting—"over reporting" in Cohen's terms; they are, in short, a creature of bad publicity. Panics of this limited scope are relatively common and have become standard fare in deviance studies. Additional examples will clarify the nature of this process.

A homophobic panic gripped the city of Boise, Idaho, in 1955 when rumors, evidently politically motivated, were circulated about homosexuals preying on the youth of Boise. The police went into high gear and staked out public restrooms and interviewed a large number of possible suspects. It was determined that, yes! there are homosexuals in Boise. The press pounced on this story like a jaguar and feasted on salacious tidbits, generally exaggerated or fictitious. The *Idaho Statesman* editorialized that "this mess must be removed" and went on to describe the "scourge that was ravaging our youth." The national news swiftly picked up on this tale of supposed rampant homosexuality. *Time* reported on "The Idaho Underground." Without convincing evidence, it was generally accepted that hundreds of boys had been ensnared. A few men abruptly left town and 15 men were tried and convicted of consensual sex and served prison sentences or were put on probation. Within months the town fathers, realizing that all this was not an image that would encourage investment in the city of Boise, allowed the panic to subside. According to John Grerassi, in *The Boys of Boise*, there is little reason to suppose that the amount of homosexual activity in Boise was in any way unusual for a city of that size. All this must be seen in the context of the prevailing attitude toward homosexuality at the time. The Federal government was enthusiastically ferreting out homosexual employees as security risks and the church—right across the spectrum—preached against this evil.

Another example draws upon the ancient wellspring of anti–Semitism. In 1969 it was rumored in Orleans, France, that Jewish shopkeepers were abducting young girls to be sold into prostitution. Variations on an ancient slander, these injurious tales were widely circulated. Many people were convinced of the truth of these accusations and were outraged and fearful. A local paper reported on this "Odious Intrigue," and there were reports of tunnels leading from Jewish shops to distant locations. A thorough police investigation found no evidence whatsoever of abductions and no tunnels. Christian church leaders publicly decried these anti–Semitic attacks quashing the atmosphere of alarm.

Although relatively transitory, moral panics are unsettling and deeply wounding and should not be regarded as merely urban legends. The headless woman who drives a yellow Volkswagen Beetle through the streets of Cleveland has harmed no one.

The model of a moral panic, when combined with the insights of conflict sociology, points the way toward an understanding of massive upheavals of deviance production. Such periods are, by definition, more enduring and destructive to status, livelihood, and life. This lies within the province of state actors for the self-evident reason that the capacity of the modern state to generate and grotesquely manipulate public fears and thereby create deviants—communists, fellow travelers, fascists, Trotskyites, capitalists, *kulaks* (i.e., rich peasants), *sub-kulaks* (not so rich peasants), adherents of the "Four Olds" during China's Cultural Revolution (Old Customs, Old Culture, Old Habits, Old Ideas), "Borers from Within," and so on—is enormous. This is unsurprising: coming from a political science stance, Murray Edelman in his *Politics as Symbolic Interaction* flatly states that "political history is largely an account of mass violence and the expenditure of vast resources to cope with mythical fears and hopes."

There is no lack of massive political persecutions for the enterprise of comparative sociology to examine. It is a matter of black-letter history that the twentieth century has witnessed the identification of tens of thousands and several instances millions of people by their governments as existential threats on the basis of improbable mythology. Indeed it can be suggested that stamping out chimerical conspiracies is one of the two things that the modern state reliably accomplishes. The other is collecting taxes.

The Great Witch Craze

It should be unsurprising that the mass production of deviance, as opposed to the ancient process of simply slaughtering people, appears

An Introduction to Comparative Sociology

prototypically during the early modern period (roughly 1480 to 1680). Some time ago I wrote a book entitled *The Politics of Demonology* in which I examined the journalistic chestnut that modern purges closely parallel the social process that fostered the European Witch Craze. It does.

Early modern Europeans did not invent witchcraft. They drew upon a surprisingly consistent suite of notions and sentiments about the nature of wickedness and evil found throughout the world, and probably within all cultures. All societies have "theories of misfortune" and witches and witchcraft were, and still are, fundamental to such theories; that is, the existence of malevolent magic (*maleficium* in the parlance of European witch hunters) and preternaturally dangerous people who employ such harmful magic—witches—are a constant part of theories of misfortune worldwide. Witchcraft feeds upon the vicissitudes of life and the abrasiveness of social relations. E. E. Evans-Pritchard who studied the Azande in Africa states this with elegant efficiency: "Sufferers from misfortune seek for witches among their enemies." Within Christendom these evil people, these witches, who embodied all that was immoral, came to be seen by ecclesiastical dignitaries as servants of the devil. Skeptics of this menacing worldview were, as a practical matter, nonexistent.

The Great Witch Craze of the early modern period took the lives of, conservatively, 50,000 people, mostly women and mostly by fire. Given the horrors of the twentieth century, it is all too easy to look upon this slaughter with an indifferent eye, but given the relatively small population of Europe of this time, that would be a mistake. At different times and different places, the pace of witch hunting became so intense as to be demographically unsustainable—too many women of childbearing age were going up in smoke. (Doubters are encouraged to read H. C. Erik Midelfort's *Witch Hunting in Southwestern Germany*.)

Europe during this period was hagridden by the specter of witchcraft. Historians and anthropologists have tallied up a long list of causes for this menacing construction of reality and the enormous increase in legal executions of accused witches (not including extralegal private vendettas). Elite insecurity, religious zealotry among powerful men, a protracted period of frequent crop failures (standardly attributed to witchcraft), all enter into this, but the most glaring reason is the rise of printing. The Great Witch Craze was fundamentally a manufacture of the printed word and a correlative rise in literacy.

An early and highly influential book, the *Malleus Maleficarum* (1486, and reprinted 26 times in succeeding centuries) reveals the hair-raising

Ten. How to Manufacture Deviance

exploits of two self-advertising and misogynistic Dominican witch hunters, Heinrich Institoris and Jacob Sprenger, who left a trail of burned witches across southern Germany. Written in formal Church Latin it reached an appreciative ecclesiastical audience, including the Pope who wrote an enthusiastic prologue in the form of a papal bull. Within a generation, sensationalistic "devil books" reached an agitated public. These books were enormously popular. The scope of this literature ranged from scholarly treatises by learned divines to luridly illustrated pamphlets displaying the Devil and his servants in compromising positions. All such publications advanced the view that the Devil's servants were ubiquitous. Clearly, *maleficium* was at the root of misfortunes, small and large.

These alarming metaphysical potboilers must have been available to all but the most isolated peasant. For the German-speaking market alone dozens of such books were written and more than 100,000 copies printed. Pamphlets and broadsheets inundated Europe. Except for the Bible, this frightening genre provided by far the most popular literature of the period. In *Europe in Crisis*, Jeffrey Parker notes that between 1550 to 1650 in France alone 235 books and pamphlets were printed fostering the impression that the Devil and his innumerable servants comprised an alternative and insidious religion which undermined Christianity and the means to salvation.

The geography of witch hunting during the Early Modern Period is revealing. There were cultural, religious, and legal differences across Europe. The starkest contrast can be found in the legal codes derived from inquisitorial law in use on the Continent, and common law in England. A fundamental difference is the legitimacy of judicial torture. With varying frequency and intensity, torture was applied throughout continental Europe; the official purpose of this tactic was to establish the truth—to obtain a confession. By contrast, in England under common law the use of torture was strictly prohibited. European witch hunters were little bridled by legal restraints. Tens of thousands were executed on the Continent but only a few hundred in England. Finer comparisons may be made by examining the differences in the pace of executions across Europe. Those Continental regions unrestrained in the use of torture, largely within the regions of modern-day Germany, executed by far the largest number of witches, perhaps as many as in all other regions combined. Those regions with modest restrictions on the use of torture (requiring two accusers, for example) produced witches at a slower pace. And in France it was slower still, since French law required careful examinations by judicial authorities and the judgment of an advisory council before torture could proceed.

An Introduction to Comparative Sociology

Without exception, among the questions put to accused witches was a demand that witches reveal their accomplices in the work of the Devil. In the context of a regimen of torture, such forced revelations had the potential to produce an exponential increase in witches. The hazards of this potential crept dimly into the minds of witch hunters when the pace of executions during a witch panic began to accelerate—and the wrong sort of people were being executed, that is, high status men. In one German town civic leaders called a halt (unfortunately not permanent) to executions out of concern that there would be no women left in the town. In another town an exasperated judge complained that they would sooner run out of wood before they ran out of witches. It is a matter of historical record that many towns executed hundreds over the course of a few decades.

It would be absurdly simplistic to argue that the use of torture entirely explains the witch craze. For one thing, torture was legal long after the witch craze ended. The demand by those in power to produce witches because of enhanced fears and threats to their security varies by time and place. Social disruption and hardships greatly augmented the menace of witchcraft, as happened during the English civil war when English society was disrupted along almost any dimension you can name, especially the legal system. In this violent setting, broadsheets graphically proclaiming an onslaught of witchcraft helped establish a fearful social reality enabling Matthew Hopkins, England's self-styled "Witch Finder General," to unleash a witch hunting campaign of Continental proportions. Dozens were hanged for the crime of witchcraft in the span of a few months.

Witch hunting by the powerful served the interest of the growing apparatus of social control of the early modern state just as the Inquisition enhanced the social control of the medieval state. (The *Malleus Malificarum* was the successor text to the *Malleus Hereticorum*, Hammer of Heretics.) The extraordinary powers of the Inquisition, and inquisitorial procedure generally, were necessary because heretics were under the protection of the Devil. Torture overrode the powers of the Devil and allowed the accused to confess. It was said with confidence that a "witness" who died under torture had been killed by the Devil to keep him from testifying.

The nineteenth-century historian George Lincoln Burr neatly encapsulates the seamless transition from hunting heretics to hunting witches. "When in the lands where the Inquisition had found entrance, heresy was rooted out—when the souls of the faithful were safe and the hands of the inquisitors were idle—then, as was natural the hungry organization cast its eyes about for other victims."

Ten. How to Manufacture Deviance

The productivity of an apparatus of social control is partly influenced by the value that is placed upon ferreting out and punishing deviants. When this demand for deviants is enabled by a social control system that is essentially unrestrained, the pace of deviance production will be high—as it was in German-speaking areas that were dominated by powerful zealots.

But the utility of this scheme lies in the light that can be shed on the catastrophic purges of the twentieth century. The lethality of an unrestrained system of social control in the context of bureaucratic efficiency cannot be overestimated. Stalin's purges—the Great Purge especially—must be seen in the perspective of the vast system of brutal and very deadly labor camps, the Gulag Archipelago, and his campaign to murder his perceived enemies, whom Stalin defined in the broadest possible terms. This huge campaign was carried out by Stalin's all-controlling political police. Historians wrangle bitterly over the human cost of Stalin's regime. Minimally, the Great Purge alone took the lives of millions.

The callous barbarity and bureaucratic efficiency of the Holocaust similarly proceeded without restraint to destroy European Jews and their culture. Across the breadth of China, Mao Zedong's Cultural Revolution demonized whole categories of people in what may be described as a vast Orwellian brawl between status groups. Hundreds of thousands died at the hands of an ideologically besotted youth movement, the Red Guards. Guided by Chairman Mao's Little Red Book, to which magical properties were ascribed, these youthful zealots sallied forth in their millions to root out the Four Olds and "all things opposed to the thought of Mao Zedong." Once identified by means of their past associations, their social position, the revelation of incorrect thoughts, or the accusations of jealous neighbors, such people were subject to violent public rebuke during "struggle sessions" which often took place in theaters and which, in actual fact, were brutal humiliations accompanied by beatings and outright torture. Death was common for such "monsters and freaks" (literally, "ox ghosts" and "snake spirits"). Many were imprisoned for years in Spartan work camps. The Cultural Revolution, directly or indirectly, brought the death of millions and shredded the social fabric of China. Mao emerged from this maelstrom serene and all-powerful.

The Holocaust

In each of these enormous purges, the state employed its resources to manufacture a social reality of great menace and to make convincingly real the source of this menace. The Third Reich was a comprehensively racist state founded upon a barbaric worldview—a sort of Wagnerian Biology—which was all about the protection of blood and race. A national cult of purity demands, perforce, a source of pollution. For this Hitler drew upon Europe's wellspring of anti–Semitism. Hitler's words and the words of Joseph Goebbels, the Reich Minister of Propaganda, harped endlessly on rats, vipers, maggots, "defilers of race, the ferment that causes peoples to decay," and so on. It must be appreciated just how all-encompassing this campaign was. Almost from infancy, German children were relentlessly exposed to this ideology of defilement versus purity in such books as *The Poisonous Mushroom* or, conversely, in a more hopeful genre, an inspiring tale about a pure blooded prince who rescues an equally pure blooded Cinderella. German adolescents were socialized in school and brutally in Hitler Youth camps, into fascist ideology and hatred for those who threatened the nation's racial purity. In all manner of state controlled media, greater and greater emphasis was placed on those "unworthy of life" and "useless eaters"—those people, often children, who were severely disabled. It led to a relentless program of "euthanasia," the necessity of which was presented in state-produced films.

The Nazi dictatorship, headed by a sacred cult of leadership, was dominated by a unified system of social under the control the Reichsführer SS, Heinrich Himmler, which ruthlessly and efficiently controlled an assortment of secret police agencies, the regular uniformed police, the concentration camps (of which there were thousands), and its own military branch, the Waffen SS. It answered only to Hitler; there were simply no countervailing institutions. It also staffed the euthanasia centers. Soon after the beginning of the Second World War Hitler authorized the killing of "useless eaters," and doctors, many of whom were members of the SS, were ordered to screen all hospital patients to determine the usefulness—or lack of it—of their patients and report their findings on a standard bureaucratic form. A check mark in the appropriate box meant death.

The Holocaust began with a massive campaign of open-air executions. This was carried out, as a matter of routine, by special battalion-sized units and brought about the death of hundreds of thousands. The learning curve of the SS in the matter of mass murder was very steep. The apparatus of the euthanasia program in combination with the burgeoning camp system set the stage for the death camps.

The Death Camps were factories which applied the machinery and techniques of mass production to exterminate a culture and murder many millions. This campaign of extermination was pursued at the highest level of priority by a bureaucracy that never hung back, but always did its utmost. A complex of camps like Auschwitz (the death factory, a part of Auschwitz, was Birkenau) could kill and consume the bodies of people as fast as they could be shipped in by rail. On a *routine* day, trains bearing several thousand people would arrive at the Birkenau rail platform and by nightfall the majority would be dead, their bodies cremated, and their clothes and hair stored away for shipment back to Germany. The overall death toll at Auschwitz alone was well over a million.

The Holocaust was not a secret; the nature of the camps was known: many thousands of Germans worked in the camp system, the German railways cooperated fully, and profited from the transport of Jews, Gypsies, homosexuals, dissidents, Seventh Day Adventists. No German institution registered objection or sought to interfere, and those few individuals who vocally objected were silenced. The camp system continued until the very end of the war, and the euthanasia system—for such is the nature of an embedded bureaucracy—for some weeks after the end of the war.

The Great Purge

Perhaps the only Czarist institution to be carried over and embraced by the Bolshevik regime was the secret police. Direct continuity between the Czarist Okhrana was limited, but the necessity for such an organization of social control within the Bolshevik government was immediately apparent to its leaders. Within months the All Russian Commission for Combating Counterrevolution and Sabotage (acronym Cheka, which means linchpin) was established and soon became a law onto itself. It had the power to investigate, hold trials by three-judge panels, and to summarily execute. Often these trials were carried out on the basis of "class morality." It was generally perceived as an utterly ruthless government within a government and was very unpopular. The Cheka was relabeled but continued on as before.

The rise of Stalin brought about a far more comprehensive apparatus of state control which would make Stalin unassailable. First was the development of the show trial to destroy Stalin's political enemies and, as this theater was perfected, to advertise the insidious nature of the Soviet Union's enemies, both internal and external. Second came the dramatic growth of the camp system, the Main Administration of Corrective

An Introduction to Comparative Sociology

Camps, acronym GULAG—Solzhenitsyn's Gulag Archipelago. Third there was the reorganization and expansion of the system of social control into an organization of almost unlimited power, the Peoples' Commissariat of Internal Affairs (NKVD). It has been characterized as having the combined powers of the FBI, IRS, and the Holy Inquisition. It was impregnable to any other Soviet institution and dominated every facet of Soviet life. It was in every way as ruthless and effective as the SS. If it lacked the bureaucratic efficiency of the SS, it made up for it in brutality.

NKVD military battalions destroyed the *kulaks* (Russian for Fist, meaning tight fisted) who were moderately prosperous peasant farmers and stood in the way of Stalin's program of collective farms. And when that proved ineffective the uniquely arch and inclusive category of *Podkulachniki*—"sub-kulak" or "kulak henchman"—was employed. They too were shipped off to marginal lands to starve or sent to the camps.

In the spring of 1936 Stalin abruptly announced that the Soviet Union was infested from top to bottom with internal enemies. Lists compiled by Stalin brought about the arrest of a majority of ranking party members. Less focused was the tactic of establishing quotas (often in the thousands) of enemies of the state for regional offices of the NKVD. These quotas had to be met and provoked a flood of arbitrary arrests. Numerous and enthusiastic denunciations added many more to NKVD prisons and camps. The camp system was brutal—the arctic camps were lethal—and readily kept pace with this enormous influx. A train with NKVD guards, prisoners, and supplies would stop at a siding in a remote region. Whereupon, the prisoners would be informed that this was the location of their camp and that they were to build it. Escape into the taiga was possible but suicidal.

Under N.I. Ezhov, the head of the NKVD and a ferocious sociopath, prisoners were routinely beaten into confessions and promptly shot. "Arrest chains" followed from the practice of naming names under torture and because family members automatically fell under suspicion and were, anyhow, guilty of "lacking vigilance."

By now the full menagerie of anti–Soviet deviants was on display—enemies of the people (a new category), fascists, capitalists, masked plotters, and "wreckers." In Russian, the term wrecker is rendered as *vreditel* and denotes crop pests, insects, or vermin, and when applied to humans shaped the public image of numberless, insidious conspirators who insect-like bored from within. Such deviants were said to infest key industries and collective farms and thus served to explain all that was wrong

Ten. How to Manufacture Deviance

with the chaotic and unproductive Soviet economy—a tall order requiring a deviant of preternatural capabilities.

Show trials, large and small, revealed to Soviet citizens the iceberg tip of this malevolent reality. Such trials should in no way be regarded as suborned or degraded legal proceedings. Show trials were unalloyed theater, produced and scripted by the NKVD and given wide publicity in lively newspaper articles, complete with leaden sarcasm, transcripts, and photographs of the accused in suitably hangdog poses. Smaller trials, held throughout the Soviet Union, were populist in nature and have been described as quite similar to the struggle sessions of Mao Zedong's Cultural Revolution. They were carnivals of indignation often fueled by issues of vodka. The infamous Moscow show trials were staged to demonstrate just how high the conspiracy had reached within the communist hierarchy. To this end, they provide a stage for elaborate, well-rehearsed confessions of the culprits—"men who had worn masks all their lives"—and for sententious and floridly outraged prosecutorial speeches. The detailed confessions were obtained by means of savage beatings—the confession of Marshal Tukhachevsky is spattered with blood—and threats to family.

The effect of this terror upon the Soviet citizen was profound. Stephen Klotkin, in his magisterial *Magnetic Mountain: Stalinism as a Civilization*, writes of the necessity of not only "speaking Bolshevik" but of not allowing one's private thoughts to stray in an environment of intellectual terror.

Toward the fall of 1938 the NKVD began to feed upon itself. Its personnel began to appear in the camps to join the men and women they had imprisoned. The pathological Ezhov was removed, allowed to linger for weeks knowing that he would be executed, and then was. The pace of arrests was reduced to a more manageable level. This was necessary because the Great Purge had made severe inroads into the Soviet economy and had left the Soviet military without leadership—the upper ranks of the officer corps was all but annihilated—and in ineffectual chaos.

The matter of Stalin's motivation for this catastrophic assault on Soviet society (and it was only *one* of his many purges) is better left to historians and psychiatrists. It is anyhow not sufficient to say as Khrushchev did, that Stalin was "sickly suspicious." Moreover, Khrushchev was adamant that Stalin was not a "giddy despot." According to Stephen Klotkin in *Stalin: Waiting for Hitler 1929–1941*, "[Stalin] just decided, himself, to approve quota-driven eradication of entire categories of people in a *planned* indiscriminate terror known as 'mass operations.'" Of direct importance from the standpoint of sociological analysis is the fact that even Stalin had to manufacture the social reality of a vast internal conspiracy to obtain his goal. It is likewise a cold historical fact that Stalin emerged from this period into a position of absolutely impregnable leadership, and was all but deified.

The Red Scares

It would be wrong the regard the brief career of England's Witchfinder General, Matthew Hopkins, who by cautious estimate, was directly responsible for the death of a significant percentage of all the people executed for witchcraft in England, as merely a brutal quirk of history. Hopkins was a creature of dangerous and profoundly unsettled times during which diabolical activities and especially the menace of witchcraft were widely advertised.

The plain case is this: normally restrained legal systems will be overridden when confronted by a deeply menacing social reality. American Red Baiting during perilous times is an example of this social process. The Palmer Raids, named after A. Mitchell Palmer, the Attorney General under President Wilson, and the McCarthy Era during which Senator Joseph McCarthy was the face of the crusade to root out communists during the early years of the cold war. Both periods saw a restrained legal system tilt toward a lack of restraint under the bidding of a coalition of powerful interests, both state and private.

The Red Scare sprang from an already fevered wartime atmosphere which saw the passage of two sedition acts that would have been regarded as unconstitutional during calmer times. The Bolshevik Revolution had come as a shock to most Americans and by war's end showed every sign of spreading. International communism saw this as the *Biennio Rosso* (the Two Red Years) and fully expected its global ambitions to be realized. In the United States the communist movement, largely foreign-born, alienated, and committed to doctrinal squabbles, stridently proclaimed the need for a revolution. In an environment of intense racial and labor unrest, the specter of Communism loomed in the public mind. This godless menace, luridly publicized in the newspapers, was used by business interests to control the genie of organized labor which had momentarily escaped confinement.

The anti-radical forces of the federal government, particularly the

Ten. How to Manufacture Deviance

General Intelligence Division under J. Edgar Hoover, spearheaded the search for all species of radicals but especially communists. An ambitious series of bomb plots targeting industrialists and government officials galvanized the campaign to control radicals. In June 1919 the Washington residence of A. Mitchell Palmer was bombed. Scattered among the body parts of one Carlo Valdinoce were broadsheets signed by The Anarchist Fighters. Palmer was not harmed but emerged from this attempt on his life highly motivated. The ensuing crusade for ideological hygiene under Palmer, now styled as the "Fighting Quaker," was enthusiastically supported by Congress.

The Justice Department's threatening construction of reality was disseminated to the press, corporate leaders and law enforcement agencies and greatly magnified public fears. One congressman urged that all aliens in Arlington National Cemetery be disinterred. There was a proposal to establish a penal colony on the island of Guam. The newly formed American Legion readily adopted paramilitary trappings. Liberals generally, and educators especially, were said to be "parlor pink" and, as in later years, the accepted remedies were loyalty oaths and a purge of anonymously accused educators. One respected commentator compared the national hysteria to the Tulip Mania of seventeenth-century Holland.

Another tempting remedy was to simply arrest and deport aliens in their many varieties, especially communists. On November 7, 1919, agents of the Justice Department raided supposed radical organizations in 12 cities. The nature of these raids can be gathered from events in New York City when anyone in or around the headquarters for the Union of Russian Workers was summarily arrested. Altogether roughly 250 people were taken into custody. State and local authorities arrested hundreds more. All were forcefully interrogated, the "third degree," a common practice of the time.

In testimony before the Senate, and likely to have been written by J. Edgar Hoover, Palmer outlined the nature of the twisted evil facing America. Cesare Lombroso could not have said it better: "Out of the sly and crafty eyes of many of them leap cupidity, cruelty, insanity, and crime; from their lopsided faces, sloping brows, and misshapen features may be recognized the unmistakable criminal type."

Scapegoating is a ritual of biblical origin. Nations continue to use it. On December 21, 1919, the USS *Buford* departed New York harbor, bearing away 249 radicals and the sins of the nation to Finland (Soviet ports were closed to U.S. shipping). Most of those deported had been arrested

An Introduction to Comparative Sociology

without warrant and held without benefit of counsel. Gleeful headlines such as "All Aboard for the Soviet Ark" reflect the public mood of the time.

Palmer then ordered far more ambitious raids, designated in suitably bland Aesopian language as an "inquiry dragnet." In raids closely coordinated with local authorities roughly 4,000 aliens were arrested in 34 cities. Including American born "radicals," often just citizens who were in the wrong place at the wrong time, a total of 8,000 to 10,000 "detainees" were generated. Too many; the system began to clog. Prisoners were held in local jails, Federal buildings, and warehouses. Detainees from the Boston area were marched through town and then held on Deer Island in Boston harbor. American detainees were culled out to be charged under the "syndicalist laws," a category of deviance so expansive as to defy concise definition. Interrogation was very harsh. Some aliens signed confessions written in English, a language they did not understand. An additional five or six hundred aliens were deported. Typical of the government's draconian actions during this period, exact figures are not available. Summary data on American citizens swept up in these round ups are entirely lacking.

As the war hysteria subsided and the nation returned to "normalcy" it became clear that Palmer had overreached. His patently extralegal policies were deemed extreme and out of place. The coalition of institutions that had once supported him unraveled and was replaced by countervailing powers. Publishers were concerned about censorship; prestigious jurists argued that the Bill of Rights had been ignored; and now that the labor movement had been cowed, business leaders feared that the anti-alien campaign was drying up the source of cheap labor. In a twinkling, the Fighting Quaker went from being a defender of red-blooded Americanism to an unreasoning fanatic who saw danger wherever he looked.

However brief, the Red Scare had enduring and baleful effects. Isolationism and a distrust of organized labor followed in its wake. The KKK reappeared and by 1924 attained a membership of four and a half million. The FBI maintained and disseminated lists of subversives. Everything from birth control to civil rights was tarred by the brush of communism.

The apocalyptic vision of international communism reemerged with the cold war and was most harrowing during the Korean War. Just as during the Red Scare, the danger to internal security was exaggerated by the strains of postwar life and manipulated by coalitions of powerful groups that perceived their interests to be threatened.

This is not to suggest that the McCarthy Era was a lockstep reprise of the Red Scare. The paramount difference being that the threat presented

Ten. How to Manufacture Deviance

by the Soviet Union during this period was genuine and grave. There were abundant reasons for this atmosphere of doomsday foreboding. The Iron Curtain had descended. In 1949 China had been "lost" to a communist regime under Mao Zedong, and many postcolonial societies found communism attractive. A communist guerrilla war raged in Indochina. The Soviet Union exploded an atomic bomb, several years before it was expected to. Espionage was suspected. But it was the sudden and unanticipated outbreak of the Korean War which crystalized these events into a hard-edged image of, in the words of Joseph McCarthy, "a conspiracy so immense."

McCarthy was a mountebank—ruthless, calculating and alcoholic. That he achieved such notoriety and influence is an indication of public discontent and fear during the cold war. Long out of power the Republicans found the attraction of a witch hunt irresistible. Few in either party allowed themselves to doubt and fewer still questioned the existence of a communist master plan. Only a few months into the Korean War, Congress passed the Internal Security Act which required the registration of "communist organizations" and authorized the detention of "potential spies and saboteurs." Congress then appropriated money to establish six detention camps. Both parties enthusiastically supported these measures.

Members of the Communist Party, and they were few during this period, found themselves under FBI surveillance, moreover the party was lumbered with paid informants. At the start of the cold war a frenzied commerce in vigilance sprang up in the United States. The perception of an immense internal conspiracy was grotesquely overblown by a powerful coalition of interests, including the American Legion, the Veterans of Foreign Wars, the Daughters of the American Revolution, The Catholic Church and many Protestant denominations, the Knights of Columbus, the American Federation of Labor, and the U.S. Chamber of Commerce, which published *Communist Infiltration of the United States*. This tract was sent to every Catholic bishop in the country and to nearly 80,000 Protestant clergy. The unwavering message was that the Kremlin lurked behind organized labor. With less specificity, much of the business community, Eastern Block ethnic groups, and the political right wing fervently supported the social reality of a vast internal conspiracy. Often bridged by common membership, these interest groups constituted an overmastering claims-making lobby. A measure of the Chamber's influence is provided by the fact that the structure of the Federal Employee Loyalty Program conforms in many particulars to its demands.

The stresses of the time fostered all manner of oddities. Fluoridation was widely considered to be a communist plot, "a Red Weapon" by one account. Parochial students in Detroit were told that in the event of a communist invasion they were to go to their church and consume the Eucharist. Visitations of the Virgin Mary included anticommunist warnings. The apogee of patriotic battiness was reached when, inspired to provide an object lesson to their fellow citizens, American Legionnaires, in the guise of Russian soldiers, staged a mock invasion of Mosinee, Wisconsin, kidnapping the mayor and clergy at gunpoint and then frog marching them to holding pens. The library was purged, newspapers closed, local restaurants limited to black bread and soup, and townspeople harangued. Days later, the mayor, who had not been warned, died of a heart attack. The national press had been informed ahead of time of this stunt and was supportive.

Other developments, institutionally pervasive and profoundly threatening to American liberties, shaped the times. The ritual of the loyalty oath swept the nation. This touchstone of patriotism was required at all levels, from the merest local school board to every nook and cranny of the Federal government. Few would openly say that this pressure to conform was an infringement on liberty. As before, educators were centered in the crosshairs of the ideologically pure patriot and many were denounced and forced to resign. Local school boards were the chief venue for these anonymous attacks. At the university level, senior academics, with feigned reluctance, denounced their colleagues to the FBI. Social scientists of all categories came under suspicion, especially anthropologists who went to strange places and encountered strange ideas. Every sociologist in the United States was interviewed by FBI agents as the Bureau under J. Edgar Hoover honed its skills of intimidation. With little fear of censure, the FBI routinely operated beyond the bounds of legality.

The American Communist Party was then very small, around 5,000 members who were for the most part either innocuous true believers or FBI informants. It is hard to avoid the impression that Hoover kept this feeble organization alive, rather like a weakened virus, to inoculate the American people against the plague of communism. However that may be, Hoover, in his ghost-written jeremiad *The Masters of Deceit*, focused on the dangers presented by "fellow travelers," a suitably vague and comprehensive category that could be plausibly said to lurk in their hundreds of thousands.

Both the House and Senate held show trials. The House Committee on Un-American Activities (usually referred to as HUAC) held numerous

Ten. How to Manufacture Deviance

televised hearings grilling citizens on their past sins. As is the universal practice, the names of past associates were demanded of the witnesses under pain of being charged with contempt of congress. HUAC meetings, which were indeed show trials, provided a stage for congressmen to display their anti-communist *bona fides*, and steely-eyed vigilance. Ostensibly investigating bodies, neither the House nor the Senate committees uncovered much, if anything, beyond what was already known to the FBI, which maintained a steady flow of information to committee members. Some witnesses (e.g., the Hollywood Ten) were obligingly hostile and became the public face of the sinister, hardcore commie.

Joseph McCarthy flourished in this charged environment. He waved lists, supposedly, of subversives before the press, launched baseless attacks on the loyalty of citizens, organized a cabal of ruthless investigators, and intimidated his congressional colleagues. Only Senator Margaret Chase Smith of Maine spoke in condemnation—*Declaration of Conscious*—in the early stages of McCarthyism.

Toward the end of 1953 the ground abruptly shifted beneath McCarthy's feet. An armistice was signed ending the Korean War, Stalin suddenly died, and the Marshall Plan was bolstering Europe's economic recovery. The world seemed to be moderately safer and the holy war atmosphere at the crest of McCarthyism subsided. Oblivious, McCarthy then overreached and maligned a decorated Army general during an investigation of the Signal Corps for supposed subversives. The Senate, with the support of President Eisenhower, held televised hearings exposing McCarthy as a bully and a thug. By this time countervailing institutions, especially the media, had become emboldened. His downfall was swift. He was condemned by the Senate and swiftly descended into acute alcoholism.

No one, as I have written elsewhere, would argue that the cost of the McCarthy Era is in any way directly comparable to the cost of the Great Purge or the monstrous tragedy of the Holocaust. All the same, the cost of the McCarthy Era was not small. It was not small in that many thousands lost their livelihoods, and many times that number lived in fear of that private calamity. Beyond that, the imposition of the narrow moral boundaries of the Fifties fostered an era of political and intellectual conformity at a time when wisdom and flexibility were required. The State Department suffered a crippling purge of its wisest and most experienced Asia hands at the precise point in time when such expertise was needed. Ignorance and fear and the consequent rigidity of thought led directly to that vast and futile expenditure of life and treasure known as Vietnam and to an arms race of such unusual insanity as to defy the drawing of historical parallel.

The critical lesson of this comparative examination of the several processes associated with the mass production of deviance is that democracies, despite being cradled within the protections of a restrained legal system, will swiftly abandon legal restraints when faced with a menacing reality, whether genuine, grossly exaggerated, or wholly chimerical. The potential for the mass production of deviance to be put in service to further the political interests of the leaders of the modern nation-state is significant and predictable.

Eleven

Collective Behavior

Collective behavior includes a variety of mass processes that appear suddenly in times of widespread stress. Mobs, riots, mass hallucinations, rumors, and financial bubbles all fall under this general term. Episodes of collective behavior cost life and fortune and, sometimes, change the course of history. Charles MacKay's (1841) *Extraordinary Popular Delusions and the Madness of Crowds* introduced collective behavior (a term not then in use) to a broad public. In this classic and endlessly fascinating text a host of seemingly bizarre occurrences are examined such the European Witch Craze, the impetuous "animal spirits" revealed by financial swindles, financial bubbles such as the Dutch Tulip Mania, which briefly saw the price of a single tulip bulb of a prized variety rise to the that of a fine house, and, without at all exhausting the list, the Children's Crusade.

Because of the upheavals of the French Revolution, the behavior of mobs became a topic of scholarly interest in the nineteenth century. **Gustave Le Bon**, who did not look on the French Revolution with fondness, argued that mobs reduced men to the lower levels of existence. He also argued that mobs were susceptible to "contagion" of emotion and under the control of a "collective mind." To the modern reader this suggests something out of *Tobin's Spirit Guide*, a sort of ectoplasmic cloud hovering over a mob. This is certainly not what Le Bon intended, and if you look beyond his flamboyant language and discussion of "racial influences," it does not seem dramatically different from the Herbert Blumer's **emergent norm theory**. Relying on symbolic interactionism, Blumer argues that in excited or stressful situations there is a certain aspect of "contagion" of understanding. People adopt a common definition of the situation, determine leadership, and reach agreement as to the proper action to be followed. Such actions might range from the noble to the ignoble, from taking back a highjacked plane from terrorists to the lynching of an innocent man.

Neil Smelser's **value added model** has drawn on an economic term to explain the genesis of collective events. Rather like a product moving along an assembly line, each stage of the process brings a qualitative change and adds value. Smelser identifies six stages each building on the transforming changes of the previous stage leading to a collective event—a riot, social movement, or revolution. **Structural conduciveness** defines a political structure allowing outrage or alternative views to be expressed. A society is said to be undergoing **structural strain** when there are perceived inequities or outrages that cause hardship, frustration, and anxiety. When these sentiments are unfocused the stage is not set for further community action. However when there are **generalized beliefs**—an explanatory ideology, a common understanding of who is behind the prevailing social circumstance—the stage is set for societal action. This stage may be followed by a **precipitating event**, a catalyst which provides the motivation for collective behavior, a "let's roll" event. Sustained action, in accordance with all models of social movements requires organization and leadership. Finally, the actions of the apparatus of social control may forestall or cut short collective action. Or, as the Ferguson, Missouri police have so effectively demonstrated, may itself be the catalyst for violent collective action.

The utility of Smelser's model may be readily examined. The Watts riot in Los Angeles during August of 1965 clearly reveals the stages of the value added model. Watts was then a neighborhood of predominantly single-family dwellings initially purchased by blacks who left the South for jobs in the California defense industry. Residents were understandably angry about a variety of conditions but leading the list were: a policy of segregated housing, a lack of public transportation to allow people to commute to jobs, and a police force whose traditional approach to law enforcement was that of an army of occupation. These factors in combination fostered both social strain and a clear understanding of who was causing the hardship among the residents of Watts. The precipitating event is well documented. The police arrested a young black man in Watts for drunk driving. A rather jovial crowd soon gathered. Suddenly into the crowd plunged an excited and belligerent woman who worked in a beauty shop across the street. She was wearing, as it happened, a green smock. The police are trained to isolate any such belligerent person in a crowd situation and they promptly bundled her into a squad car. What people in the crowd "saw" was the police manhandling a pregnant woman. The crowd immediately turned hostile and the rumor of a police attack on a pregnant woman—"The police hit a lady and she was pregnant"—swiftly spread the anger. The police left the scene of the arrest, probably the only wise decision made by the LAPD for the next several days.

Eleven. Collective Behavior

The riot in Watts, once started, was hard to control because Watts had an open suburban setting. Furthermore the chief of the LAPD issued a number of idiotically inflammatory remarks which added to the anger. Within days the National Guard in large numbers had to be called in to restore order. Thirty-four people were killed and many dozens were seriously injured. There are modest variations in the reporting of the Watts riot but the account above seems to be substantially correct. An investigation by a commission headed by John McCone, a former director of the CIA, issued a damning report and recommended a number of corrective policies. In the result, changes to the city structure and the police department were feeble and cosmetic.

Other collective events have been transforming. The fall of the "Anti-Fascist Rampart," the official name for the Berlin Wall, in retrospect should have been predicted. In fact, it caught everybody by surprise, especially the East German government. Even in the realm of imagination, it would be difficult to conjure up a more creepily drab and confining society than the German Democratic Republic (GDR). It could be described as Orwellian but for its extreme inefficiency. The GDR's leaders were inflexibly committed to ideology and impervious to innovation, relying instead on the ruthless Ministry of State Security (Stasi) to control its dissatisfied citizens. With one Stasi agent for every 180 people, no other security apparatus was so comprehensively present. By comparison, in the USSR there was one for every 600. In addition, the Stasi had long cultivated a host of toadying snitches to round out the fearful atmosphere of state watchfulness. The amount of money lavished on this ponderous bureaucracy was enormous.

The prevailing reaction to life in the GDR was flight to the West, and this became an ever-increasing problem. At one point, people were driving to areas where the border was easy to cross, abandoning their cars among the acres of abandoned vehicles already there, and walking into the West. Periodically the Stasi towed the cars away to be resold. It had branched unwillingly, perhaps, into the used car business. The sale of furniture from abandoned apartments was another source of revenue.

The Anti-Fascist Rampart was of course designed to keep citizens in East Germany, not to keep fascists out. No one wanted to get into East Germany. The wall extended all along the East German border and was a formidable (and dangerous) barrier, especially in Berlin. It was patrolled by savage dogs and Stasi guards were handsomely rewarded for shooting anyone attempting to escape. Laws controlling legal border crossing were

An Introduction to Comparative Sociology

very restrictive requiring protracted dealings with the GDR's sclerotic bureaucracy. Over time these laws became increasingly confusing, if not contradictory.

Demonstrations against the government were well organized, peaceful, and huge—numbering a half million in one instance. Then suddenly the law was revised, perhaps with the intent of reducing the "pressure" so that all could emigrate with a proper stamp requiring multiple mid-level approvals. The GDR politburo passed on the wording of the new law without even a glimmer of what the likely consequence would be. The politburo member in charge of media relations, Gunter Schabowski, held a news conference which Western reporters attended. That meant that questions would be asked, something not in Mr. Schabowski's experience. Furthermore he had not troubled himself to read the announcements ahead of time and droned through a series of mundane proclamations. Then Mr. Schabowski found himself reading to the assembled reporters about "travel possibilities."

Questions! What about the "travel possibilities"? What were they? Without a passport? Visibly befuddled, Mr. Schabowski responded with a rambling answer which the reporters probed further. Could every citizen leave? Mr. Schabowski said, "Yes, with justification." When does this take effect queried the reporters? "Right away," responded Schabowski blandly.

The pandemonium was instantaneous as reporters raced to file copy. The news spread with electronic speed and rumors seem to have sailed ahead of the media: "you don't have to go to Czechoslovakia to cross the border!" The passport control units of the Stasi were the gatekeepers to the West, and within hours they were confronted by large crowds. The Stasi men were without instructions and could not contact anyone who would tell them what to do. By 11:00 p.m. the crowd in front of the Bornholmer gate was enormous and began to chant, "Open the gate. Open the gate." The choice facing the guards was brutally simple: open the gate or open fire.

They opened the gate. What followed has been described as the largest block party in history. The wall itself was immediately attacked by "wall peckers" with picks and sledgehammers. After laborious assault, whole sections were being pulled down under the bemused gaze of Stasi guards. In three days as many as three million people crossed into West Berlin, some to visit, many to stay.

When the GDR collapsed not long after, one of the first things accomplished was the occupation of Stasi headquarters so that the voluminous records maintained by the Stasi could not be destroyed. What these records revealed is chilling. There was a file on virtually every citizen. The number of informants was staggering. These records also revealed in great detail the events leading up to the fall of the Berlin Wall. In her book, *Collapse*, Mary Elise Sarotte has made use of this resource to describe this amazing event.

The Berlin Wall shared much the same fate as the Bastille. The wall is gone, almost entirely. Most of it has been used to resurface roads. Hundreds of sections have been sold, mostly those with the most colorful graffiti. Pieces of the wall are now found in dozens of countries. A section of the wall is now in the restroom of a Las Vegas casino. The urinals have been installed into it.

Rumors

"Enter RUMOUR painted full of tongues" (*Henry IV Part 2*). Rumors fill a vacuum. During times of crisis those in charge will attempt to disseminate as much information as they have to check the spread of rumors. I grew up during the cold war, a cauldron of rumors if ever there was one, and one night the local fireworks company blew up with a gigantic explosion. People for many miles around were convinced that the Russians were bombing and headed for their cellars. The next morning the papers and airways were filled with the reassuring news that we were still at peace. I suppose a few diehards were coaxed out of places of refuge by friendly neighbors. No stranger to planting rumors, J. Edgar Hoover wrote in his hair-raising, and ghost written, *Masters of Deceit* that there were more than 200,000 communists and "fellow travelers" just waiting to take over. Actually he gave an exact number—a common propagandist's trick. He also advised the watchful patriot to keep their eyes peeled for those who were "driving like a communist."

Rumors betray collective fears, common aspirations, and people's suppressed outrage at their position in society. Shakespeare was right to "enter rumour" during times of war. Marc Bloch, a founder of the Annales School of social history, and later as a member of the French underground, murdered by the Germans, wrote of the skepticism of official reports he shared with other soldiers in the trenches of the First World War. This pervasive skepticism provoked an "approximation of the popular psychological atmosphere of the Middle Ages, where rumor was not borne as now

An Introduction to Comparative Sociology

by ration-parties but by peddlers, jugglers, pilgrims, beggars." The literary critic and social historian Paul Fussell calls the First World War a "world of reinvigorated myth." One rumor, grown to the status of a full-fledged myth, is the appearance of the Angels of Mons. In the early months of the war the retreating British turned to delay the German advance at the village of Mons. British soldiers were just on the verge of being overrun, when the Archangel St. George, the patron saint of England, suddenly appeared along with angelic bowmen—the ghostly dead of Agincourt—who began killing Germans with magical arrows. Nothing could have been better calculated to have demonstrated to the English the righteousness of their cause than the active intervention of Henry V's long dead bowmen and St. George. It became, writes Fussell, "unpatriotic, almost treasonable, to doubt it." This myth now leads a resurgent life on the internet.

The Vietnam War produced its own spate of rumors. Predictably there was the hopeful "Our division is going to stand down," or the NVA (North Vietnamese Army) is going to use poison gas. There was the curious (and racist) notion that NVA soldiers didn't bleed. The insight and resentment held by infantrymen for their callous treatment and higher-level indifference to their mortality was expressed in the myth that after you were killed, the Army freeze dried your corpse before shipping it home, thereby saving valuable cargo space. Once stateside, they added water. This was expressed with absolute conviction.

Twelve

Sociology of War

When Napoleon Chagnon was studying the Yanomamo, a large warring tribe in Venezuela, he attempted to explain to these violent men why his father, a World War II veteran, had gone to war against "Germany-teri" (teri meaning place). The Yanomamo warriors were baffled. Was it not over women? No. Was it over food? Not exactly. The Yanomamo do not risk their lives for abstractions. But it is clear that both the Yanomamo and their ethnographer had a common idea of what war is. It is a cultural activity centered on organized violence and the preparation for violence. It is not football, nor is it simple thuggery. The purpose in war is to destroy the enemy. Warfare is a species of coalitional violence that is dedicated to lethality. It is violence that is embedded in notions of tribal "we-ness" and the state. We defend or attack. And we do so by means of a particular sort of institution that is readily distinguished from other social institutions by a consistent set of characteristics that even the Yanomamo would have recognized.

It is a predominantly male activity. Although this is changing, even today the direct participation of women is limited, excepting in guerrilla armies in which women are frequently found. Success in war is a means to status. It is a means of gaining resources. Warfare protects the group and what the group—whether tribe or nation—thinks to be in its interest. It protects their god or gods and extends such pieties to their benighted neighbors. As the means to these ends evolved—as armies evolved—complexity of organization necessarily increased as a result of circumstance and, especially, competition from other groups. What principally separates us from the Yanomamo is that we are much better at killing people.

The study of *war* (proto–Indo-European, * wers, to mix up, confuse) involves the examination of the steady rise of an institution, the military, which is devoted to the bureaucratization of lethal violence. Warfare, and the military, have been shaped by society and, in turn, have shaped society. It is not a topic that should be treated as extraneous to the discipline of

An Introduction to Comparative Sociology

sociology. Quite the opposite, the history, organization, emotive rituals, and politics of war is revealing of the development of complex societies. It is part and parcel of the state and fundamental to the origin of the state.

Evidence for coalitional violence is found as early as the end of the last ice age at *Jebel Sahaba* along the upper Nile. At that location the skeletons of 59 individuals (men, women and children) were uncovered. Of these nearly half showed evidence of trauma caused by arrows. Whether this was a battle or a massacre, who can say?

Nineteenth- and early twentieth-century archaeologists, who were often soldiers, colonists, or both, were quick to ascribe any major change in material culture to violent conquest. The abrupt appearance in the archaeological record of high-status males buried with their favorite things, chiefly weapons, would seem to suggest this. The ability to read ancient genomes—genetic archaeology—has reinforced this picture. In *Who We are and How We Got Here*, David Reich has analyzed the genetic evidence for prehistoric mass migrations and the mixing of populations (what we call a "race" is just the most recent mixture). In some instances the newly mixed populations reveal a very pronounced sex bias, meaning that the X chromosome persists at a high frequency but the Y chromosome of the men of the "host" population all but disappears. Credulity is strained when it is supposed that this demographic shift was accomplished without the agency of organized violence. All the same, there is still occasional resort to peaceful, and fanciful, explanations.

However, there is no doubt about the existence of warfare among the city-states of Mesopotamia. Whatever ambiguity there may have been vanished in a flash when the Standard of Ur was unearthed during the excavation of that city, the biblical Ur of the Chaldees. Dating to around 2,500 BC, the Standard—in fact a small box of unknown purpose—displays in semi-precious stone inlay scenes of a celebration and on the other side soldiers, men similarly garbed and carrying weapons. They appear to be in formation. There are also scenes of spearmen riding in solid wheeled chariots pulled by donkeys or onagers, a larger species of donkey. These chariots are clearly doing what chariots are supposed to do—run over the enemy.

It would be incorrect to dismiss this as a quaint picture of the Model T of chariots. In fact it betrays a sea change in the overall organization of society and in military organization. This comprehensive change is a consequence of the reciprocal relationship between the military and society.

The early appearance of city walls in ancient Mesopotamia reflects a

Twelve. Sociology of War

hostile environment and the hierarchical social structure capable of the social control required to build a city wall such as surrounded the city of Uruk which was as much as 30 feet wide at the base and ran for miles. Boring, that is to say, tedious and methodical, archaeology is often the most revealing of prehistoric cultures. A common, and boring, artifact found about Sumerian city states is the "beveled rim bowl," an object that is almost serene in its drabness. These are ration bowls used to feed a large and likely conscripted workforce.

The "wheel complex" (it isn't just the wheel, but also the wagon, the axel, and the team) developed on the Eurasian Steppes shortly after 4,000 BC, diffused rapidly and was swiftly developed into a weapons system. Military technology, once developed, diffuses very quickly. What may have taken decades in the Sumerian world now takes a matter of years or months. Cutting-edge technology is invariably utilized to make weapons, bronze, iron ... computerized guidance systems. It is often invented for military purposes and reciprocally adopted by the larger realm of society. The breech loading Hall rifle (1819) was initially manufactured for the U.S. Army using a pioneering and highly successful application of interchangeable parts. Radar .is another such example.

Discipline is the hallmark of the Greek phalanx, a dense formation of spear wielding men, and the more open Roman legion requiring every man to "hold the line." Such close-knit groups of disciplined men, men who trained together and were subject to shame or corporal (in extremis, capital) punishment if they failed in "their duty," had a major political impact in both societies. In the Hoplite Revolution of Athens middling well-off men who could afford the armor and weapons of a Greek hoplite soldier—men who carried the Hoplon shield—not only trained together and fought together, but also voted together. "No man," said Julius Caesar, "is really rich unless he can afford and army." Such client armies, loyal to only one man, dominated Roman politics from the Late Republic on.

Surprisingly simple gadgets can have far-reaching consequences. Greek and Roman cavalrymen had saddles but no stirrups, rendering them rather ineffective; they tended to fall off. The stirrup diffused into Europe from the Eurasian plains around 700 CE and was rapidly adopted. The clear advantage was the ability to stay firmly on your horse while flailing about with the gruesome weapons of the feudal period. Any horseman with a lance charging a solid line of men without the advantage of stirrups would be propelled right off the back of his horse. The armed and armored aristocratic horseman is made possible by the lowly stirrup. This horsey aristocracy persists in language: chevalier, cavalier, caballero. No one would argue that feudalism was solely caused by the stirrup, but it was revolutionary in its impact. Lynn Townsend White, in *Medieval Technology and Social Change*, writes that "few inventions have been as simple as the stirrup, but few have been so catalytic an influence on history.... The new mode of warfare ... found expression in a new form of Western European society dominated by an aristocracy of warriors endowed with land so that they might fight in a new and specialized way." To this I might add that it was an expensive form of warfare. The endowed lands had to support the knight, various servants, horses (especially the highly trained warhorse, the *destrier*), arms, and armor. And, the freedom to train; it was generally acknowledged that a boy had to start training by the age of 16, "otherwise he was fit only for the clergy." It is worth noting that in Switzerland, rugged geography and the rise of disciplined pike men undercut the dominance of the mounted warrior. This was (and is) reflected in Swiss society, which from medieval times on was less burdened by aristocracy.

If technology fostered the supremacy of the mounted knight, it also in subsequent centuries served to bring low that status. This was the effect of the Gun Powder Revolution because even the primitive guns of the time could reliably defeat armored horsemen. Guns made holes in even the best armor, and in the man wearing it. This was deeply unsettling to European society. The armored aristocrat was now at grave risk of being killed by the meanest peasant. In Japan guns so threatened the social hierarchy that they were outlawed. And they remained outlawed until a benevolent West reintroduced firearms centuries later.

Guns and cannons were hideously loud in a heretofore quiet world. They were clearly of the black arts, works of the devil, and were railed against as sacrilegious by theologians. When it was discovered that cannons could knock down castles of the time in just a span of days, this sacrilege was universally ignored. Gunpowder, guns, cannon, and the drive to improve them had great impact on science, especially metallurgy. Hitting something at a distance, even for the savviest master gunner, required measurement and, in time, mathematics. The science of ballistics (from the Greek "to throw") challenged mathematicians for generations, including Isaac Newton, and was the impetus for developing the first American computer in order to calculate the ballistics of artillery shells.

The military institution and nationalism have always been intertwined. Armies are a source of national pride. Battlegrounds and the cemeteries they feed are sacred. The red blood that links nationalism and the military is propaganda; the ability by any and all means to convince the enemy of the hopeless folly of their course of action, that their defeat is inevitable. For domestic consumption propaganda dehumanizes the enemy and magnifies the wisdom, gallantry, and humanity of our soldiers. Nations are, with few exceptions, born in violence and the propaganda that attends it.

As a general rule, propaganda has only a limited effect on the enemy but it is a potent means domestically of generating a bellicose worldview. J. A. Hobson understood the connection between bellicose nationalism and the popular media, such as music halls, theaters and widely sung ditties. Jingoism, the unvarnished support for militarism, derives from a popular song in Victorian England: "We don't want to fight but by jingo if we do / we've got the ships, we've got the men, we've got the money too."

According to Sinisa Malesevic, in *The Sociology of War and Violence*, "propaganda is essentially a device of self-legitimization." By extension it attempts, usually with less success, to delegitimize the enemy's society and undermine the enemy's war making capacity. From the third millennium BC on, rulers have celebrated themselves in victorious attitudes while also revealing the puniness of their enemies. During World War II the Allies had whole units dedicated to dropping leaflet-filled containers, virtually papering the Third Reich. Soft feminine voices—Tokyo Rose—warn soldiers of calamities ahead. The North Vietnamese had shells filled with leaflets showing a black American soldier crawling through rice paddy crud; the intention, judging from the caption, being to drive a wedge between black and white soldiers, which, in rear areas, required little prodding.

It is difficult to identify a means of communication that has not been exploited to disseminate propaganda. The highly disciplined and overpowering armies of the Inca Empire advertised to enemy leadership the cost of doubting their invincibility by threatening to "make a drum of you." This, by means of innovative taxidermy, is exactly what they did. The flayed leader was stuffed and a drumhead installed in place of his stomach.

Shortly after the United States declared war on Germany during the First World War, Americans—less some of German heritage—acquiesced to the vision of the iniquitous Hun disseminated by the Committee on Public Information. Taken in hand by the journalist George Creel, the committee saw its mission: "sell the war." It was, opined Creel, "the world's greatest adventure in advertising." With the enthusiastic participation of the print media, it was wildly successful. The linguist Noam Chomsky writes that the Creel Commission "succeeded within six months, in turning

An Introduction to Comparative Sociology

a pacific population into a hysterical, war-mongering population which wanted to destroy everything German, tear the Germans limb from limb, go to war and save the world." Dictatorships are no less successful.

Unit cohesion and loyalty are fundamental to success in war, and over the centuries such qualities have been honed to near perfection. Until recently, the spoils of war—in other words, loot—was the predominant reason for leading military adventures. In the summer (horses need grazing) armies would sally forth to claim the wealth of their neighbors. This would be repeated annually until the distance proved too great or there was a dearth of things to steal. If you could baptize people along the way, so much the better. This was the reliable pattern in Western Europe from Clovis to Charlemagne to William the Conqueror. Napoleon's armies sent whole caravans of loot back to France, filling, among other places, the Louvre.

There are more refined methods of enhancing morale (as it came to be called). The Janissaries of the Ottoman Empire were organized into regiments composed of men who had been selected between the ages of eight and 14 from Balkan Christians. They were converted to Islam and trained in what was in every way a total institution. Initiated in the late fourteenth century, the Janissaries—which translates as new soldiers—were Europe's first standing army. From boyhood on these men were subjected to the strictest training from which they emerged intensely disciplined and well-armed. They were utterly devoted to their regiments and had little life beyond.

Although still practiced today, it is not necessary to kidnap children to maintain a loyal and tightly knit unit. The trappings of military flummery are surprisingly potent in this regard. Unit history is much touted, distinctive uniforms, and particularly unit symbols are embraced. Sometimes this attachment can be all but totemic. In *Totemism*, the structural anthropologist, C. Lévi-Strauss has noted that during the First World War men from the Rainbow Division—so called because the men in it were from all over the United States—would refer to themselves by saying, "I'm a Rainbow." The division insignia was, naturally, a rainbow. Napoleon had a genius for manipulating such symbolism. The Grand Army's Imperial Eagles were no less sacred than those of the Roman army. In a ceremony of the utmost solemnity, he bestowed each battalion with its own flag. With similar intent, he instituted military medals. Further evidence that "men are ruled by bits of ribbon."

The British regimental system likewise fostered loyalty. Long-term

Twelve. Sociology of War

enlistments, pride in regimental history (coded upon revered battle flags), and distinctive uniforms of a remarkably flamboyant and impractical design—whatever suited their Colonel's fancy—all served the cause of high morale. From the Napoleonic wars until the brutal lessons of the First World War there was intense international competition in the display of bright colors and gold braid (which still lingers vestigially). The importance of this panoply is best encapsulated by the no doubt sincere statement of a nineteenth-century British general, "I hate war, it spoils the army."

Over and above just regimental tradition, nations and armies have a culture that profoundly influences their conduct of war. Robert M. Citino examines how the German conduct of warfare hails back to the Prussian king, Frederick the Great, who out of necessity sought and usually achieved quick victories. The Prussian state in the eighteenth century was both small and poor and could not sustain a long drawn-out war. This same policy was disastrously attempted by Germany in the First World War. Undaunted, Hitler stuck to the same strategy against Poland, the Netherlands, and France. It worked. But after that it did not work.

France, even after repeated defeats by Germany, harkened back to Napoleonic spirit and rested its honor upon the *arme blanche* (the sword and bayonet). French soldiers went to war in 1914 waving edged weapons and wearing their traditional pantaloons rouge. The American army still draws upon its experience in the Civil War and following Grant is expected to smash its way to victory. Some 80 years later, General Eisenhower's mission statement was succinct and direct: "You shall enter the Continent ... and undertake operations striking at the heart of Germany and destroy her forces." Only recently has the U.S. Army recalled its origins in a guerrilla war. Japanese soldiers were inculcated with a strict (and suicidal) code of strict military honor known as *Bushido*.

In *The Allure of Battle* Cathal J. Nolan has exhaustively examined our belief that conflicts are invariably determined by a "decisive battle." By Nolan's detailed analysis it is the application of superior resources over the long haul that typically determines victory. The case is overstated: of course there have been decisive battles; the Battle of Hastings comes to mind. Nolan draws upon the example of the Battle of Tours during which Charles Martel an eighth-century French strongman defeated a Moslem raiding force. This has long been presented as a great turning point in the history of Europe, indeed its salvation. It has been a matter of historical gospel that had the Franks not been victorious, Europe would have fallen to Islamic hordes. On the authority of the great historian of Rome, Edward

An Introduction to Comparative Sociology

Gibbon, "the interpretation of the Koran would now be taught in the schools of Oxford, and her pulpits might demonstrate the truth and sanctity of the revelation of the Mahomet." This message has been parroted to a dozen generations of schoolchildren.

In point of fact there is no reason to suppose that the Battle of Tours was anything other than a "grubby little skirmish" which had no impact whatsoever on the course of history. How many captains have endeavored to "bring the enemy to battle"? That was the stated purpose of General Westmoreland's Khe San strategy during the war in Vietnam. It achieved nothing. Well after the war ended a thoughtful dialogue was recorded in Hanoi between an American colonel and his counterpart, a Vietnamese colonel. "You know you never defeated us on the battlefield." To which the Vietnamese office responded, "That may be so, but it is irrelevant."

In the eighteenth and nineteenth centuries, depending on the country (England, for instance), the enlisted soldier, or press-ganged sailor, was regarded as the dregs of the nation. Such men were according the French Secretary of War, "the slime of the nation and of all that is useless to the nation." "Men who have enlisted solely for drink," in the Duke of Wellington's resolute opinion. The Duke was a disciplinarian, a believer in neck stocks—stiff leather collars to keep a soldier's head erect—and whipping. He could be abruptly severe, as in, "Inform me in ten minutes time that that man has been hanged." But in fact, apart from a certain terse facility with words, he was typical for commanders of the time.

Increasingly, conscript armies were filled with "ordinary men" who had been drafted, and such citizens were not to be regarded as slime or useless to the nation. Ordinary citizens were "called up" in huge numbers. Conscription under the Emperor Napoleon was universal and bled the nation. His glorious victories combined with his catastrophic defeat in Russia cost France 800,000 men. The American Civil War saw men drafted in even greater numbers. The levies of the First World War were greater still and carried correlatively massive bills of mortality. People daily checked the newspapers for the names of loved ones. The Second World War, beginning only 21 years later, mobilized tens of millions and killed a far greater number. The United States alone put 12,500,000 men in uniform, expanding so rapidly from the puny 200,000 man prewar army that an army-wide command reveille was ordered, requiring, as much as possible, on a particular day in 1944 that every man be identified by name and counted. This was necessary to ascertain just how many men were in the army. Within surprisingly broad limits, the army didn't know. Always

Twelve. Sociology of War

during that conflict the numbers were staggering. Towards the latter part of the war within the relatively narrow confines of Western Europe over 10 million men were directly engaged in battle.

Military and domestic economies were comprehensively interwoven during the Second World War to such a degree that it is misleading to suggest that there was any significant separation at all. Spending reached unheard of levels. By some accounts over 15 percent of Britain's GDP (Gross Domestic Product) was devoted to developing and maintaining their heavy bomber force. The cost of the American B-29 program was greater than the Manhattan Project which developed the atom bomb. Ford's Willow Run factory which turned out heavy bombers using assembly line technology employed 40,000 workers and 250,000 more people settled in a nearby town which emerged from the Michigan woods. The mobilization of the Soviet economy during the Great Patriotic War was total; that of the Third Reich turned to an enormous force of slave laborers.

Paul Fussell's magnificent study of the poets of the First World War, *The Great War and Modern Memory*, makes clear the degree to which the social fact of war has shifted the tumblers of reality within our collective brains. Militarism has captured our worldview and our discourse, both metaphorically (e.g., "capture") and concretely. The language of war is commonly used in sports, particularly the more violent sports. Likewise among businessmen who are fond of the aphorisms found in Sun Tzu's *The Art of War*. It might seem strange that contemporary management students should study the thoughts of an ancient Chinese philosopher general, initially written on bamboo strips, but that is the world we live in.

We have moved on since the days of bamboo strips. Indeed, warfare has taken on a new dimension with the advent of the digital species of asymmetrical warfare. Multiple and intimate media have the ability to influence the public opinion of an enemy power. There is now the power to influence, distort, terrify, and generally hoodwink a credulous public in ways unimaginable to George Creel.

Images of war and terrorism in vivid detail are all but unavoidable. What used to be presented in grainy illustrations on newsprint is now seen in bright clarity in a variety of electronic media. As I write, a white nationalist has live-streamed his slaughter of worshipers within a mosque. Such horrific scenes, real or imagined, are common and unremarkable fare to all, including the very young. Even the merest glance at the typical video game reveals militaristic plots that challenge the player to rack up a high virtual body count.

An Introduction to Comparative Sociology

It should not be overlooked that the Iranian Revolution was triggered by the circulation of Ayatollah's Khomeini's sermons on what are now quaintly archaic eight track tapes. The ability of contemporary media to exercise, in Galbraith's terms, conditioned power in the furtherance of militarism is far beyond what could have been imagined only a few decades ago. Today such messages have come unmoored from any existing state or ethnicity. Only ideology is served. Terrorist entities exist in virtual reality but influence genuine slaughter.

That often quoted but seldom read book by the Prussian General Carl Philipp von Clausewitz, *On War*, contains his philosophy that war is an extension of politics. It is "a true political continuation of political intercourse, carried on with other means." Perhaps so, but it is now much more than that. The consequences of *rolling the iron dice* are far-reaching.

Thirteen

Social Change

Geographical, climatic, and pestilential events are obvious sources of change, and their impact can be so massive and so sudden as to override any cultural response. The increasing toxicity of human society to its habitat is potentially another source of collapse.

From the perspective of macrosociology four major revolutions have occurred within the genus *Homo*. The first revolution was a florescence of culture and social organization beginning around 50,000 or 60,000 years ago in Africa. This dramatic transformation came about because of a confluence of cultural traits, including language, which has a genetic basis and may have been a longstanding part of society. The ability to generate symbolic constructions and communicate them from person to person and from generation to generation (these were the first people to have grandparents) contributed greatly to this revolution in our species. The archaeology is clear. Quite suddenly art, symbolic exchange (xharo), complex alliances to buffer hard times, and the ability to adapt to new environments, became the ordinary condition of humankind. The spread of our species across the globe was not a gradual process. People were in Australia by 40,000 years ago; from an ecological standpoint it was a blitzkrieg.

The contrast to what went on before could not be starker. In the underlying Neanderthal levels found in European cave sites tens of thousands of years pass with almost no discernable change in the stone tool industry. It is monotonous in the extreme. It is a picture of small groups, parochial in their outlook. The African immigrants who replaced them left a record of comparatively rapid and innovative change. These were modern people, superlatively skilled as hunters and gatherers, from which everyone alive today is descended.

If it took two million years for the first revolution to come about, the next one followed in only 40,000 or 50,000 thousand years. This was the **neolithic revolution** a term derived from a new type of stone tool (*neo lithic:* new stone). People as early as 12,000 years ago were beginning to

An Introduction to Comparative Sociology

grow crops (grains) and raise animals—ruminants at first, goats, sheep, and later cattle—beginning a symbiotic relationship between humankind and plants and animals. This happened in several parts of the world and the result was a dramatic increase in population. Where the archaeology is fine-grained enough, food production and settled life can be seen to have specific points of origin, for example, Çatal Höyük.

The tag end of the **industrial revolution** is within living memory and its beginnings stem from only a few generations before that. Complex and reliable machinery in combination with fossil fuels brought about a massive change supporting large-scale production of commodities, including weapons, rapid communication, and great cities.

We are now living the fourth revolution. The "computer age" has harnessed much of the fabric of the industrial revolution and transformed the shape of things into a globalized, highly interconnected world now dominated by **global cities**—New York, London, and Tokyo—that are world-dominating hubs of finance, manufacturing, and communication.

Anciently, the world changed according to the whims of the gods, who might be pleased, angry, or just indifferent. People studied the gods and especially how to please them. Only recently have people come to the view that change occurs according to patterns found in nature and society. Less than two centuries separate us from a time when the majority of the Western world accepted the date calculated by Bishop Ussher in the seventeenth century of 4,004 BC for the beginning the world. He did this on the basis of scripture, which would have been quite reasonable in that century. A contemporary of his examined scripture more closely and refined the date to 4,004 BC on October 23 at 9:00 in the morning, which was a Sunday. This is my favorite example of spurious precision.

The pioneering work of early geologists argued convincingly that the earth was far older than 6,000 years allowing Darwin the time depth to postulate his theory of organic evolution. He got it right, mostly, even though he had only the murkiest notion of how mutation drove the process of evolutionary change. Darwin was a gradualist. That is, he saw the formation of new species as a relatively steady, gradual process. But that is not what, by and large, is found in the fossil record. The pattern that is found in the fossil record is described by Stephen J. Gould as **punctuated equilibrium** meaning that the pace of evolutionary change is essentially a herky-jerky process whereby there are long stretches of little or no change followed abruptly in the geological record by the appearance of new descendant species. There are exceptions. There are fish swimming about

Thirteen. Social Change

today, long known to residents of Madagascar, which are all but identical to their fossil ancestors of hundreds of million years ago. But horseshoe crabs (another example) and coelacanths aside, organic evolution generally follows a pattern of stability punctuated by rapid speciation. The point of this sidebar is that in the modern world social change often proceeds in a similar manner—innovation, discovery, invention, social movements, and new connections all have a point of origin in time and space. The "winds of change" do not waft softly over the landscape. Change in complex societies can be swift.

Notions of social evolution predate Darwin's theory of organic evolution by two generations, if not more. Human society was seen as progressing through three stages: savagery, barbarism, and civilization. There are several versions of this notion reaching back to the Scottish Enlightenment and Adam Ferguson's discussion of "rude nations" in his *History of Civil Society*. All of these schemes saw social evolution in terms of "progress" to a higher state of society, the evidence being that you could look about and see savages and elsewhere you could see barbarians (barbarians have horses, savages don't), and then there were civilized people like us. This approach to social change is called unilinear evolution. It is subjective and without any objective merit.

Nineteenth-century social scientists tended to use the terms development, progress, and evolution coterminously. The contemporary usage of the term evolution recognizes that societies do evolve, in the sense that they have moved from a state of little complexity as revealed by their material culture to a state of greater complexity. This process is now termed **multilinear evolution** since it is abundantly clear that there is no single line of stages to pass through. There are different paths to complexity; more importantly, the concept of multilinear evolution recognizes the fact of **devolution**. The world is littered with the remains of great cities and states that have collapsed. Devolution may become a fruitful area of scholarship in years to come.

Grand Theories

Marx's analytical scheme, **historical materialism**, argued for social progress through stages driven by the **dialectic**. No part of Marxist scholarship is more lumbered with abstruse terminology than the concept of the dialectic. Marx saw tension arising from conflicting interests between opposing classes or groups: the tension between master and slave fostered reorganization toward feudalism, in which the tension between the feudal lord and his serfs dominated the social dialectic. Feudalism gave way to capitalism and the opposing bourgeoisie and proletariat. The final stage in which the means of production were controlled by the state did not come about as he predicted and Marx would have found the twentieth-century communist reality appalling. All this was seen as following the Hegelian process of thesis, anti-thesis, synthesis (but not in Hegel's realm of ideas).

The majority of nineteenth-century sociologists developed concepts that describe the reorganization of social relationships brought about by industrialization: the shift from traditionally organized society to the rational-legal (Weber); from mechanical to organic solidarity (Durkheim); from *Gemeinschaft* to *Gesellschaft* (Ferdinand Tonnies); and Comte's progress from theological to metaphysical to positive thinking. Although hardly identical these are all solid concepts describing the shift from rural, elder-dominated, kinship based societies with traditional morality to urban, industrial, and social complexity of often isolated and alienated people bound together only by the formal obligations of secondary groups. Just how overwhelming this transformation came to be would have astonished the originators of these concepts.

The twentieth century produced its own set of grand theories of social change. Beginning in 1912 Oswald Spengler wrote *The Decline of the West* in gloomy apprehension that a great European war was looming. Spengler's perspective on the course of history was that civilizations follow a life cycle much like an organism. His book was not published until just after the war was over and it found a receptive audience. Spengler's cogitations became very influential in the 1920s and spread the view that Western Civilization was in an unpleasant dotage. Pitrim Sorokin, a brilliant scholar with unorthodox ideas, was born in Russia and had the good fortune to be exiled (not shot) in 1923. He is responsible for a sociological study of saints and a quite interesting one at that. Most saints, by the way, are from the upper classes. In *Social and Cultural Dynamics* (1935) he describes a pendular swing in which civilizations shift from an "ideational state" (otherworldly, ascetic, rigidly moral) to a "sensate" state (worldly, materialistic, hedonistic). I suppose the present Iranian theocracy would be described as ideational but some aspects of Iranian society strike some observers as indulgent. In short, this is all pretty subjective.

Arnold Toynbee, who wrote a massive multivolume history of the world, developed the concept of **challenge and response**, arguing that

Thirteen. Social Change

societies challenged by geography and circumstance often respond in such a way as to expand and prosper. This, as Toynbee points out, worked well for Prussia under Frederick the Great but not so well for other societies.

So comes the dawn. Robert Merton gazed upon these grand notions of social change and called for **theories of the middle range**, *theories with narrower scope conditions* that did not try to explain everything; theories which were documented, quantifiable, and open to falsification.

Innovation, discovery, and invention all introduce something new into the cultural pool that influences, sometimes dramatically, other social elements. I used to mention an extreme example as a sort of thought experiment which was: what would happen if machine guns were introduced into a society that had only primitive weapons? That was foolish. In the contemporary world there is no need to speculate as this has already happened many times over. The lethality of violence increases, strong men appear, and the life of that society is rendered more precarious. The British placed themselves at the vanguard of this process by introducing tribesmen to the advantages of machine guns by shooting them. An activity nicely captured in 1898 by Hilaire Belloc in his sardonic poem *The Modern Traveler*, "Whatever happens, we have got the Maxim gun and they have not." Other nations soon followed this example.

One innovation connects with and influences other innovations. Take a simple example from a world that was not burdened with many innovations. The invention of bronze which also happened independently in different locations had dramatic consequences. Bronze is an alloy of copper and tin, two elements that do not naturally occur together. This geographic fact necessitated long-distance trade, Britain being one far-flung source. Since bronze is far harder than copper, it was in high demand, especially for weapons. (It is almost always true that new technologies are first used for weapons.) But it was also used in art. Small frequently quite exquisite objects of art were—and are—cast using the lost wax method. The technique is quite straightforward: fashion an object of wax, surround it with clay and then heat the clay so that the wax flows out of what is now a mold into which molten bronze may be poured. Weapons may be fashioned in the same way. For this, beeswax was critical. This practice added to the value of bee keeping which provided the only source of sweetener in the ancient world. Honey was in great demand for the brewing of mead—a sort of strong honeyed beer—which high status males and their bronze-equipped chums would imbibe in staggering quantities. Mead was also imperative for status-reinforcing funerals. The archaeology

An Introduction to Comparative Sociology

of the Bronze Age burial mound at Hochdorf provides evidence of just how mead soaked and jolly such occasions were. So here are the connections associated with bronze metallurgy: extensive trade in both bronze artifacts and the elements from which the alloy was made, effective and high-status weapons along with the establishment of a military hierarchy, and bee keeping for the strong beer that any leader needed to provide to his followers. The list of connections can be extended to new crafts, metalwork, smelting, fancy goods, and markets.

This simple, and a bit contrived, example makes the central point that innovations foster other innovations, both technological and social, and that the more innovations there are the more connections to new innovations appear. James Watt did not sit as a hermit in a Tibetan cave and suddenly have a vision of his steam engine. His innovation depended on preceding ideas and it answered a particular need. Watt's engine was needed to drain coal mines that were reaching depths that were prone to flooding. And, of course, the steam engine, endlessly refined, has brought about a cascade of change.

Sometimes innovations can be catastrophic. Eli Whitney is known for his invention of the cotton gin which had the immediate effect of making slavery profitable and encouraging its enthusiastic justification. In the slave-holding south, profitability determined the interpretation of God's will. Eli Whitney also, with modest chicanery, demonstrated the advantages of interchangeable parts. Not long after, in 1819 John Hall employed genuinely interchangeable parts and the techniques of mass production to produce his patented breech loading rifle for the U.S. Army.

William Ogburn highlighted the problems generated by rapid technological change with his concept of **cultural lag**. The pace of change in technology outstrips the ability of culture to adjust to the consequences of new technology. Material culture changes more rapidly than non-material culture. The problem with machine guns, for example, was driven home when it was discovered that machine guns kill Europeans just as effectively as their colonial subjects. At times, the glacial pace of enlightenment in the military mind is revealed by the statement of one British general (in 1915!) that the machine gun was a vastly overrated weapon. Technological change in this century and the past century has been dizzying. All sorts of new technologies have been developed which have side effects that are hard or impossible to manage. Thermonuclear weapons are terrifying to all.

A particular concern of Ogburn was the automobile, which was first seen as a solution to a gigantic urban problem. It was clear to all that

Thirteen. Social Change

automobiles did not do what horses did, in their tens of thousands on the streets of cities, creating a monumental problem. Manhattan is said to have been home to 100,000 horses. No one anticipated that the automobile would change the shape of American cities, clog the streets and freeways with stationary cars, and kill tens of thousands of people a year. As with all major innovations, automobiles affect society in hundreds of ways. Some have speculated that a major source of the feminist movement was the invention of the Bendix Automatic Starter (the thing that starts your car when you turn the key). When a car was so equipped young women did not need to ask dad, big brother, or hubby to crank-start the car and drive them somewhere. They could just hop in and go, and unsupervised, do what they pleased. Farfetched? The ability to move yourself and do what you want is not only freedom, it is power. The early feminists saw the bicycle in just such terms, and as an excuse, oh dear! to wear bloomers.

An interested observer in outer space would have been surprised to see a sudden blossoming of electro-magnetic energy emanating from the Earth. In earth time, this would have begun in 1899 when Marconi started transmitting radio waves over long distances. It presaged the modern world of electronic communication. Only a couple generations before that, Ada Lovelace conceived the intellectual basis for the computer.

The need for rapid computation was recognized in Victorian times. The Babbage "Difference Engine" was an elegant and massive mechanical creation of Victorian design. But by modern standards this hand-cranked machine didn't do much, and it did it only unreliably. Probably the first computer was the Colossus which was used to decode German encryptions. The first American computer, ENIAC, was commissioned by the Army with work commencing at the University of Pennsylvania in 1943. It used vacuum tubes arranged in groups of 10—ENIAC did not use the binary system—and when delivered in 1946 it consisted of a series of large cabinets in a room that had to be air conditioned because the heat given off by 17,000 vacuum tubes (the rumor that ENIAC browned out neighborhoods in Philadelphia is untrue). ENIAC did what the Army wanted it to do: it calculated the trajectory of artillery shells. Programming ENIAC meant rewiring it, and took weeks. Your smart phone has far more computational power than ENIAC. EDVAC used the binary code and followed in1949; UNIVAC came in 1951 and the public marveled at the power of this "electronic brain." From that point forward exponential leaps in computer power, availability and social dependence have followed, in ever-diminishing spans of time.

An Introduction to Comparative Sociology

Diffusion

Ralph Linton illustrated the importance of diffusion by penning a short essay portraying the morning routine of a typical American man. Everything he touches has been borrowed from another culture, from his cotton pajamas to his morning coffee and cigarette. Cultural traits have the potential to diffuse from one culture to another in a manner loosely analogous to the physical process of diffusion. The Romans were great borrowers, and this may have been the key to their success. What they couldn't steal they borrowed, everything from ship building, to weapons, to writing. It has been said that the Romans never met a god they didn't like, or at least tolerate. Diffusion in the modern world is far more comprehensive than Linton could have imagined when he was writing in the 1930s. It is not only more comprehensive, it is now all but instantaneous. In the nineteenth-century scientific discoveries traveled by the Victorian internet, a very efficient postal service. Now scientists communicate by the click of a mouse.

There are three types of diffusion. **Stimulus diffusion** takes place when contiguous cultures borrow from one another. The Canadians have adopted (and adapted, as is often the case) American football; we play hockey. We also wear moccasins, paddle about in canoes, and play lacrosse. The extent to which we have absorbed cultural traits is hard to appreciate. We are the only society where a statement such as "Donald is the boss of a powwow of meshugas" is likely to be understood. The nouns are respectively Scot, Dutch, Algonkian, and Yiddish. **Demic diffusion** fosters change when a population bearing different culture traits, including language, migrates. Archaeological, genetic, and linguistic evidence argues that we speak Indo-European because of the rapid migration of pastoralists from the Eurasian plains into Western Europe. These proto–Indo-European speakers had a variety of domestic animals, especially horses, wheeled vehicles, a tolerance for lactose, and an enduring penchant for violence. People throughout western and southern Africa speak Bantu because of the Bantu Expansion. Much of this process was historical. The process cuts both ways as the migrants also borrowed; Bantu spoken in South Africa contains Khoisan click consonants. The Crusaders carried their cultural traits to the Middle East—none of which were adopted because they were heretical or useless. For their part, the Crusaders readily took to Middle Eastern practices such as bathing and practical garments.

There is also **hierarchical diffusion,** by which traits diffuse to large population centers first and then to smaller centers. An innovation arising in New York City is likely to spread to Los Angeles before it arrives in Possum Walk, Alabama. Only rarely is Possum Walk, Alabama more fashion forward than Los Angeles.

Although often broadly used, **acculturation** may be viewed as a type of diffusion. This arises when the culture of a dominant society forces cultural traits upon a dependent society. The Marxist sociologist Antonio Gramsci, who wrote for years from a prison cell provided by Mussolini, railed about how the condition and world view of the **subaltern** society was manipulated, sometimes subtly and sometimes violently, by a dominant, **hegemonic,** society. Language is a big part of this. Why should the northern dialect of Florence be the official language taught to Italian school children asked Gramsci, if not to impose upon the poor south? In his Marxian abstruse, many-thousand-page *Prison Notes*, Gramsci might have discussed the Romanization of half the world by means of conquest and the agency of Latin. Hegemony is nothing new.

Social Movements

Except for those closely involved with a social movement, the common sense view is that (1) there is a folly or injustice in the land which clever, right-thinking people identify and (2) these people apprise Congress of this "problem" and enthusiastic congressmen pass a law fixing the problem. *This rarely happens.* No matter how immoral, cruel, vile, and disgusting a social condition is, there are groups, and often powerful groups, that favor such a condition because it is in their self-interest and spend lavishly to ensure its continuation.

The study of social movements tries to determine how social movements organize and overcome the opposition of other groups. Social movements have limited goals, they seek to change attitudes and especially laws. A good example is Mothers Against Drunk Driving (MADD), which changed attitudes that tolerated drunk driving and brought about the passage of severe penalties. Revolution has as a goal a dramatic transformation of society.

To be successful a social movement must transform *individual* problems into a *social* problem. People with common concerns join together into a **movement organization** which seeks redress. Social movements

An Introduction to Comparative Sociology

are social organizations; they have rules, a recognized structure, offices, property, and so on. One influential theory argues that the sole determinant of the successful social movement is its ability to gather together resources, meaning money, skilled people, committed workers and supporters and so on. The nature of the cause does not matter. In fact, this is far from true. The nature of the cause does matter. Many cause are likely to attract widespread popular support in the form of donations, committed membership and skilled specialists—resources. MADD is a clear case in point. Some social movements even when well-heeled will fail. Elliot Rudwick, a scholar of social movements—especially the civil rights movement—lectured on circumstances of one such failure. A small but wealthy group in New York City took up the cause of forbidding the exposure of naked animals in public. If you took your dog or cat or horse or any animal out for a walk on the streets of New York, it must be modestly covered. Predictably this righteous cause, though well-funded, was greeted by public indifference and the proposed legislation was disdained by the city council.

Successful social movements consistently follow similar stages: **Incipient, coalescence and organization, institutionalization, demise**. Initially there is a growing awareness of a common cause and a sharing of a common condition. The second stage brings the beginnings of formal organization and authority. The fundamental effort at this stage is to *advertise* the problem as something that is a **social problem**. Unless the public perceives a particular problem to be a social problem, the movement will fail. It will be starved of mobilizing resources. Often a book has a galvanizing effect on the public sentiment: *Uncle Tom's Cabin, The Passing of the Great Race, The Feminine Mystique*. Sometimes a widely reported collective event such as the 1969 Stonewall Riots in Greenwich Village, a response to police harassment of homosexuals, can kick-start a movement. With more forethought, the Gay Liberation Movement also put pressure on the American Library Association to change the catalog designation of books on homosexuality from "deviant behavior" to "lifestyles."

For some the commitment to the social movement is total; it is their life. For most the commitment is far less compelling but they still provide important support. The structure of leadership varies. The NAACP (National Association of Colored People), established in 1909, has always employed a conservative, legalistic strategy, and because the turnover of leadership was slow it tended to remain very conservative. The Congress of Racial Equality (CORE) had a rapid turnover of leadership and swiftly became radicalized in the 1960s. Entertainers—Dick Gregory for one—would donate their time, and funds would be raised in nightclubs. It took the mobilization of a charismatic leader, Martin Luther King, Jr., and the legislative genius of Lyndon Johnson to bring about a change in the law.

The goal of a social movement is institutionalized when legislation is passed to place the movement's view of the world into the social fabric. Demise usually follows the success of a movement organization because the goal has been achieved. Continuation of the movement, as in the case of the March of Dimes, depends on a change in goals. The March of Dimes was organized to provide funds for the development of a vaccine for polio, once a terrifying disease. The Salk vaccine brought success. Rumor has it that the March of Dimes officials tried keep the vaccine off the market. This was not true. What did happen was an unseemly squabble between developers of rival vaccines. The March of Dimes now raises funds for the prevention and treatment of birth defects.

On the Status of Women: The Long View

The status of women is inextricably tied to notions of gender equality, the right to equal employment, and the right to control their own bodies. Cross-culturally the status of women varies because of two predominant influences: (1) the degree to which women can form coalitions and (2) the level of violence within a particular society. Stated directly, the status of women is low in very violent societies and it is likewise low in societies in which it is difficult for women to come together and exert political power.

As a group, Iroquois matrilineages controlled productive land. Despite the high level of *external* violence invested by men in tribal wars, *internally* coalitions of women dominated lineage activities and greatly influence tribal politics. Critically they chose the men who sat on the Council of the Iroquois Confederation. It is true that the Iroquois Confederation, *in the form that Benjamin Franklin understood it*, was the guiding idea for the Articles of Confederation, but Franklin left out the high status of Iroquois women.

Conversely, among the Yanomamo who have no lineage structure, women do not and cannot form large or lasting coalitions. The status of women in this very violent male dominated culture is low and women are often subject to beatings. Students who have watched Chagnon's classic film, *The Feast,* will have noticed that Yanomamo women are *not* seen

An Introduction to Comparative Sociology

in groups and will often sit with their backs to the central plaza where men are active. Later in this film, a group of men are seen planning a raid. Yanomamo women do not like being married to a man from another village because she will have no male relative to protect her from beatings by her husband. Judith Schapira, who studied the Yanomamo in a different area, witnessed men from different villages engage in a violent tug of war using the arms of a young woman as a substitute rope to determine which village the girl would marry into. This tactic resulted in a dislocated shoulder. Such an activity was unthinkable among the Iroquois.

To be an "out of status woman," that is a woman without a man to protect (and control) her, in many cultures is to be a lightning rod for accusations of deviance, especially a charge of witchcraft. This applies also to an independent woman. In Nigeria, Nupe women traders are often the target of accusations of witchcraft: "Women alone are evil witches," it is said. Suspicion is often cast on women in coalitions, such as in the witches' Sabbat, once regarded as a regular activity. Midwives, who had a certain degree of independence, were often accused.

Unlike many tribal societies, the status of women in nineteenth-century industrial societies was low, and once married their status diminished to something approaching chattel or by one description, a *perpetual juvenile*. Of course some women achieved a certain degree of status and career success. Harriet Martineau was one such, despite being hard of hearing and supposedly not attractive, a considerable deficiency in Victorian England. Harriet Taylor Mill, the wife of John Stuart Mill, was a philosopher in her own right and the couple worked closely together. John Stuart Mill was a strong advocate of female equality. The generally low status and powerlessness of women, particularly married women, can be gauged by the difficulty of women to divorce for *any* reason—not adultery on the part of husband, nor physical cruelty, unless that was judged (by men) to be life threatening. Upon marriage a woman ceded her fortune to her husband and upon divorce would lose any right to regain it. She would lose her children and could be legally prevented from seeing them again. With some variation, such legal hazards and privations could be found throughout the "civilized" industrial world.

By the same token, it was remarkably easy for a man to incarcerate his wife in an insane asylum. This could be accomplished on the basis of the feeblest assertions of mental incompetence. The most celebrated case is that of Elizabeth Packard, the wife of Theophilis Packard a strict Calvinist divine. They were a disputatious couple by most accounts, but it

Thirteen. Social Change

was when Mrs. Packard began to publicly disagree with the wisdom of her husband's orthodoxy that the Reverend Packard had his wife incarcerated for insanity. This was easily accomplished because Illinois law did not require a public hearing when a wife was admitted to an insane asylum. There she remained for three years until her children obtained a writ of habeas corpus. Following her release she promptly penned *Marital Power Exemplified, or Three Years Imprisonment for Religious Belief*. A result was the Illinois law changed so that a public hearing was required for all—even wives. But few cases in which wives were dragooned into asylums had such a happy outcome. Most ended badly and, and without adjudication, often resulted in long-term incarceration under dreadful conditions. A review of the admittance reports at a California asylum in the early twentieth century is revealing. For both men and women these brief reports, about a paragraph or two, list a variety of symptoms—hearing voices or otherwise "odd" behavior. Other reports are extremely vague and would not be a basis for admittance today. In one admittance statement it was noted by the woman's relatives that, among a number of modest idiosyncrasies, "she no longer crochets."

By the middle part of the twentieth century, Western society had turned upside down—or better, right-side up. Now divorce was comparatively easy but the task of incarcerating one's wife was very difficult. Involuntary admissions now cannot be done without clinical appraisal and legal permission. This is a massive change. The lives of an entire category of people have been profoundly altered.

The Second World War vaulted women into an important role: war work. Who has not heard of Rosie the Riveter? Women were employed in a broad spectrum of tasks which were physically demanding and required very technical skills, lens grinding for example. Factories and government facilities magically began to provide day care. All this was abandoned upon victory. Women were expected to go back to crocheting and raising children. Not all did.

By the late 1940s and early 1950s it was widely accepted that if you had a husband, a car, a washing machine, a vacuum cleaner, and you were not, like the wives you saw on television, deliriously happy, there was something wrong with you. There were pills for that. By the mid–1960s that had changed. As with many social movements, there was a catalyst. This, as in other movements, was a book. The *Uncle Tom's Cabin* of the equal rights movement was Betty Friedan's *The Feminine Mystique* (1963). It wasn't the woman's fault anymore. The sources of injustice and inequality were in the open, and clear. Often clarity was obtained in consciousness raising sessions. The Civil Rights campaign also turned women into feminist activists because the exploitation of women—sometimes sexual—was bitterly resented.

Beginning early in the nineteenth century, the first women's rights movement fought for a number of social goals—laws against the exploitation of children was one successful campaign—but fought chiefly for women's suffrage, the right to vote. Upon passage of the 19th Amendment, the movement lost steam and was further enfeebled by the Great Depression. The postwar feminist movement(s) which had coalesced by the 1960s, skillfully employed social movement know-how (recalling that many women had been active in the civil rights movement) to engage injustice in employment rights, equal pay, educational rights, birth control, abortion rights, and the right to an harassment-free workplace. Organization skills, determination, and the strong support of women have largely prevailed, despite the opposition of well-financed conservative groups and religious fundamentalists.

Change Forestalled

Social movements fail for a variety of reasons. **Repression, decapitation,** and **co-optation** are the principal causes for failure. In this country the labor movement was repressed, often brutally, for decades. Organizers were jailed under syndicalist laws, written so broadly as to permit the arrest of anyone who talked of the union movement or attended a rally, or simply annoyed the local sheriff. Just after the First World War the Universal Negro Improvement Association (UNIA) founded by Marcus Garvey, provided hope and pride to many thousands. Harlem was host to huge, prideful marches which, although entirely peaceful, alarmed the authorities, none more so that J. Edgar Hoover who was soon to take control of the FBI. A goal of the UNIA was to return black Americans to Africa. To this end funds were solicited and the Black Star Line was established. This enterprise was poorly organized and sloppily run giving the FBI the chance to arrest and incarcerate Marcus Garvey on a variety of trumped-up charges. He was then swiftly deported. Without Garvey's commanding figure, the UNIA folded. An unknown, but likely sizable, number of embittered members went underground only to emerge during the depression as far more radical groups, the Black Muslims among them.

Thirteen. Social Change

During the depression when urban blacks were starving and lynching on the rise in the cotton south, it was not hard to convince blacks that they were being oppressed by "white devils."

During the depression the Townsend Plan, initiated by Dr. Francis Townsend, became a powerful political force—for a while. It proposed a quick fix for unemployment: all retired people over the age of 60 would receive a monthly check for $200 from the Federal Government, the only stipulation being that you had to spend it that month. People over 60 thought it an excellent plan and they flocked to the movement, and the polls, in large numbers. The Townsend movement grew like Topsy and the organizational skills capable of running a large organization were lacking. How much would it Cost? Dr. Townsend did not know but he insisted it wasn't much of a problem. A more conservative plan (but very radical for some in Congress) undercut Dr. Townsend's scheme. It is known as Social Security. The Townsend Movement's followers were largely co-opted; their self-interest and their loyalty had been taken over. For a time, members of the Townsend Movement continued to meet in their homes. They would carefully consider the minutes of the last meeting, and then get down to the real purpose of the meeting which was to play cards.

History, to borrow a phrase from Stephen J. Gould, is massively contingent. Whether or not the dialectics of Hegel and Marx are a valid understanding of history is questionable, but in a much more narrow sense it is useful. The cascade of connections brought about by new ideas, technologies, and cultures fuel the process of **syncretism**, a term which can be used in the sense of a reconciliation of opposites or just a merging and reorganization of ideas and technologies. This process can be marvelously creative. Consider the renaissance (rebirth) of art, and science that blossomed after the discovery of classical learning and art. Nowhere was this more impressive than in Florence, Italy where a curious misconception prevailed. Artists, musicians, and city fathers thought of classical Greek and Roman theatre as something along the lines of a Judy Garland musical. Instead of speaking or chanting their lines, the Florentines supposed classical actors sang them. A committee was formed and opera was born. We can readily see this new sort of theatre growing in sophistication and spectacle through the centuries. The most extravagant, moving, and lengthy operas were staged by Richard Wagner. It is from Wagnerian staging that we get the stereotypical image of a Viking as a shaggy ruffian in a horned helmet. There is an American version of Wagner in an entirely new medium. It is found in the brilliant work of the cartoonist Chuck Jones. In the visually impressive *What's Opera Doc,* a Siegfried-like Elmer Fudd tragically shoots the impishly clever Bugs Bunny and is dramatically remorseful. No one in sixteenth-century Florence anticipated any of this.

Fourteen

Globalization

Some time ago I received a phone call from the student newspaper wondering if I had time for a photograph in my office. I did. Flattered, I picked lint off my sport jacket, combed my hair, and put on the tie that I keep in my desk drawer for grand occasions. The photographer arrived, politely asked me to move aside, snapped a digital picture of my old manual typewriter, and departed. It was one of life's little epiphanies, and I reflected on how much had changed. There is a word for it: **globalization**. This multifaceted sea change is justifiably the subject of a huge amount of scholarly research and literature by social scientists of every variety. Economists are very interested in this field, unsurprisingly since globalization makes some people lots of money and impoverishes others. Globalists, by the way, wear different hats. There are hyper-globalizers, who see an end to the nation-state (foreseeing the transnational state), and just plain globalizers. Both camps spar about how far-reaching and comprehensive globalization will be. There are no globalism deniers.

According to the *New York Times* (March 12, 2019), the continents are linked together by 750,000 miles of underwater cable that transmit untold amounts of information at something marginally less than the speed of light. This and other remarkably efficient means of communication—there are now five hundred commercial satellites in orbit—are the sinews of globalization.

Communication sustains and drives globalization; its efficiency can be measured by invoking a term employed by economists: information friction. Crude comparisons can be informative. The first transatlantic cable was laid in 1858. With great pomp, a suitably pious telegraph message was sent by Queen Victoria to President Buchanan. Two weeks later the cable broke down, sizzled by the high voltage it carried. After several unsuccessful tries, finally in 1866 a durable cable, weighing several thousand pounds per mile, established reliable telegraphic communication. Transmission was slow and expensive, no less than five Gilded Age dollars

An Introduction to Comparative Sociology

a word. But the price was paid because the timely availability of commercial data enhanced profits. In contrast transatlantic communication by ship usually took a week to 10 days—if all went well. In the preceding century it was a matter of months. In the sixteenth and seventeenth centuries transatlantic travel was not only very slow, it was lethally unreliable.

It is idle but interesting to speculate about when globalization began. Was it, as the poet John Keats describes, the moment of wonder when Balboa (not Cortez) "star'd at the Pacific—and all his men look'd at each other with wild surmise—Silent upon a peak in Darien." That was in 1513. Or was it when Magellan's fleet, or what was left of it, completed its circumnavigation of the globe, a feat of navigation that provoked many a wild surmise, particularly about trade and making money. Galileo's telescope was initially sold to Venetian merchants so that they could spot the identity of arriving ships hours before their competitors. Timely information meant profit.

Precious objects and manufactures are relatively immune to distance, whether overland or by sea. This has been true since prehistoric times. Fancy flint and obsidian (natural glass) were traded over great distances in both the Old and New Worlds. Cowrie shells in Africa, and spondylus shells, a colorful mollusk, sometimes called "spiny oyster," was harvested in the Aegean, traded throughout Europe and made into beads. An extensive trade in Baltic amber was established prehistorically and continues undiminished to this day.

The Silk Road carried great quantities of precious commodities via a passage of months linking China, across central Asia, to Anatolia. From there goods flowed into Europe. This trade was sustained by that remarkably durable animal, the camel, and a system of *caravanserai* (Persian for caravan inn) stationed at intervals of a day's march. In a sense this great interconnected network of towns and *caravanserai*—communities of rest and commerce—constitute a vast disparate city laid out across much of the Old World. Upon this, "ceaselessly flowing stream of life," not only goods but ideas, tales, philosophies, and religions moved along the Silk Road. Caravans provided a sense of community, mutual assistance and safety in regions where the Silk Road attracted brigands who would be delighted to kill you for your sandals, much less items of great value. Might this long distance trade be the beginning of globalization?

A far greater volume of commerce traveled over the cruelest sea. The Middle Passage, carrying enslaved Africans to the New World, was the fulcrum of the Triangle Trade. For centuries by means of routes that

Fourteen. Globalization

crisscrossed Africa, slaves would be brought to the coast, shipped to the plantations of the New World, which then shipped the products of the slave labor, principally sugar and tobacco, to Europe. Once there ships set out for Africa laden with—guns, rum, and other manufactures. The profits to be made were enormous, the risks relatively small—for the slavers, that is. Estimates of the number of Africans enslaved and transported to the Western Hemisphere compiled by the Trans-Atlantic Trade Data Base run to well over 12 million, of whom nearly two million died at sea. Four hundred thousand arrived at North American ports.

Abstruse cogitations by economists aside, money, in its several forms, has value. And the ability to move it about safely is essential to long distance commerce. The Knights Templar—an international order of warrior monks—which, upon being made wealthy by crusader donations, diverted their talents to banking. The Templars devised a method whereby a traveler, especially a pilgrim, could deposit valuables at one Templar House, obtain a letter (likely in code) that could be redeemed at another Templar House, in, say, the Holy Land. The Knights Templar has been characterized as the Western Union of the Middle Ages.

Globalization becomes a fair description of the world when the most essential commodity is the rapid transmission of information. Eric Sheppard, in *A World of Difference*, states that the "dynamic of globalization [is] the increased range, speed, and intensity of human induced connections between different parts of the world." Anyone who has discussed their computer problems with a friendly voice in India, moved money about with the click of a mouse, or had an image of their innards examined by a consulting doctor in another state (or country) has a sense of this new international world.

The globalized world now functions as one great cosmopolitan metropolis seamlessly connected by the speed of communication and transportation. Think in terms of the container revolution in ocean transport, of the supertanker, or the speed of commercial aviation. By some lights the largest business in the world is tourism, not an unreasonable assertion if the many-tentacle connections—food, housing, transport—of tourists are taken into account in their search for "sun, sand, sea, and sex." More prosaically, museums, and ancient ruins may be added to this. The capabilities of commercial aviation are very great; it should not be forgotten that the United States transported the soldiers of an entire army to southeast Asia largely by means of commercial aviation.

There are many facets to this transformation. The penetration of

An Introduction to Comparative Sociology

boundaries is consistently thought to have to have magical properties. If so, there is much magic hovering about this new globalized world. If that analogy seems a bit lightheaded consider what the present world would look like to someone viewing it from the vantage point of the nineteenth century. Transnational companies which span distance and national boundaries are the leading agents of this boundary jumping. Such companies are nothing new. The British East India Company is a prime example. It controlled directly or indirectly most of what is now Pakistan, Bangladesh, and India; it maintained its own armies (the training ground for the young Duke of Wellington); and made great fortunes by extracting the wealth of that region. Agriculture was transformed to produce crops useful to the home country. Instead of food, cotton and that great moneymaker opium was grown to the detriment of the local population. That sets the pattern: early transnational companies were an adjunct to colonial conquests.

By the early twentieth century there were a number of large transnational companies such as the Shell Oil Company based in the Netherlands (its home country) and the United Fruit Company which at one time controlled nearly all of the growing, harvesting and export of bananas. It could call on the Marine Corps when its interests were threatened. The growth of transnational companies since the end of the Second World War has been enormous. By the estimate of the United Nations, there are now well over 70,000 transnational companies. "Capitalism," according to Sheppard, "flourishes by expanding into new areas of social life and new places." Coca-Cola-guzzling GIs spread that product, by design, around the globe. It was not so much weapons, as gadgets, soft drinks, and Hollywood that made up the vanguard of American hegemony.

Transnational corporations are not moored to any particular place and can seek the holy grail of production: cheap labor. Benefits accrue to host countries in the form of technology transfers as plants are constructed, labor hired (skilled and unskilled), and subcontracts parceled out. Patent rights and copyright laws are frequently ignored and knockoff products—fashions, computer technology, films, records, your uncle's $75 "Rolex"—flood the world.

Operating within a seven and a half billion strong sea of humanity, transnational agencies are both a cause and conduit of insight and innovation, typically entrepreneurial. The interconnections, individual, corporate, state, are so numerous as to be ungraspable, or at any rate uncountable. Connections fostered by the multiplier effect now spin off new

Fourteen. Globalization

ideas, technologies, etc., which are then taken up by transnational corporations and spread around the world.

With modest variations there are two production and marketing patterns employed by transnational corporations. One being, so to speak, is linear. An innovation can arise in one country, be sent to another to be evaluated, sent to another to be designed for production, sent to another to be manufactured, and then transferred to markets worldwide. The other pattern is solar in that the parts of a complex product, an automobile, an airplane, a refrigerator, are assembled at one central point but that central assembly point draws the constituent parts—in some cases thousands of different parts—of that product from around the globe drawing upon a network of subcontractors. Industrial innovations can be immensely valuable, as in nanotechnology and artificial intelligence, and attract a correlative activity: industrial espionage. Many companies and countries exploit this source of information transfer as a matter of routine. The Soviet Union which was not known for innovation except in the realm of weapons relied heavily on this practice.

Cross-cultural exchanges provoke syncretism and creativity. The opening bars of "Rhapsody in Blue" by George Gershwin show the influence of the music of the East European *shtetel*, klezmer, on the classically trained Gershwin. A spectacular example of this is provided by the interconnections and creativity by which a popular song in the 1920s, "Black Snake Moan No. 2," may be found in the remote ancestry of rock and roll: Mississippi blues to Memphis, by the Illinois Central Railroad to Chicago to be influenced by jazz and commercial "race music," and soon to receive infusions from folk and country music. The complexity of this genesis can be gauged by the fact that Paramount Records began as a subsidiary of the Wisconsin Chair Company which also made record players—so, then, why not records? Rock and roll has been described as a creature of "loud." It is only because of amplifiers and electric guitars, that such music is loud enough to be heard in an auditorium full of ticket purchasing (and record buying) teenagers. A youthful Van Morrison was introduced to this musical synthesis because of his father's records, acquired while in Detroit, and by recordings carried by merchant mariners to his native Belfast.

Transnational corporations can also bring hardships and costs to the host countries. Traditional cultural patterns long attuned to local conditions may be undercut. Rural people can be pitchforked into impoverished urban environments, straining resources. The ballyhooed advent of the Green Revolution which offered super productive seeds provided a new

An Introduction to Comparative Sociology

market for the petrochemical industry. But the wonder seeds required fertilizer, pesticides, and irrigation pumps, which were expensive and beyond the means of rural farmers throughout the Third World. People are invariably enchanted to see Balinese men herding flocks of ducks to rice paddies so that they can feed on the insects infesting the young rice shoots: much better than pesticides which kill the useful fauna in the paddy and can harm the local hydrology. And you can always eat the ducks. In the end, because of the Green Revolution many Third World farmers—from the Philippines to Indonesia—fell into debt and were displaced from the land.

It isn't only transnational corporations that are active globalizers. State run organizations, or affiliated organizations, transfer information and culture: the North Atlantic Treaty Organization (NATO) formed after the Second World War to counter the Soviet threat is a prime example, as are the Peace Corps, or the Saudi sponsored *madrasas* which proselytize Wahhabism throughout much of the world. The World Trade Organization (WTO) is fundamental to global economics; likewise the International Monetary Fund (IMF).

In vital ways, the harsher attributes and consequences of globalization are blunted and softened by the activities of non-governmental organizations (NGOs) which are often nonprofit. Big and small, there are thousands, and possibly millions, of NGOs with international connections. One familiar example would be the National Geographic Society. NGOs are nothing new: missionary societies to help the benighted non-believer, the Red Cross founded to nurse the appalling numbers of sick (cholera) and wounded of the Crimean War, and the Salvation Army mustered to succor the urban poor of Victorian England. The term Transnational Organization is found in the Charter of the United Nations and now refers to, locally and internationally, millions of non-profit organizations that have as their purpose social aid and the mitigation of structural violence inherent in globalization.

Likewise inherent in globalization is the process of cultural exchange along many avenues: print, film, literature, fashion, fast food chains, scholarly exchange, medicine, political values. John Lennon and Ronald McDonald are more recognizable than any public leader. Newborns in the Amazon are named after Princes Diana. Any widespread trading sphere is likely to develop a trade language such as Mobilian among the Native Americans in the Southeastern United States or Swahili throughout much of East African. In the globalized world, English may well be thought of as such a language. However that may be, the use of English in cross-cultural

Fourteen. Globalization

communication is standard. It is the language of international trade, scholarship, and a second language in many countries. The planes you ride in are likely to be guided to a safe landing in English.

If cultural homogenization is a consequence of globalization, it is most pronounced among the elite of all nations. As has been the case for centuries the elite have a great deal more in common and are far more comfortable, with their counterparts in other nations than with the lowly *hoi polloi* of their own country, and little if any among the very poor with whom they would have trouble communicating.

It is difficult to envision with confidence what globalization will look like a generation forward. Perhaps the twenty-first century is to be the meth lab of social change, and globalization the agent of impoverishment and economic inequality, benefitting only a minute elite; or globalization may be subject to humane control, limiting hardship and expanding the benefits of communication, commerce, and science.

Of course there is another aspect to this process: nature has a vote!

Coda:
The Consolations of Sociology

Sociology is driven by curiosity and, fundamentally, by women and men who are willing to invest the time and effort to learn the skills to obtain reliable knowledge about how society *really* works. It is not too much to say that without the enterprise of sociologists the world would be a poorer place. To take just one important example: how we understand the class system and its inequities has been shaped by sociology. The power elite is a familiar concept to the merest freshman; we know that many of the homeless, if not the majority, are children; we recognize that women are uniformly shortchanged by a male dominated social system; "separate but equal," once the law in many states, is rightly dismissed as a racist dodge intended to diminish and control; sociologists have tabulated the disparity by class among the casualties of the war in Vietnam. They have examined the influence of father's status and wealth on his son's social mobility and, belatedly, mother's influence on her daughter's mobility ... and on and on. Such studies along with a host of other fine-grained studies on all facets of American society probe and reveal in detail, much as a CAT scan does the human body. The more such knowledge becomes general, the more difficult it is for the powerful to grab, steal, manipulate, and distort. As Paul Sites, the author of *Control Theory* has said, "The certain thing about sociology is that you know when you are being ripped off."

Sociologists investigate anything that involves humans in groups, which as you are now well aware of is a very great deal. One of the advantages of the discipline of sociology is indeed its breadth. The impact of this advantage is twofold. First, the breadth of sociology derives from the fact that sociology can be described as a bridge discipline. One of the strengths of sociology can be found in the fact that sociology is at home in both history and anthropology and can be said to link, to bridge, the two disciplines. Comparative studies in sociology draw upon both history and anthropology and are enriched by them. Our understanding of the long-term processes of society rests on this broad, multidisciplinary foundation. Second, sociology requires training across a broad spectrum of skills. One certain consequence of the scope of the sociological enterprise is that students of this discipline will graduate with extensive knowledge of (1) how society really works, (2) research skills, and (3) the ability to write clear English. These are valuable skills; moreover these are skills that are surprisingly scarce. Women and men so equipped are welcome in business, government, and research. Equally, such skills, the red meat of the sociological enterprise, provide good footing for graduate studies in any discipline.

Principal Sources and Further Reading

Chapter One. How to Explain Society: Different Views. A compendium of social theory and theorists can be found in Don Martindale's *The Nature and Types of Social Theory*. *Theoretical Sociology* by Randall Collins and *The Discovery of Society* by Randall Collins and Michael Makowsky are both solid and accessible. The theoretical writings of Robert Merton present the case for functionalism; see especially *On Social Structure and Science* edited by Piotr Sztompka.

All of the theorists discussed are the subject of biographies that also examine their theoretical stances. Karl Marx is the subject of many biographies, see *Karl Marx: A Nineteenth Century Life* by Jonathon Sperber. Works on Marxist theory are legion and frequently recondite in the extreme. One book that I have not put aside in frustration is *The Worldly Philosophers* by Robert Heilbroner which contains an especially clear discussion of Marx's perspective. On power see John Kenneth Galbraith's *The Anatomy of Power*. On conflict theory, contemporary views see Randall Collins, several works.

Max Weber is also the subject of numerous biographies, one of which was written by his wife Marianne Weber. *Max Weber: Politics and the Spirit of Tragedy* by John Diggins is a detailed, clear and entertaining examination of this complicated man. *The Iron Cage* by Arthur Mitzman remains the classic study. Weber's *Economy and Society*, while valuable, is an assemblage of drafts, notions, and ideas that hint at what he would have produced had he lived.

Émile Durkheim's works are still fresh and provide a firm basis for functionalism. Steven Lukes is the author of the definitive biography of Émile Durkheim: *Émile Durkheim*. For an anthropological perspective there is *Cultural Materialism* by Marvin Harris. For systems theory see *General Systems Theory* by Ludwig von Bertalanffy. On symbolic interac-

Principal Sources and Further Reading

tionism see *Symbolic Interactionism* by Herbert Blumer. See also *Symbolic Interactionism* by Bernard N. Meltzer et al. Charles Horton Cooley's views are found in *Human Nature and the Social Order*. Examples of total institutions are found in Erving Goffman's *Asylums*. C. Owen Lovejoy's (1988) perspective on bipedalism is found in "Evolution of Human Walking," *Scientific American* 259. On the life of C. Wright Mills there is *Taking It Big* by Stanley Aronowitz. Henry Chapin (1926), "Family vs Institution," The Adoption History Project. For the studies of René Spitz, see René Spitz (1949), "The Role of Ecological Factors in Emotional Development in Infancy," *Child Development* 20, no. 3.

Chapter Two. Reliable Knowledge. Books on both qualitative and quantitative research are legion. A fine grounding in research can be found in *Reliable Knowledge* by John Ziman. For an introduction to statistical methods, see *Figuring Anthropology* by David Hurst Thomas which provides an exceptionally clear discussion of statistics. Brilliant applications of participant observation and ethnography are to be found in *You Owe Yourself a Drunk* by James P. Spradley and *The Broken Fountain* by Thomas Belmonte. James O. Finckenauer's study of the Scared Straight program is found in *Scared Straight: The Panacea Phenomenon Revisited*. Elton Mayo's reflections on the Hawthorne Study can be found in *The Social Problems of an Industrial Civilization*.

Chapter Three. Culture. The number of definitions and explanations of the concept of cultures is equal to the number of introductory texts. On the sudden appearance in the prehistoric record of what may be taken as evidence for modern culture see *The Dawn of Human Culture* by Richard Klein. What Noam Chomsky meant by deep structure is highly technical see *Current Issues in Linguistic Theory*. On the Cheyenne see E. Adamson Hoebel, *The Cheyenne*. David Anthony's discussion of Indo-European is found in *The Horse, the Wheel, and Language*. The aboriginal concepts of totemism and Dreamtime are classically found in W. E. H. Stanner's *The Dreaming and Other Essays*. On symbolism, see Rodney Needham's *Symbolic Classification*. On culture as a tool, see Paul Sites, *Control: The Basis for Social Order*. And see also his introductory text.

Chapter Four. Social Organization and Stratification. The study of kinship is the red meat of anthropology and a Cliffs Notes review can be found in any introductory text. More specialized studies can be found in *Kinship and Marriage* by Robin Fox and *The Elementary Structures of Kinship* by Claude Lévi-Strauss. On life chances see Ralf Dahrendorf, *Life Chances: Approaches to Social and Political History*. *American Kinship*

Principal Sources and Further Reading

by David Schneider focuses on kinship within industrial societies. The standard source for bureaucracy is found in *Economy and Society*. The request for quantities of gold braid is mentioned in *Stalin: The Court of the Red Tsar* by Simon Montefiore. The classic (and dated) account of the Indian caste system is found in *Caste in India* by John Henry Hutton. Other sources are *On the Indian Caste System* by M. Madhok and *The Western Foundation of the Caste System* edited by Martin Farek. See also David Gilmore's (2018) *The British in India: A Social History of the Raj*. The classic accounts of supposedly enfeebled American lineages are *The Kallikak Family* by Henry Goddard and *The Jukes* by R. L. Dugdale. The highly influential *The Passing of the Great Race* was written by Madison Grant. On lynching see *The Tragedy of Lynching* by Arthur F. Raper. A more fine-grained account (county by county) is found in *A Festival of Violence* by Stewart E. Tolnay. On the convict leasing system see "Punishment After Slavery" by Christopher R. Adamson (1968), *Social Problems* 30, no. 5. For a searing examination of slavery and slave owners see *Our Man in Charleston* by Christopher Dickey. For the rise of Jim Crow, there is *The Strange Career of Jim Crow* by C. Vann Woodward.

Chapter Five. Economics. On xharo, see Polly Wiessner (1977), *A Regional System of Reciprocity for Reducing Risks Among the Kung San*, University Microfilms. For Monte Testaccio, "Sorting Through a Mountain of Pottery to Trace the Roman Oil Trade," *Archaeology*. Bronisław Malinowski's description of the Kula Ring is found in *Argonauts of the Western Pacific*. For the Yanomamo, see Napoleon Chagnon's introductory standard *Yanomamö: The Fierce People*. For the world system, Immanuel Wallerstein, *The Modern World System*. Dependency theory presented in "The Development of Underdevelopment," by Andre Gundar Frank (1966), *Monthly Review* 18, no. 4. Daniel Chirot applies Wallerstein's theory in *How Societies Change* (1st edition). Gerhard Lenski's discussion of levels of social complexity can be found in *Power and Privilege: A Theory of Social Stratification*.

Chapter Six. Strategies of Political Control. Only technically short of deification and the various grandiose titles for Stalin can be found in Joel Carmichael's *Stalin's Masterpiece*. For the power elite see, C. Wright Mills, *The Power Elite*, and note how little has changed. For a discussion of framing see Erving Goffman's *Frame Analysis*. For a broad comparative discussion of fundamentalism see Karen Armstrong, *The Battle for God: A History of Fundamentalism*. For a view that is closer to home see *The Evangelicals* by Frances FitzGerald.

Principal Sources and Further Reading

Chapter Seven. Demography. For a detailed introduction see *Demography: The Study of Human Population* by Jennifer Hickes Lundquist et al. John Graunt, as quoted in *An Introduction to Population Ecology* by G. Evelyn Hutchison. On the demographic transition as first introduced by Warren Thompson in 1929 see "Population" *American Journal of Sociology* 34, no. 6. On cohort analysis see Peter Lowenberg (1971), "The Psychohistorical Origins of the Nazi Youth Cohort," *American Historical Review* 76, no. 5. Aaron V. Cicourel (1967), "Fertility Planning and the Social Organization of Family Life, Some Methodological Issues," *Journal of Social Issues* 23, no. 4. And see Gail Kligman (1992), "When Abortion Is Banned," *The National Council for Soviet and East European Studies.*

Chapter Eight. Urbanism. On Çatal Höyük, *The Leopard's Tale* by Ian Hodder. On urban sociology see Mark Abrahamson's *Urban Sociology: A Global Introduction.* Herbert Gans, *The Urban Villagers.* On the vibrant city of Miletus, see John Freely, *The Flame of Miletus.* The classic account of the early city is Gideon Sjoberg's *The Preindustrial City.* For a global perspective on squatter's Settlements see Robert Neuwirth's *Squatter Settlements.* On Pruitt-Igoe and its end, see Rowan Moore's film *Pruitt-Igoe: Death of American Urban Dream.*

Chapter Nine. The Sociology of Religion. On millenarian religions see Norman Cohn, *Pursuit of the Millennium* and *The Trumpet Shall Sound* by Peter Worsley. On civil religion see Robert Bellah, *Varieties of Civil Religion.* A critical view on studies of shamanism is provided by Alice Kehoe, *Shamans and Religion.* See also *The Earth Is Weeping* by Peter Cozzens. On ritual in the Soviet Union see *Ritual in Industrial Society—The Soviet Case* by Christel Lane. Regarding the maintenance of Lenin's corpse, see Ilya Zbarsky and Samuel Hutchinson, *Lenin's Embalmers.* And also Katherine Verdery, *The Political Lives of Dead Bodies.* On Shinto see Helen Hardacre's *Shinto: A History.*

Chapter Ten. How to Manufacture Deviance. Cesare Baccaria's philosophy is found in his *Crimes and Punishments.* The Marxist view on deviance was expanded by Willem Bonger in *Criminality and Economic Conditions.* Murray Edelman's quote is found *Politics as Symbolic Action.* On the concept of stigma contests, see Edwin M. Schur's *The Politics of Deviance.* E. E. Evans-Pritchard's discussion of the Azande is found in *Witchcraft, Oracles, and Magic Among the Azande.* For a general introduction to witchcraft, Lucy Mair's *Witchcraft.* Christina Larner's *The Enemies of God: The Witch-Hunt in Scotland* is brilliant. On the Spanish Inquisition, see Henry Kamen, *The Spanish Inquisition.* Robert Merton's introduction to

Principal Sources and Further Reading

strain theory, 1938, is found in "Social Structure and Anomie," *American Sociological Review* 3, no. 5. On the mass production of deviance see my *Politics of Demonology*. The classic account of the Great Purge is by Robert Conquest, *The Great Terror*. For a more tempered view of the purge see J. Arch Getty's *The Road to Terror* and Stephen Kotkin's *Stalin*. For life in the Soviet Union see *Everyday Stalinism* by Sheila Fitzpatrick. See also George Leggett, *The Cheka: Lenin's Political Police*. On evolutions of Stalin's political police see Simon Wolin and Robert M. Slusser, "The Evolution of the Soviet Secret Police," in *The Soviet Secret Police*. There is also Arkady Vaksberg's *The Prosecutor and the Prey: Vyshinsky and the 1930s Moscow Show Trials*. Also Robert Tucker and Stephen F. Cohen, *The Great Purge Trial*. An excellent overall source is Adam Ulam's *A History of Soviet Russia*. Raul Hilberg's magisterial *The Destruction of the European Jews* (2nd edition) is the classic—and most detailed—account of the Holocaust. On the Palmer raids, see Robert K. Murray's *Red Scare: A Study in National Hysteria*. And also Constantine Panuzio, *The Deportation Crisis of 1919–1920*, and NGPL, *Report on the Illegal Practices of the United States Government*. Protecting the Eucharist from invaders: Jean Johimsthal, personal communication. For the best account of the McCarthy Era see David Oshinsky's *A Conspiracy So Immense*. And there is Edward Schneier's "White Collar Vigilantism: The Politics of Anti-Communism in the United States" in *Vigilante Politics*, H. Jon Rosenbaum. See also Peter Irons' "*The Cold War Crusade of the United States Chamber of Commerce*" in *The Specter*, edited by Robert Griffith and Athan Theoharis. Among the many biographies of Mao Zedong see *Mao: The Unknown Story* by Jung Chang and Jon Halliday. Reference to Ox Ghosts, etc., see Richard Solomon's *Mao's Revolution and Chinese Political Culture*.

Chapter Eleven. Collective Behavior. A standard source is *Collective Behavior* by Ralph Turner and Lewis M. Killian. Gustave Le Bon's cogitations can be found in *The Crowd: A Study of the Popular Mind*. Herbert Blumer's *A New Outline of the Principles of Sociology*. On value added theory see Neil Smelser's *Theory of Collective Behavior*. The Watts riot is detailed in *Fire This Time* by Gerald Horne. On the angels of Mons see David Clarke's *The Angels of Mons: Phantom Soldiers and Ghostly Guardians* and Paul Fussell's *The Great War in Modern Memory*. A detailed discussion of the GDR, the Stasi, and the fall of the Berlin Wall is found in Mary Elise Sarotte's *Collapse: The Accidental Opening of the Berlin Wall*.

Chapter Twelve. Sociology of War. Military historians are increasingly concerned with the cultural and social aspects of military conflict.

Principal Sources and Further Reading

See especially Max Hastings, Robert Citino, and Cathal J. Nolan. Focused treatments on the sociology of warfare are few, but see Miguel Centeno and Elaine Enriquez, *The Sociology of War*, and *The Sociology of War and Violence* by Siniša Malešević. For prehistoric warfare and tribal conflicts see Lawrence H. Keeley's *War Before Civilization*. On Sumerian society see J. N. Postgate's *Early Mesopotamia*. For Japan's outlawing firearms see *Giving Up the Gun* by Noel Perrin. On the Hall Rifle and John Hall see Jon Oplinger in Bernard Fishman's *The Story of Maine in 112 Objects*. For the Hoplite revolution see *Athens* by Christian Meier. On Inca propaganda see Alfred Métraux's *The History of the Incas*. A history of the Janissaries can be found in Godfrey Goodwin's *The Janissaries*. On totemism, see C. Lévi-Strauss.

Chapter Thirteen. Social Change. On Paleolithic tools see Richard Klein, *The Human Career*. The term Neolithic Revolution was coined by the venerable V. Gordon Childe; see his *Man Makes Himself*. For a more recent account, see Steven Mithen's *After the Ice Age*. On punctuated equilibrium see Niles Eldredge's *Pattern of Evolution* and also Stephen J. Gould's *Punctuated Equilibrium*. On multilinear evolution see Julian Steward, *Cultural Change*, and Leslie White's *The Evolution of Culture*. On ENIAC, see Scott McCartney et al., *ENIAC*. For resource mobilizations see John McCarthy and Mayer Zald (1993), "Resource Mobilization and Social Movements." *American Journal of Sociology* 99. On social movements see Armand Mauss, *Social Movements as Social Problems*. For a much older social movement see *How to Plan a Crusade* by Christopher Tyerman.

Chapter Fourteen. Globalization. On the transatlantic cable, *A Thread Across the Ocean* by John Steele Gordon. Giddens et al. has an excellent section on globalization. See also *Globalization* by Manfred Steger. There are several histories of the Silk Road but see Valerie Hansen's *The Silk Road*. Although not directly focused on globalization, I have relied on Eric Sheppard, *et al*'s *A World of Difference* which is especially strong on the structural violence associated with globalization. On the tangled connections of rock and roll see *The History of Rock and Roll* by Ed Ward and *The Birth of the Loud* by Ian S. Port. On the consistent absence of altruism among the elite see *Collapse* by Jared Diamond and *Warning* by Richard A. Clarke and R. P. Eddy.

Bibliography

Anthony, D. W. (2010). *The Horse, the Wheel and Language.* Princeton: Princeton University Press.
Armstrong, K. (2004). *The Battle for God: Fundamentalism in Judaism, Christianity and Islam.* New York: Harper Perennial.
Bellah, R. N., & Hammond, P. E. (2013). *Varieties of Civil Religion.* Eugene, OR: Wipf and Stock.
Bertalanffy, L. (2015). *General System Theory: Foundations, Development, Applications.* New York: George Braziller.
Blumer, H. (1969). *Symbolic Interactionism: Perspective and Methods.* Englewood Cliffs, N.J.: Prentice-Hall.
Centeno, M. A., & Enriquez, E. (2017). *War & Society.* Cambridge, UK: Polity.
Chagnon, N. A. (1997). *Yanomamo.* Fort Worth: Harcourt College.
Clarke, R. A. (2018). *WARNINGS: Finding Cassandras to Stop Catastrophes.* New York: Ecco.
Cohn, N. (1993). *The Pursuit of the Millennium: Revolutionary Millenarians and Mystical Anarchists of the Middle Ages.* London: Pimlico.
Collins, R. (2004). *Theoretical Sociology.* New York: Wadsworth.
Collins, R., & Makowsky, M. (2010). *The Discovery of Society.* Boston: McGraw-Hill Higher Education.
Dickey, C. (2016). *Our Man in Charleston.* New York: Random House.
Diggins, J. P. (1997). *Max Weber: Politics and the Spirit of Tragedy.* New York: Basic Books.
Eldredge, N. (2000). *The Pattern of Evolution.* New York: W. H. Freeman.
Várek, M., Jalki, D., Pathan, S., & Shah, P. (2017). *Western Foundations of the Caste System.* Cham: Springer International.
Fitzpatrick, Sheila (1999). *Everyday Stalinism.* New York: Oxford University Press.
Freely, J. (2018). *The Flame of Miletus: The Birth of Science in Ancient Greece and How It Changed the World.* London: I. B. Tauris.
Galbraith, J. K. (1985). *The Anatomy of Power.* London: Transworld.
Getty, J. A., Naumov, O. V., & Sher, B. (2010). *The Road to Terror.* New Haven: Yale University Press.
Gordon, J. S. (2003). *A Thread Across the Ocean: The Heroic Story of the Transatlantic Cable.* New York: HarperCollins.
Hardacre, H. (2017). *Shinto: A History.* New York: Oxford University Press.
Harris, M. (2001). *Cultural Materialism: The Struggle for a Science of Culture.* Lanham, MD: Rowman & Littlefield.
Heilbroner, R. L. (2000). *The Worldly Philosophers.* London: Penguin.
Hilberg, R. (2003). *The Destruction of the European Jews.* New Haven: Yale University Press.

Bibliography

Hodder, I. (2011). *The Leopard's Tale: Revealing the Mysteries of Çatalhöyük.* New York: Thames & Hudson.
Keeley, L. H. (1995). *War Before Civilization.* New York: Oxford University Press.
Klein, R. G., & Edgar, B. (2002). *The Dawn of Human Culture.* New York: Wiley.
Kotkin, S. (2014). *Stalin.* New York: Penguin Press.
Lenski, G. E. (1966). *Power and Privilege.* Boston: McGraw-Hill.
Lévi-Strauss, C. (1969). *The Elementary Structures of Kinship.* Boston: Beacon Press.
Loewenberg, P. (1971). *The Psychohistorical Origins of the Nazi Youth Cohort.* The American Historical Review.
Lovejoy, C. O. (1988). Evolution of Human Walking. *Scientific American* 259, no. 5.
Lukes, S. (2018). *Émile Durkheim, His Life and Work: A Historical and Critical Study.* Harmondsworth: Penguin.
Lundquist, J. H., Anderton, D. L., & Yaukey, D. (2015). *Demography: The Study of Human Population.* Long Grove, IL: Waveland Press.
Madhok, M. (2014). *Indian Caste System.* Lanham: Centrum Press.
Mair, L. (1976). *Witchcraft.* New York: McGraw-Hill.
Malinowski, B. (2014). *Argonauts of the Western Pacific: An Account of Native Enterprise and Adventure in the Archipelagoes of Melanesian New Guinea.* London: Routledge.
Mauss, A. L. (1975). *Social Problems as Social Movements.* Philadelphia: Lippincott.
Merton, R. K., & Sztompka, P. (1996). *On Social Structure and Science.* Chicago: University of Chicago Press.
Métraux, A., & Ordish, G. (1988). *The History of the Incas.* New York: Schocken Books.
Mitzman, A. (1971). *The Iron Cage.* New York. New Brunswick: Transaction Books.
Oplinger, J. (1990). *The Politics of Demonology: The European Witchcraze and the Mass Production of Deviance.* Selinsgrove, PA: Susquehanna University Press.
Oshinsky, David M. (2019). *Conspiracy So Immense: The World of Joe McCarthy.* New York: Free Press.
Perrin, N. (1999). *Giving Up the Gun: Japan's Reversion to the Sword, 1543–1879.* Boston: David R. Godine.
Postgate, J. N. (2017). *Early Mesopotamia: Society and Economy at the Dawn of History.* London: Routledge.
Sarotte, M. E., & Rodgers, E. S. (2015). *The Collapse.* New York: Perseus.
Schur, E. M. (1980). *The Politics of Deviance: Stigma Contests and the Uses of Power.* Englewood Cliffs, N.J.: Prentice-Hall.
Sheppard, E. (2009). *A World of Difference: Encountering and Contesting Development.* New York: The Guilford Press.
Sjoberg, G. (1967). The Preindustrial City. *Peasant Society* (January 1): 15–24.
Smelser, N. J. (2014). *Theory of Collective Behavior.* New York: Free Press of Glencoe.
Sperber, J. (2014). *Karl Marx: A Nineteenth-Century Life.* New York: Liveright.
Stanner, W. E. H., & Manne, R. (2011). *The Dreaming & Other Essays.* Collingwood: Black.
Thomas, D. H. (1976). *Figuring Anthropology: First Principles of Probability and Statistics.* New York: Holt, Rinehart and Winston.
Tolnay, S. E., & Beck, E. M. (1995). *A Festival of Violence: An Analysis of the Lynching of African-Americans in the American South, 1882–1930.* Urbana: University of Illinois Press.
Wallerstein, I. M. (1976). *The Modern World System.* New York: Academic Press.
Worsley, P. (1974). *The Trumpet Shall Sound.* New York: Schocken Books.

Index

Abel, Theodore 88
Aborigines, Australian 46, 97
abortion 79, 87, 158
abstract history 17
acculturation 153
achieved status 65
adaptivity (culture) 51
affective action 16
affinal kinship 52
Africa 44, 51, 68, 145
age cohort 88
agrarian societies 69–70
Alger, Horatio 62
Algonkian language 47
Aliens and Dissenters (Preston, William) 111
alliance (kinship) 53
Allure of Battle (Nolan) 141
altricial 20, 41
Amaterasu 103
American Communist Party 125, 126
American Library Association 154
American sociologists 18–30
ancien régime 60, 70, 81, 88
ancient warfare 136–138
Angels of Mons 134
animatism 99, 101
animism 99, 101
Annales School of Social Science 47, 133
L'Année Sociologique 14
anomie 15, 107
Anslinger, Harry 110
Anthony, David 46
anthropology 3, 35, 49, 52, 81, 168–169
Anti-Fascist Rampart 131, 133
Anti-Malthusians 85–86, 87
anti-Semitism 112–113, 118–119
antithesis 8
archaeology 90, 136, 137, 145, 146, 149
aristocracy 59, 60, 61, 70, 77, 78
arme blanche 141
Arminius 81
arrest chains 120
The Art of War (Sun Tzu) 143
Arunta 97
ascribed status 65

Astorix (comic) 81
Athens (Greece) 137
Auschwitz 118
Ayatollah Khomeini 144
Azande tribe 114

Baccaria, Cesare 106
bailouts (financial) 72
ballistics 138
banking 71–72, 163
Bastard Feudalism 60
Battle of Tours 141–142
Becker, Howard P. 99, 110
beehive soccer 28
Belgian Congo 74
belief systems 99–100
Bellah, Robert 103
Belloc, Hilaire 149
Berlin Wall 131, 133
Bierstedt, Robert 33
Big Men 70
Bills of Mortality 84
birth control 79, 85, 86, 87, 124; *see also* contraception; fertility
birth rate 86, 88
Bloch, Marc 133
Blood Banner 104
Blumer, Herbert 25, 27, 129
Boas, Franz 63
Boer War 74
Boise (ID) 112
Bolshevism/Bolshevicks 75, 119, 122
Book of Mormon 98, 99
bourgeoisie 8, 61
The Boys of Boise (Grerassi) 112
Brahmins 57
Braudel, Fernand 47
Brave Heart (film) 83
Britain 74, 86, 111, 134; *see also* England
British East India Company 58, 74, 164
Brown, Peter 18
Brown v. Board of Education 38
Buddhism 99, 100, 101
bureaucracy 16, 54, 56, 119
Burkumin 58

179

Index

Burmese Supernaturalism (Spiro) 101
Burr, George Lincoln 116
Bushido 141

Caesar, Julius 137
capitalism 71–72, 75, 93, 164
caravanserie 162
career lines 54
cargo cults 100–101
Carlyle, Thomas 9
caste systems 57–59
Çatal Höyük (Turkey) 90
Ceauşescu, Nicolae 87
Chagnon, Napoleon 135
Chambliss, William 38
Chapin, Henry 22
Charcot, Jean-Martin 31
chariots 136
charter myths 82, 83
chattel slavery 70, 73–74, 79–80, 156; *see also* slavery
Cheka (USSR) 119
Cheyenne Dog Soldiers 18
Cheyenne Sun Dance 45
Chicago (IL) 93–94, 111
Chicago School of Sociology 19, 35, 94
children, homeless 95
Children's Crusade 129
China 65, 76, 77, 87–88, 111, 117, 125
Chirot, David 72
Chomsky, Norm 43–44
Christianity 101, 102, 115
churches and denominations 97, 98
Churchill, Winston 81
Cicourel, Aaron 86
cities: functional density 91–92, 96; origins and development 90–91; primate cities 95–96; rapid growth of 93–94; squatter settlements 92–93, 95; urban renewal 94
Citino, Robert, M. 141
Citizens United v. FEC 78
civil religion 103
Civil War (U.S.) 80
class systems 61–67
Clausewitz, Carl Phillip von 144
Cloaca Maxima 91
Clovis (Merovingian) 83, 140
coalitions and coalitional power 77–78, 83, 125, 135
Coca Cola 164
coffee 73
cognitive development 25, 30–31
Cohn, Norman 100
Cohn, Stanley 111, 112
Colbert, Jean-Baptist 13
cold war 122, 125
Coleman Report 38
Collapse (Sarotte) 133

collective behavior 129–134
collective conscience 15
collective events 129–130, 131, 154
collective mind 129
Collingham, Lizzie 76
colonialism and colonies 73–74, 75
commodities 68, 69, 73–74, 91, 146, 162
communications 96, 139, 146, 151, 161–162, 166–167
communism 9, 38, 73, 87, 124–125, 126
Communist Infiltration of the United States 125
communists 102, 109, 111, 113, 122, 123, 133
comparative sociology 11, 35, 113
compensatory power 11–12, 70, 111
computer development 151
Comte, August 4–6, 13
concentration camps 118
condign power 11–12, 70, 77, 111
The Condition of the Working Class in England (Engels) 9
conditioned power 11–12, 33, 78, 111, 144
conflict perspective of religion 102–103, 105
conflict sociology 113
conflict theory 4, 7–10, 14, 18
conflict vs. functionalism 13, 18
Confucianism 101
Conrad, Joseph 74
consanguineal 52
consciousness 15, 25, 29, 72, 158
conscription 142
conservation of volume 30
conspicuous consumption 65
construction of reality 13, 45–46, 123
contraception 87; *see also* birth control; fertility
control group 36, 37, 39
control theory 11
convict leasing program 80
Cooley, Charles Horton 19, 25, 53–54
CORE (Congress of Racial Equality) 154
core states 73, 74, 76
corvee labor 59
cotton 73
cotton gin 150
Council of Forty-Four (Cheyenne) 70
Cours de Philosophie Positive (Comte) 5
The Court Society (Elias) 59–60
cowrie shells 162
cradle of sociology 20, 54
Creel, George 139, 143
The Criminal Man (Lombroso) 106
The Criminal Woman (Lombroso) 106
cross cousins 53
cross cultural exchanges 165
crossbows 60
Crusades 59
cults 98

Index

cultural diffusion 152–153
cultural lag 150
Cultural Revolution 111, 117, 121
culture: characteristics 41–45, 49–51; digital revolution 146; industrial revolution 146; neolithic revolution 145–146; paleolithic change 145; social construction of reality 45–46, 114
culture vs. society 51

Dahmer, Jeffrey 44
Dalits 57
Darwin, Charles 4, 62, 63, 85
Davis, Kingsley 21, 23
Dawn Cave 68
Dawn of Human Culture (Klein) 68
Death and Rebirth of the Seneca (Wallace) 100
death camps 118–119
death rate 88
decisive battle 141–142
Declaration of Conscience (Smith) 127
deep structure 42
demic diffusion 152
democracy 73, 77, 78
demographic transition 86–87
demography 84–89, 136
dependency theory 74
dependent variable 36
descent (kinship) 53
deviance, manufacturing: conflict theories 108; criminology 106–107; defective people theories 107–108; labeling theory 108–110; moral entrepreneurs 110; nation states and 109–110
deviance, mass production: Great Purge 119–122; Great Witch Craze 113–117; Holocaust 117–119; McCarthy era 124–128; moral panics 111–113; nation states and 111; Red Scares 122–124
devolution 147
Dewey, John 25
the Dialectic 8–10
dialectical materialism 4, 8, 9
diamonds 11
dictator 77, 87, 111, 140
differential association 108
digital revolution 146
Dirty War (Argentina) 110
The Discovery of France (Robb) 82
disease 90–91
divorce laws 156
dog whistle politics 80
Domesday Book 12, 84
drapetomania 80
Dreamtime 46, 97, 99
Durkheim, Émile 14–15, 19, 36, 97, 101, 107
Dutch Tulip Mania 123, 129

dynamic process (culture) 50
dysfunctional behavior 107

Early Modern Period 114, 115
East Germany 131–132; *see also* German Democratic Republic
ecclesia 98–99
ecology 47, 51, 71
The Economic Consequences of Peace (Keynes) 17, 75
economic determinism 61
economic development 16, 72, 73–74
economic relationships 8–9
economics 17, 68–76, 85
economies: agricultural 69–70; capitalist 71–72; industrial 70–71; World System Theory 73
Edelman, Murray 113
ego 31–32
Eisenhower, Dwight D. 78, 127; mission statement 143
The Elementary Forms of Religious Life (Durkheim) 14, 97
Elias, Norbert 59–60
emergent (culture) 50–51
emergent norm theory 129
enculturation 41, 50
endogamy 57
Engels, Friedrich 9, 71
England 62, 63, 71, 84, 115; *see also* Britain
English class system 63
English language 166–167
Erikson, Kai 38
An Essay on the Principle of Population (Malthus) 85
estate systems 59–61
ethnocentrism 80–81
ethnomethodology 48–49
eugenics 63
Europe in Crisis (Parker) 115
European Union 83
European Witch Craze 113–117
euthanasia 118–119
Evans Pritchard, E.E. 114
Everything in Its Path (Erikson) 38
exchange 68–69, 145
exogamy 57
experimental group 36, 37, 39
extended family 52
Extraordinary Popular Delusions and the Madness of Crowds (MacKay) 129
Ezhov, N.I. 120

false consciousness 10, 32
falsification 36, 108
famine 67, 77, 85–86, 88; *see also* starvation
fasces 45, 77
fascism 38
The Feast (film) 155

181

Index

Federal Bureau of Investigation (FBI) 107, 124, 126, 127, 158
Federal Bureau of Narcotics (FBN) 110
Feminine Mystique (Friedan) 154
feminist movement 151, 157–158
Ferguson, Adam 147
fertility 85; *see also* birth control; contraception
feudalism 59–60, 138
finance 76, 178
financial swindles and bubbles 129
Finckenhauer, James 37
Finland 123–124
Folk Devils 112
Folk Devils and Moral Panics (Cohn) 111
folkways 44–45
Folkways (Sumner) 44
foot binding 65
fossil fuels 71
framing 79
France 70, 82, 87–88, 115, 141
Franklin, Benjamin 155
Franks 83
Frederick the Great 141, 149
French Revolution 4, 60, 129
Freud, Sigmund 31–32
functional density 91–92, 96
functionalism 4, 6, 13–14, 18
functions (society) 5, 6, 101–102
fundamentalism 79
Fussell, Paul 134, 143

Galbraith, John Kenneth 12, 111
Galileo 162
Galton, Francis 62–63
game stage 27–28
Gandhi, Mohandas 57
Gans, Herbert 94
Garvey, Marcus 158
Gastonia (NC) 102
gay liberation movement 154
Geary, Patrick 81, 82
Geertz, Clifford 13
generalized beliefs 130
generalized other 28–29
gentrification 94
German Democratic Republic (GDR) 131–132; *see also* Germany
Germania (Tacitus) 81
Germany 75–76, 88, 115, 119, 141; *see also* German Democratic Republic (GDR); Third Reich
ghettoes 92
Ghost Dance 100
Gibbon, Edward 141–142
Gilded Age (Twain) 71
Gillen, F.J. 97
global cities 146

global warming 77
globalization: communications 161–163; trade and trading 162–163; transformations due to 163–165; transnational agencies and organizations 165, 166–167; transnational corporations 164–166
Goebbels, Joseph 81, 118
Goffman, Erving 33–34
gold 75
Gould, Stephen Jay 17, 146, 159
Gourney, Jean 54
grammar 43–44, 46
Gramsci, Antonio 82, 153
Graunt, John 84–85
Great Being 5
Great Depression 92
Great Purge (Russia) 110, 119–122, 127
The Great War and Modern Memory (Fussell) 143
Great White Race 62
Great Witch Craze (Europe) 113–117
Green Revolution 165–166
Grerassi, John 112
Gulag Archipelago (USSR) 117, 119–120
Gun Powder Revolution 138

Hall, Edward 47–48
Hall, John 137, 150
Handsome Lake religion 100–101
Harijans 57
Harris, Marvin 79
Hawthorne Study and Effect 39
health 85
Heart of Darkness (Conrad) 74
Hegel, Georg 7–8
Henry VIII 102–103
Heroditus 92
hierarchical diffusion 153
High Church 99–100
Hill, Joe 102
Himmler, Heinrich 118
Hindu/Hinduism 58, 98, 99, 100
historical linguistics 45–46
historical materialism 8, 147
History of Civil Society (Ferguson) 147
Hitler, Adolf 76, 88, 104, 118
Hitler Youth Camps 88, 118
Ho Chi Minh 104
Hobson, John A. 74–75, 139
Hodder, Ian 90
Holocaust 110, 117–119, 127
Homo sapiens 41, 50, 51
homosexuality 38, 112, 119
Hoover, J. Edgar 110, 123, 126, 133
Hopkins, Matthew 115, 122
Hoplite Revolution 137
The Horse, the Wheel and Language (Anthony) 46

182

Index

horses 136–137
horticultural societies 69–70
How the Other Half Lives (Riis) 71
Hunger Plan 76, 86
hunting and gathering societies 69–70

the I and the Me 29–30, 32
I Have a Dream (speech) 80
id 31–32
ideal types 16, 54, 55
idealists and ideology 8, 38, 104, 118, 130–131, 144
Ifugao culture 10
imagined communities 81
immunities 90
imperialism 75–76
Imperialism, a Study (Hobson) 75
Inca Empire 71, 139
independent variable 36
India 57–59, 67, 87
indigo 73
Indo-European language 46
industrial espionage 165
industrial societies 53, 55, 61, 69–70, 71–73, 146
informal rules 56
information friction 161
Institoris, Heinrich 115
institutions 9–10, 15–16, 33–34
interactionist perspective 108–110
Internal Security Act (U.S.) 125
internet 35, 79, 134
IQ testing 63
Iranian Revolution 144
Irish Potato Famine 85, 86
Iron Age 91
Iron Cage 17, 83
Iron Law of Wages 61, 85
Isenberg, Nancy 63
ISIS (terrorists) 80
Islam 97, 99, 101, 140
Islamophobia 80
isolates 20–24

Jainism 100
James, William 19
Janissaries 140
Japan 58, 60, 76, 101, 103, 138
Jati 58
Jebel Sahabi 136
Jews 74, 117, 119
The Jigalong Mob (Tonkinson) 97
Jim Crow laws 64
jingoism 75, 139
John Frum cult 100
Johnson, Lyndon 80, 100, 155
Jones, Chuck 160
Jones, William 46

Judaism 98, 99, 100
judicial torture 115
junk science 38, 75, 76, 82

The Kallikak Family 62
kami 103
Das Kapital (Marx) 4
Kennedy, John F. 73
Keynes, John Maynard 17, 72, 75
Khoisan hunters 16–17
King, Martin Luther, Jr. 80, 155
kinship 52–53, 70
Kipling, Rudyard 75
Klein, Richard 44, 68
kleptocracy 77
Klotkin, Stephen 121
Kluckhorn, Clyde 49
knights 59, 138, 163
Knights Templar 163
Korean War 124, 125
Kornblum, William 28
kratos 77
Kroeber, A.L. 49
Kruschev, Nikita 121
Kshaytriya 57
Ku Klux Klan (KKK) 124
Kula Ring 69
kulaks and *sub kulaks* 113, 120

labor 59, 61, 102, 124, 125, 158, 163–164
labor camps (USSR) 117, 119–120; *see also* Gulag Archipelago
Lakoff, George 47
language 41–42, 46–47, 82, 83, 166
LAPD (Los Angeles Police Department) 130
latifundia 70
laws 44–45, 61, 64, 70, 115, 132
LeBon, Gustave 129
legitimate racket 13
Lemert, Edwin 108
Lenin, Vladimir Ilyich 75, 104
Lenski, Gerhard 69, 71
Le Pen, Jean Marie 83
Lévi-Strauss, Claude 7, 52, 140
life chances 57, 61
limpieza de sangre 74
lineages 53, 70
linear production 165
lines of action 27
linguistic determinism 42
Linton, Ralph 152
Little Red Book (Zedong) 104, 117
Little Red Songbook (IWW) 102
logos 5
Lombroso, Cesare 106, 123
London (England) 84
longue durée 47
looking glass self 19, 26

Index

loosely coupled system 18
Louis XIV 13, 59–60
Lovelace, Ada 151
Loving v. Virginia 64
low income housing 94
Lowenberg, Peter 88
loyalty oaths 123, 126
Lumpenproletariat 9, 61, 94–95
Lyndon Johnson Cult 100–101

Mackay, Charles 129
madrasas 166
Magellan, Ferdinand 162
magic 100, 101, 104, 114, 134
Magnetic Mountain: Stalinism as a Civilization (Klotkin) 121
Malesevic, Sinesia 139
Malinowski, Bronislaw 69
Malleus Maleficarium 114
Malthus, Thomas 61, 84, 85
mana 99, 101
mantle of sacredness 103
manufacturing 71, 73, 74
Mao Zedong 12, 104, 117, 121, 125
marasmus 22
March of Dimes 155
Marconi, Guglielmo 151
Marijuana Tax Act 110
Marital Power Exemplified (Packard, E.) 157
marriage 52, 53, 57, 58, 64, 104, 110
Martineau, Harriet 156
Marx, Karl 4, 6–11, 71, 94–95, 107
Marxism 6–10
mass operations 121
massively contingent 17
Masters of Deceit (Hoover) 126, 133
material culture 150–151
materialist and materialism 8–9, 147
matrilineage 53, 155
Maxim gun 149
McCarthy Era 110, 122, 124–128
McNeill, William 38, 90–91
Mead, George Herbert 25–30
means of production 61
media and war 143–144
medieval cities 92
Medieval Technology and Social Change (White) 138
The Mediterranean and the World in the Age of Philip II (Braudel) 47
megapolis 96
Meiji Restoration 103, 104
Melanesia 100
Mencken, H.L. 102
Merton, Robert 107–108, 149
Mesopotamia 136
metaphors 44, 47, 49, 50, 110
Metaphors We Live By (Lakoff) 47

metaphysical thinking 5
method of difference 36
Middle Passage 162–163
Midelfort, H.C. Erik 114
migration 47, 85, 92, 95, 136, 152
Miletus (Turkey) 91–92
the military 137, 138–139, 150
military-industrial complex 78
military morale 140–142
military technology 137–138
Mill, Harriet Taylor 156
Mill, John Stuart 36, 156
Mill Hands and Preachers (Pope) 102
Millenarinism 100
Mills, C. Wright 32–33; 78
Mind, Self and Society (Mead) 26
Mines and Collieries Act of 1842 (England) 62
Ministry of State Security (Stasi) 131–133
mobs 129
Modern Traveler (Belloc) 149
The Modern World System (Wallerstein) 73
modernization 78
Mods 111
monarchy 77–78
money 11, 78, 163
monogamy 52
monopoly and monopolies 12, 57, 72, 77
monotheism 99, 101
Mons (France) 134
Monte Testaccio (Italy) 70–71
mores 44–45
morphemes 43
Morrison, Van 166
mortality rates 84, 85, 86
Mosinee (WI) 126
Mothers Against Drunk Driving (MADD) 153, 154
Moyers, Bill 80
multilinear evolution 147
Muskogean language 47
Muslims 74, 99, 101
Mutually Assured Destruction (MAD) 56
Myth of Nations (Geary) 81
mythogenesis 80–81
myths 46, 50, 83, 100, 134

NAACP (National Association of Colored People) 154
Napoleon Bonaparte 105, 140, 142
Napoleon III 81
nation-state 83, 98, 110–111, 128, 163
national religion 103, 104
national strategies (military) 141–142
nationalism 75–76, 81, 83, 104, 138
Nats 101
Nazis (National Socialist Workers Party) 81, 82, 104, 118, 124
Neanderthals 106, 145

Index

Negro Removal 94
nepotism 55
New Deal 66
New Guinea 69, 70, 100
New Malthusians 85–86
New Testament 98
Nixon, Richard 80
NKVD (Peoples Commissariat of Internal Affairs) 110, 120, 121
Nolan, Cathal J. 141
nongovernmental organizations (NGO) 166; *see also* transnational organizations
nonsignificant gestures 26–27
norms 44–45, 107
North Vietnamese Army (NVA) 134, 139
nuclear family 52

Ogburn, William 150
Okhrana (Russia) 119
oligarchy 77, 78
On the Origin of Species (Darwin) 4
On War (Clausewitz) 144
one child policy 87
operational indicator 36
opium 73–74, 164
Oplinger, Jon 114
organicism 5
organization of symbols 50
organized structure of religion 98–99
organizing space/personal space 47–48
Ottoman Empire 140

Packard, Elizabeth 156–157
Packard, Theophilus 156
paleoanthropology 44
Paleolithic era 47, 101
Palmer, A. Mitchell 122, 123, 124
Palmer Raids 111, 122
parallel cousins 53
paramilitary 123
Parker, Jeffrey 115
participant observation 35, 39
particular other 27
Passing of the Great Race (Grant) 154
patrilineage 53
patterns (culture) 47, 50
peripheral States 73
Philip II 47
phoneme 43
phonology 43
Piaget, Jean 30–31, 32
Pivot of the Four Quarters (Wheatley) 91
place names 47
Plagues and Peoples (McNeill) 90–91
Plains Indians 70, 100
plantation system 70, 163
play stage 27
Pledge of Allegiance 103

Pleistocene era 51
plutocracy 77, 78
The Poisonous Mushroom 118
Political Action Committees (PACS) 78
political control 77, 83
Politics as Symbolic Interaction (Edelman) 113
Politics of Demonology (Oplinger) 114
polyandry 52
polygamy 52
polygyny 52
Polynesian societies 99
polytheistic 100
Pope, Liston 102
Popper, Karl 36
population pyramids 88
populations 84–85, 86
positivism (Comte) 5
post-colonial world 72
post-industrial society 71
poverty 66–67
power 11–12; *see also* power elite
power elite 78, 110, 168; *see also* power
pre-industrial city 93
Preston, William 111
primary deviance 109
primary groups 19–20, 53–54
primary production 71
primate cities 95–96
primitive culture 97
Primitive Culture (Tyler) 41
printing 114–115
Prison Notes (Gramsci) 153
pro-natal programs 87–88
productivity 71, 117
proletariat 8–9, 61, 71
propaganda 81, 111, 118, 139–140
The Protestant Ethic and the Spirit of Capitalism (Weber) 16–17
Protestant Reformation 79
proto–Indo-European language 46
Pruitt Igoe Housing Project 94
punctuated equilibrium 146–147
The Pursuit of the Millennium (Cohn) 100

qualitative research 35–36
quantitative research 35–36
Quran 98, 142

racial imperialism 75, 76
racial memory 16
racism 63–64, 75, 76, 79–80, 107, 118
Rahway State Prison (NJ) 37
Rainbow Division (U.S. Army) 140
random samples 36
Raper, Arthur 64
reciprocity 69, 136
Red Cross 166

Index

Red Guards 117
Red Scares 122–124
red tape 56
reductionism 14
Reefer Madness (film) 110
reflexive self 19
regulation 72
Reich, David 58, 136
reliability 37
religion 74, 79, 97–105
research methods and methodology 35–40
resocialization 33
Ricardo, David 85
Rig Vedas 58
rigid hierarchical structure 54
Riis, Jacob 71
rites of passage 104
rituals 97, 99, 103, 104, 123, 126
Robb, Graham 82
Rockers 111
Roman Catholic Church 55, 56, 59, 98
Roman Empire 18, 56, 81–82, 98
Romance languages 46
Romania 87
Rome 18, 70–71, 91
Roosevelt, Franklin 72
Roosevelt, Theodore 72, 93
Rostow, Walt 73
rule-bound 54, 55
The Rules of Sociological Method (Durkheim) 14
rum 163
rumors 130, 132, 133–134
Russia 75, 110, 142, 148

sacred beliefs 97
St. George (England) 134
Saint-Simone, Henri de 5
Salk vaccine 155
Salvation Army 166
samples and sampling 36, 39
San bushmen 18
Sanskrit 42, 46
sanskritization 58
Sapir-Whorf, Benjamin 42
Sapir-Whorf, Edward 42
Sapir-Whorf Hypothesis 42
Sarotte, Mary Elise 133
scapegoat 64, 123
Scared Straight Program 37, 39
Schapira, Judith 156
Scott, Walter, Sir 83
secondary deviance 109
secondary groups 54
sects 97, 98
the self 25, 29
self as a social process 29
self-awareness 19
semantics 43
semi-peripheral states 73, 74, 75, 76
Seneca Indians 100
Septuagint 98
serfs 59, 60
shamanism 101
shared culture 50
shells 68, 70, 162
Sheppard, Eric 163, 164, 165
Shinto 101, 103
show trials 119–120, 121, 126
shtetel 165
significant gestures 26–27
Silk Road 91, 162
simony 55
Sites, Paul 11
Sjoberg, Gideon 92
skill monopolies 71
Skype 96
slavery 70, 73–74, 102, 162–163; *see also* chattel slavery
Smelser, Neal 129–130
Smith, Adam 19
Smith, Margaret Chase 127
social action 16
social change, grand theories of 147–148
social change, middle range theories 149–151
social construction of reality 13, 44, 45
social control 116, 117, 130, 137
Social Darwinism 62–63, 75, 106
social fact 14–15
social interaction 26, 27–28
social mobility 60–61
social movements 130; Black Muslims 158–159; Civil Rights movement 158; failures of 158–159; feminist 158–159; MADD (Mothers Against Drunk Driving) 153; stages of 154
social organization 52–56
Social Pathologies (Lemert) 108
social problem 19
social psychology 25
Social Security law 159
social self 19
social strain 130
social stratification: caste systems 57–59; class systems 61–67; estate systems 59–71; hunting and gathering 69–70; industrial societies 71
social structure 34, 137
Social Structure and Anomie (Merton) 107–108
socialization 20–24, 33, 41, 54, 110
societies, types of 69–73
society: American sociologists 18–30; Comte, August 4–6, 13; conflict vs. functionalism 18; Durkheim, Émile 14–15;

Index

Freud, Sigmund 31–32; Hegel, Georg 7–8; Marx, Karl 6–11; power 11–12; Weber, Max 12, 15–17
society vs. culture 51
Sociological Imagination (Mills) 32–33
The Sociology of War and Violence (Malesevic) 139
solar production 165
soldiers 142–143
Solzhenitsyn, Alexander 120
South Vietnam 73
Soviet Union 7, 55, 85, 104, 109, 119–120, 125; *see also* USSR
Spanish Inquisition 74, 116
Spencer, Baldwin 97
Spencer, Herbert 62
Spiro, Milford 101
Spitz, Rene 22–23
spondylus shells 162
Sprenger, Jacob 115
squatter settlements 92–93, 95
Stalin, Joseph 56, 78, 85, 117, 119–120, 121
Stalin: Waiting for Hitler 1929–1941 (Klotkin) 121
Standard of Ur 136
starvation 67, 77, 85–86, 88
state violence 77
status 65–66
sterilization 63
stigma contests 109
stimulus diffusion 152
stirrups 137–138
Stone of Scone 83
strain theory 107
Strategic Air Command 56
structured inequality 66, 67
sub-castes 58
Sudra 57
sugar 163
Suicide (Durkheim) 14, 15, 36
Sumeria 137
Sumner, William Graham 44
sumptuary laws 59–60
super-ego 31–32
superstructure 10
survival of the fittest 62
Sutherland, Edwin 108
Switzerland 138
symbolic exchange 145
symbolic interactionism 20, 25, 30, 129
symbols and symbolism 41, 50, 71, 83, 104, 140
sympathetic magic 100
syncretism 159, 165
syndicalist laws 124
synoikismoi 90
syntax 43
synthesis 8

System de Politique Positive (Comte) 5
systems theorists 18

taboo system 103
Tacitus Cornelius 81
take the role 27, 28, 29, 31
Taste of War (Collingham) 76
tea 73
technology transfer 164
Thales 91–92
theater state 13
theism 101
theological thinking 5
theories of misfortune 102, 114
The Theory of the Working Class (Veblen) 65
thesis 8
Third Reich 38, 63, 76, 104, 111, 118, 143; *see also* Germany
Third World 78
Thomas, W.I. 35, 45
Thompson, Warren 86
tobacco 74, 163
Tobin's Spirit Guide 129
Tonkinson, Robert 97
Torah 98
total institution 33–34
Totemism (Lévi-Strauss) 140
totemistic landscape 46
tourism 163
Townsend Plan 159
trade and trading 90–92, 162–163
traditional action 16
Trans-Atlantic Trade Data Base 163
transnational agencies and organizations 165, 166–167; *see also* nongovernmental organizations (NGO)
transnational corporations 164–166
transportation 91, 95, 130, 163
Treaty of Versailles 75
Triangle Trade 162–163
tribal warfare 135–136
tribes and tribal cultures 53, 81–82, 105
Trobriand Islands 69
Troeltsch, Ernst 97
Truce of God/Truce of Peace 59
Tudors 59
Tukhachevsky, Marshal 121
Turkey 90, 95
Twain, Mark 71, 74, 76
Tyler, Edward B. 41

The Unadjusted Girl (Thomas) 35
Uncle Tom's Cabin (Stowe) 154
unilinear evolution 147
Union of Russian Workers 123
uniqueness (human culture) 51
U.S. Army 56
United States Chamber of Commerce 125

187

Index

Universal Negro Improvement Association (UNIA) 158
universalistic 54, 55
untermenschen 76, 82
Untouchables 57
Upanishads 98
urban elite 93–94
urban renewal 94
urban underclass 94–95
"Urban Villagers" (Gans) 94
Urbanism as a Way of Life (Wirth) 90
Uruk (city) 137
useless eaters 118
Ussher, James 146
USSR 77, 78; *see also* Soviet Union
usufruct 70

Vaisya 57
validity 37–38
value added model 129–130
variables 36, 39
Varnas 57
Veblen, Thorstein 65
Vercingetorix 81
Vietnam War 127, 134, 142
violence 77, 113, 135–136, 139, 155, 166
Volksseele (folk soul) 16, 81–82
voluntary associations 54
Vonnegut, Kurt 26–27
vreditel 120

wages 61, 66, 71
Wallace, A.F.C. 100
Wallerstein, Immanuel 73
wandering tribes 81
war and warfare 135–144
warfare, genetic data 136
Warner, W. Lloyd 66
warriors 57, 59, 135, 138
Watt, James 150
Watts riots (L.A.) 130–131
wealth 60, 61, 65, 66, 70–71, 78
The Wealth of Nations (Smith) 19
weapons 67, 137, 138, 149, 150
Weber, Max 12, 15–18, 83, 105
wertrtational 16
Wessel, Horst 81, 104
Westmoreland, William 142
What's Opera, Doc? (film) 160
Wheatley, Paul 91
White, Lynn Townsend 138
white supremacy 80
White Trash (Isenberg) 63
Whitehead, Alfred North 3
Whitney, Eli 150
Who We Are and How We Got Here (Reich) 136
Wilhelm II 81
William the Conqueror 11–12, 84, 140
Willow Run factory (MI) 143
Wirth, Louis 90
Witch Hunting in Southwestern Germany (Midelfort) 114
witchcraft panics 35
witches and witchcraft 45, 114–116
Witchfinder General 116, 122
women: feminist movement 157–158; status of 45, 52, 109, 114, 155–157
World of Difference (Sheppard) 163
world redeeming religion 100–101
World System Theory 73–74, 76
World War I 63, 75, 87, 133, 134, 142
World War II 55, 56, 72, 76, 82, 103, 104
wreckers 109–110, 120
Wundt, Wilhelm 25, 26

xenophobia 80, 83
xharo exchange 68–69, 145

Yankee City (Warner) 66
Yanomamo culture 10, 18, 69, 135, 155–156
Yasukuni 103

Zedong, Mao 12, 104, 117, 121, 125
Zulu tribe 82
zweckrational 16